Word Search

Assorted Words 1

```
Y  C  A  R  I  P  S  N  O  C  Y  Z  B  R  G
M  T  R  T  Q  L  A  S  G  I  H  Q  E  B  J
E  I  E  H  R  E  A  E  E  N  M  F  I  H  Y
O  N  I  E  Q  T  W  G  L  N  I  M  T  L  N
V  K  S  R  Q  T  H  S  N  B  T  D  U  G  F
E  W  S  E  P  U  K  R  C  I  A  R  U  N  S
R  E  U  B  U  C  O  L  I  C  S  C  U  E  E
P  L  E  Y  O  E  T  L  L  D  S  W  U  C  F
L  L  D  E  V  O  U  T  N  E  S  S  O  D  R
A  S  P  I  R  A  T  I  O  N  M  W  E  D  E
Y  P  J  M  A  G  N  E  T  I  Z  I  N  G  L
F  B  P  A  S  U  K  J  D  X  Z  L  P  S  E
M  Q  D  E  L  L  E  N  N  A  H  C  R  K  R
Z  P  W  X  N  O  I  T  A  N  I  M  A  X  E
Y  T  Q  S  E  D  U  T  I  T  L  U  M  W  S
```

APPEND	DOWSING	MULTITUDES
ASPIRATION	EDUCABLE	OVERPLAY
BOOTED	EXAMINATION	REISSUED
BUCOLICS	FEUDING	THEREBY
CHANNELLED	IMMUNE	
CONSPIRACY	INKWELLS	
CURTNESS	LETTUCE	
DEVOUTNESS	MAGNETIZING	

Puzzle #2

Assorted Words 2

```
G Y Y Q I N Q D N K E M F L S
S O R D E P O L E V E D K C V
F R U E E E M B A L M I N G O
X C E G D F Y W L B L H E P E
N Y I T I U R V W S I O I X B
R D F B F N R A A G H X T D E
U E Z X F I G P Y R N I Y X I
D F V N D V R D S S O I D X E
D D X H F I N D S T T O W B I
E F L A S H I E S T O A M A Z
R M I R T H L E S S R P O E S
S M O O R H C N U L E V E L D
N R N F F P O L I S H E R O F
R A T T R A P R E P U S O H P
G R E S P E C T F U L L Y R K
```

ALWAYS
DEFRAYS
DEVELOPED
DRIFTERS
EMBALMING
EXTOLLED
FINDS
FLASHIEST

FLOATS
GOUGING
LEVEL
LUNCHROOMS
MIRTHLESS
POLISHER
PRUDERY
RATTRAP

RESPECTFULLY
ROOMED
RUDDERS
SAWING
SUPER

Assorted Words 3

```
H  O  U  S  E  P  L  A  N  T  R  B  V  R  H
R  K  E  A  R  T  H  I  N  E  S  S  C  E  O
D  E  Z  I  T  E  H  T  S  E  A  N  A  E  U
E  E  W  Z  G  J  T  S  M  F  M  X  V  N  S
V  R  V  O  O  N  E  T  C  J  E  P  E  L  E
O  O  E  A  L  Y  I  T  O  I  Z  B  A  I  B
L  U  F  F  E  F  L  T  I  L  T  V  T  S  R
U  B  V  F  R  R  D  I  N  S  B  P  T  T  E
T  C  Y  O  I  A  E  E  R  E  A  A  E  K  A
I  K  B  Q  P  C  I  B  R  A  U  R  D  S  K
O  B  A  S  E  L  I  N  E  U  T  Q  A  P  I
N  E  S  B  L  P  S  A  S  R  T  E  E  P  N
S  R  E  R  E  T  S  A  L  P  T  S  N  R  G
H  I  N  A  U  G  U  R  A  L  S  V  A  O  F
T  S  K  O  O  B  S  S  A  P  Z  Y  S  P  M
```

ANAESTHETIZED	FREQUENTING	PASTURED
BASELINE	HOUSEBREAKING	PLASTERERS
BEREAVED	HOUSEPLANT	REENLIST
BLOTTERS	INAUGURALS	REFRAINS
CAVEATTED	MONETARILY	SEPTICS
DEVOLUTION	OFFICIAL	
EARTHINESS	PARASITE	
FLOWER	PASSBOOKS	

Assorted Words 4

```
Q  Z  H  D  X  M  C  L  E  A  N  S  E  D  L
E  C  N  A  V  E  I  R  G  V  Z  R  D  U  O
T  G  N  I  Z  I  L  A  C  O  L  H  I  N  D
J  Y  G  N  I  M  I  R  G  C  Z  N  S  C  G
G  H  L  J  G  N  I  C  N  A  H  C  L  O  I
G  E  C  I  B  E  R  E  F  T  L  X  O  R  N
D  R  N  J  B  K  B  S  L  I  N  B  D  K  G
E  E  U  E  R  R  N  L  T  O  V  V  G  S  S
K  Q  R  E  R  C  E  B  E  N  E  F  I  C  E
H  A  R  E  S  A  F  T  N  S  A  Z  N  I  W
N  S  F  G  P  O  T  I  T  A  N  M  G  Y  F
P  L  X  R  B  M  M  I  X  I  M  F  R  H  I
D  Z  M  I  G  C  A  E  O  E  S  O  N  O  P
C  Q  U  I  N  T  E  T  L  N  R  T  E  H  D
E  L  G  G  A  R  T  S  G  Y  S  S  S  Y  Z
```

AVOCATIONS	GENERATIONS	QUINTET
BENEFICE	GRIEVANCE	STRAGGLE
BEREFT	GRIMING	TAMPERED
CHANCING	GRUESOMELY	UNCORKS
CLEANSED	HARES	YEOMAN
DISLODGING	LIBRETTISTS	
DORMANTS	LOCALIZING	
FIXERS	LODGINGS	

Puzzle #5

Assorted Words 5

```
N D G P X S S U O I D I S N I
A H X X S W E R B O X N W W A
S A T H D T D H O Y S O L A J
Q T C W Z E E E C O L T E N Q
U T N S I K P K W A L B M N T
I E M E F N R P N O T F M E A
N R V O M P E O A A R E N S R
T S Q F O Y A A W C L R D T T
E W F N E R A R M H I B A R N
R E H T E T G P T P C D L F E
R E G E N T S E N S E T N D S
H E F T I E S T D O N R A A S
G N I K C I S U M I N I A P H
P A N O P L I E S U R Q H G E
E N T I R E T Y W P G B P C E
```

AMPERAGE
BLANKETS
BREWS
BRIDEGROOM
CHINSTRAP
DETACHES
ENTIRETY
FARROWED

FLOORS
HANDICAPPED
HATTERS
HEFTIEST
INSIDIOUS
MUSICKING
NONPAYMENTS
PANOPLIES

PATCHWORK
REGENTS
SQUINTER
TARTNESS
TETHER
TWINE
WANNEST

Assorted Words 6

```
M  U  Y  L  E  T  A  I  D  E  M  M  I  G  S
T  H  G  I  E  W  R  E  T  N  U  O  C  W  C
B  O  Q  N  O  F  S  T  L  I  U  Q  P  C  R
I  S  G  N  I  L  F  Q  K  S  Y  V  O  P  A
W  Z  R  L  L  H  L  V  P  D  J  W  R  R  T
A  B  Z  Q  P  B  C  E  V  U  O  W  T  U  C
T  S  K  A  R  O  N  A  H  L  F  D  R  B  H
T  W  K  T  S  X  L  S  O  R  L  F  A  B  I
U  Y  A  E  I  X  H  E  Y  R  J  U  I  L  N
N  V  O  Y  W  S  F  W  V  B  B  H  T  E  G
E  Y  O  B  L  D  F  M  U  E  S  L  I  S  R
D  T  T  R  H  A  Q  F  O  N  D  E  S  T  M
I  X  Q  N  A  G  Y  B  N  P  O  S  T  S  V
S  E  I  F  I  D  I  M  U  H  P  Z  S  P  G
O  Q  H  K  Q  M  P  H  S  N  A  R  L  E  D
```

ANORAKS	HELLO	PUFFIER
ASKEW	HIGHBOY	QUILTS
ATTUNED	HUMIDIFIES	RUBBLES
BROACHING	IMMEDIATELY	SCRATCHING
COUNTERWEIGHT	MINTY	SNARLED
DEVELOP	MUESLI	WAYLAY
FLINGS	PORTRAITISTS	
FONDEST	POSTS	

Assorted Words 7

```
P  C  H  I  L  L  I  N  E  S  S  T  L  B  M
G  N  Z  Q  N  Q  Z  C  A  N  R  N  O  A  X
L  L  I  R  H  T  R  Z  S  G  I  N  O  J  A
X  G  T  M  A  L  A  R  I  A  O  N  S  F  U
P  A  N  T  H  E  I  S  T  R  A  H  E  A  W
D  G  I  P  P  L  F  A  T  E  F  U  L  L  Y
F  E  N  C  H  A  N  T  R  E  S  S  Y  T  V
O  F  H  I  U  D  I  S  T  R  A  C  T  E  D
O  K  B  C  T  G  S  I  G  N  B  O  A  R  D
H  T  S  G  N  I  E  X  H  U  M  E  S  I  P
L  H  N  H  Q  U  M  D  L  I  S  T  O  N  K
S  E  X  O  B  L  L  I  P  S  V  J  E  G  F
M  G  N  I  H  C  R  U  L  R  E  K  E  E  S
M  O  I  S  T  U  R  I  Z  E  E  V  D  I  I
G  N  D  J  S  N  O  I  T  I  R  A  P  P  A
```

APPARITIONS	HOGAN	PANTHEIST
CHILLINESS	KNOTS	PILLBOXES
DISTRACTED	LIMITING	SEEKER
ENCHANTRESS	LOOSELY	SIGNBOARD
EXHUMES	LUNCHED	THRILL
FALTERING	LURCHING	
FATEFULLY	MALARIA	
FRIZZ	MOISTURIZE	

Assorted Words 8

```
O  I  Q  J  H  O  F  I  S  H  T  A  I  L  S
N  O  T  P  Y  R  K  K  V  O  L  L  E  Y  S
X  R  A  S  G  U  E  R  G  W  O  E  F  U  L
E  E  H  H  I  R  C  R  K  N  W  U  H  M  A
V  N  A  A  E  Y  D  O  R  M  I  T  O  R  Y
H  U  R  M  N  W  S  T  E  E  R  T  S  X  O
A  M  D  E  I  G  Q  H  T  L  Z  I  T  W  S
R  B  C  F  C  E  N  T  R  A  L  I  Z  E  S
B  E  O  A  S  Y  F  I  N  U  E  R  J  P  B
O  R  V  C  P  S  H  A  R  P  E  D  O  T  O
R  E  E  E  A  P  B  R  X  I  L  B  H  J  S
I  D  R  D  B  C  L  V  D  O  F  Y  N  A  S
N  A  M  I  N  G  D  I  N  G  I  E  S  F  I
G  T  H  O  K  O  S  N  E  D  D  E  R  B  N
S  T  N  E  M  T  S  U  J  D  A  X  N  L  G
```

ADJUSTMENTS	FISHTAILS	RENUMBERED
APPLIED	HARBORING	REUNIFY
BETTING	HARDCOVER	SHAMEFACED
BOSSING	HYGIENICS	SHARPED
CENTRALIZES	JOHNS	STREETS
DINGIES	KRYPTON	VOLLEYS
DORMITORY	NAMING	WOEFUL
FIRING	REDDENS	

Assorted Words 9

```
Q S H Z D R S S S L Q K O N X
I K E C D E F E A T I S M R S
N N K V V E S S S N O S Q E H
S I Z U A E C S M R D H C S X
T G C K A P T I A A O B S J K
I H H A L B I O P G W D A P Q
G T R E T T O H E H N G N N U
A L O N F L Q E S S E B I E K
T Y C O N T O R T E D R Q W J
E D H R W W S R D I L H I N G
D Y H D Q B A S E R V T G N F
H G N I N G I S E R A A T I G
I N F U R I A T I N G T D A H
I G L G E E Z I C R O X E E B
W S Y L L A C O V I U Q E R B
```

BASER
BATTLESHIP
CONTORTED
DAVIT
DECIPHERING
DEFEATISM
ENDORSES
EQUIVOCALLY

EXORCIZE
GASSED
HEFTS
HOTTER
INFURIATING
INSTIGATED
KNIGHTLY
PAVES

RESIGNING
RETARD
SANDBANK
UPSHOTS
VETOES
WIGWAMS

Assorted Words 10

```
G  I  G  B  B  A  I  N  T  E  R  S  E  C  T
E  B  M  C  L  U  T  C  H  I  N  G  Q  O  P
M  L  I  I  G  A  R  R  U  L  I  T  Y  Y  R
B  X  L  N  C  O  M  M  A  N  D  I  N  G  O
R  R  I  J  O  R  D  E  N  W  A  P  S  A  T
O  N  T  U  S  I  E  E  L  B  W  G  U  R  E
I  O  I  R  M  E  T  T  C  E  R  N  G  A  C
D  R  A  I  E  I  X  A  T  C  S  K  L  S  T
E  M  M  E  F  D  S  I  L  A  A  S  I  H  I
R  A  E  S  I  N  W  C  S  L  H  L  E  N  O
I  L  N  O  V  T  C  E  U  M  E  X  D  E  N
E  C  O  U  O  Q  O  L  L  E  F  P  W  S  S
S  Y  T  I  L  A  R  O  M  D  Y  Q  P  S  V
T  V  B  I  D  I  R  E  C  T  I  O  N  A  L
P  V  R  Q  C  R  E  D  I  B  I  L  I  T  Y
```

APPELLATION	EMBROIDERIES	MORALITY
BECALMED	GARRULITY	NORMALCY
BIDIRECTIONAL	HATTER	PROTECTIONS
BLAMELESS	INJURIES	RASHNESS
CLUTCHING	INTERSECT	SIXES
COMMANDING	LEWDER	SPAWNED
COOTIE	MILITIAMEN	UGLIED
CREDIBILITY	MISCUE	

Assorted Words 11

```
E  N  I  N  T  E  N  S  I  V  E  L  Y  C  E
X  R  S  N  P  R  O  F  U  S  I  O  N  X  Y
S  Q  C  B  T  D  F  R  K  R  E  A  D  E  R
D  D  E  C  A  M  P  I  E  R  E  K  N  A  L
M  S  N  D  D  Z  B  G  N  I  T  E  E  L  S
T  H  T  E  B  L  O  O  K  C  F  F  K  H  M
P  A  S  A  P  S  A  O  T  K  H  Y  P  C  I
E  E  E  L  R  P  K  T  K  H  P  E  W  O  S
Z  G  D  I  A  C  A  C  I  A  E  N  S  M  C
B  G  D  I  Z  I  H  A  U  B  S  R  B  M  A
O  Y  V  O  G  O  D  Y  N  M  R  D  E  O  R
F  G  Y  C  L  R  O  M  N  M  H  O  J  D  R
D  I  V  E  R  S  E  L  Y  C  Y  C  J  E  I
M  E  Z  J  U  F  I  E  F  U  L  C  S  S  E
S  T  I  P  P  L  E  D  D  G  Z  K  J  F  S
```

ACACIA	DIVERSELY	PROFUSION
APPENDS	FINCHES	READER
BAZOOKAS	FLOOZIE	SCENT
BOTHERED	INTENSIVELY	SCHMUCKS
CAMPIER	LANKER	SLEETING
COMMODES	MISCARRIES	STARCHY
DIALS	ORBITAL	STIPPLED
DISLODGE	PEDIGREED	

Assorted Words 12

```
R  T  M  T  Z  P  E  T  T  I  N  E  S  S  R
P  E  E  S  R  E  T  T  I  S  Y  B  A  B  E
R  P  R  T  L  D  L  R  E  T  T  A  T  M  C
E  I  A  E  A  D  E  T  V  T  D  L  T  Y  O
P  D  K  X  D  G  E  P  I  S  V  K  I  X  V
O  F  H  Z  F  N  D  Y  P  T  L  B  T  Q  E
N  C  O  J  O  N  U  O  E  O  N  A  U  K  R
D  O  R  R  R  Q  S  A  O  B  R  E  D  F  S
E  L  S  E  E  R  L  G  L  L  O  P  I  E  S
R  B  E  A  T  H  V  W  N  E  F  S  N  G  M
A  Z  W  C  A  T  E  Q  U  I  P  P  I  N  G
N  X  H  T  S  P  Q  A  L  H  D  Z  Z  D  I
C  A  I  O  T  S  C  E  D  K  X  L  E  R  S
E  L  P  R  E  Y  W  H  O  I  S  T  E  D  J
M  A  S  S  E  U  S  E  Y  Y  D  K  W  G  T
```

ATTITUDINIZE	GELDINGS	PROPPED
BABYSITTERS	HOISTED	REACTOR
DISOBEYED	HORSEWHIPS	RECOVERS
ENTITLE	LAUNDERER	TATTER
EQUIPPING	MASSEUSE	TEPID
FLOODGATE	MEDALS	
FOREHEAD	PETTINESS	
FORETASTE	PREPONDERANCE	

Assorted Words 13

```
X  S  D  E  B  N  H  F  S  I  N  N  E  R  S
L  L  E  O  C  I  R  O  T  S  I  H  E  R  P
U  O  H  D  W  O  B  O  M  R  A  G  O  Y  C
U  V  C  P  A  N  S  T  N  E  G  A  E  R  Y
C  E  S  C  O  N  L  S  B  P  W  O  O  A  B
O  N  J  U  T  S  E  O  C  H  B  O  G  V  E
S  L  A  C  N  H  H  R  A  O  N  S  R  S  R
M  I  X  K  W  G  G  E  G  D  N  Z  M  K  P
O  E  K  E  Q  H  E  N  S  F  I  S  V  B  U
S  S  R  O  T  A  I  T  I  N  I  N  U  B  N
E  T  S  C  C  K  K  S  A  Y  Z  Z  G  L  K
S  T  S  I  V  I  T  C  A  N  T  H  E  M  S
E  D  N  U  O  B  E  R  N  L  O  P  I  O  V
S  E  C  N  E  R  E  F  E  R  P  D  M  N  B
I  M  E  T  A  T  A  R  S  A  L  M  P  E  R
```

ACTIVISTS	FOOTSORE	REAGENTS
ANTHEMS	GRENADE	REBOUND
CONSULS	HOMEWORK	SINNERS
COSMOSES	INITIATORS	SLOVENLIEST
CYBERPUNKS	METATARSAL	
DONATE	POSHES	
DOWNLOADING	PREFERENCES	
EMPTYING	PREHISTORIC	

Assorted Words 14

```
X  C  S  Y  Y  G  N  I  P  Y  T  E  R  F  K
F  D  Y  L  T  N  E  I  D  E  B  O  S  I  D
S  A  E  S  Q  I  V  R  Q  I  E  O  F  D  P
V  D  I  N  V  H  L  E  B  U  M  Z  I  G  A
F  I  R  T  O  G  N  I  G  N  I  R  C  E  R
A  S  Y  A  H  M  J  L  B  A  Q  E  V  T  T
E  P  E  L  O  L  I  V  Y  I  N  Q  T  S  I
V  O  E  G  B  B  E  N  S  E  D  S  A  Y  T
B  R  R  L  A  A  K  S  A  Q  V  U  N  Z  I
E  T  I  O  P  T  R  C  S  T  U  R  A  V  O
Q  S  K  U  T  M  N  O  U  L  I  O  U  F  N
B  Y  N  E  G  U  I  O  N  B  Y  N  T  P  I
W  X  Y  I  R  M  N  P  R  O  T  J  G  H  N
S  F  F  U  R  C  S  D  P  F  H  N  Y  B  G
A  E  B  R  X  K  K  C  A  S  P  A  N  K  O
```

AUDIBILITY

BUCKBOARDS

CRINGING

DENOMINATING

DISOBEDIENTLY

DISPORTS

FAITHLESSLY

FIDGETS

FRONTAGES

HONORABLY

KNAPSACK

OROTUND

PARTITIONING

PIMPLE

PURVEY

QUIET

QUOTH

RETYPING

RINSE

SCRUFFS

VEGANS

Assorted Words 15

```
Y  R  G  T  C  R  E  D  W  O  P  N  U  G  T
P  U  S  T  S  I  G  O  L  O  Y  R  B  M  E
A  S  E  E  G  A  G  T  R  O  M  C  X  M  D
F  Q  F  X  Y  Y  B  P  A  V  I  L  I  O  N
A  F  W  O  V  E  R  S  U  P  P  L  I  E  S
L  C  J  G  D  C  M  A  L  A  D  R  O  I  T
S  P  C  T  B  U  K  W  T  H  E  S  I  S  W
I  S  A  E  E  T  W  G  G  I  W  I  R  E  P
F  W  A  I  L  T  M  A  L  D  D  R  S  J  R
I  S  W  I  P  E  M  P  L  O  Y  E  S  M  Z
E  T  W  U  D  R  R  R  X  F  B  C  R  J  Y
D  Z  A  G  E  S  R  A  B  E  D  E  S  E  D
D  E  X  P  E  N  D  I  T  U  R  E  S  R  H
R  O  R  A  N  G  E  A  D  E  S  Y  G  G  E
G  N  I  Z  I  L  A  T  I  P  S  O  H  P  C
```

ACCELERATE	GUNPOWDER	PERIWIG
CUTTERS	HEREDITARY	SWIPE
DEBARS	HOSPITALIZING	THESIS
EMBRYOLOGISTS	MALADROIT	
EMPLOY	MORTGAGEES	
EXPENDITURE	ORANGEADES	
FALSIFIED	OVERSUPPLIES	
GLOBES	PAVILION	

Assorted Words 16

```
T  F  A  C  E  L  I  F  T  I  V  H  P  Y  A
C  N  E  X  O  R  B  I  T  A  N  T  G  E  N
X  A  E  B  X  M  T  R  A  N  S  M  U  T  E
L  I  F  D  U  R  P  R  V  E  Y  L  W  E  N
A  N  L  E  N  P  E  O  O  R  E  P  P  U  S
B  C  A  M  I  E  D  I  S  P  E  R  S  A  L
U  A  M  B  U  D  P  X  H  T  A  N  X  H  C
R  R  M  E  T  R  E  E  O  C  S  E  Q  I  N
N  C  A  W  L  R  K  O  D  T  T  M  S  H  L
U  E  B  G  A  P  I  I  L  O  D  A  L  E  W
M  R  I  P  Y  O  M  M  E  O  C  A  R  A  Z
S  A  L  Z  K  Q  B  E  S  R  G  I  M  C  B
N  T  I  G  H  A  B  I  T  A  T  I  O  N  S
D  E  T  A  R  T  S  U  L  L  I  A  E  O  K
W  J  Y  O  M  I  R  A  C  U  L  O  U  S  J
```

BALMS	IDEOLOGIES	SEAPORT
CODEPENDENT	ILLUSTRATED	SUPPER
COMPOSTS	INCARCERATE	TEMPLE
DISPERSAL	LABURNUMS	TRANSMUTE
EXORBITANT	MIRACULOUS	TRIMS
FACELIFT	MURKIER	
FLAMMABILITY	NEWLY	
HABITATIONS	SCRATCHIER	

Assorted Words 17

```
E  C  G  D  O  H  E  G  A  T  R  O  P  E  R
Z  Z  K  S  T  R  I  N  T  N  E  L  O  I  V
U  I  D  D  T  L  T  D  O  O  V  J  D  X  J
P  T  E  C  E  L  G  H  E  T  P  N  P  H  P
S  A  T  G  N  I  C  S  O  A  S  E  Y  H  Y
U  L  R  Z  E  D  N  H  W  D  W  E  E  W  I
B  S  A  T  I  S  E  N  E  A  O  A  M  L  J
S  S  C  T  I  B  T  C  A  R  B  N  Y  I  S
E  R  T  F  N  S  I  A  S  N  O  B  T  S  L
C  K  E  M  M  E  T  R  T  E  T  O  E  I  H
T  I  D  T  Y  A  D  E  V  I  L  S  T  D  A
I  Q  T  U  R  N  S  I  S  M  O  A  K  S  H
O  M  D  T  L  A  L  P  C  H  W  N  O  A  X
N  K  Q  N  I  X  G  M  X  C  W  F  C  C  I
W  P  L  A  N  N  I  N  G  S  A  F  M  W  L
```

ACCIDENTALS	GESTATION	SUBSECTION
ARTISTES	HIDEAWAYS	SWABBED
BONSAIS	LIMESTONE	TURNS
CHEROOTS	NANNIED	VIOLENT
COALESCED	ORTHODONTIA	
DETRACTED	PEELS	
EVILS	PLANNINGS	
GARTERS	REPORTAGE	

Assorted Words 18

```
Y  Z  G  D  A  E  W  C  L  D  G  D  K  D  W
H  T  R  N  R  D  M  R  R  E  W  D  J  A  B
C  H  I  E  I  E  Y  R  A  I  D  F  U  Z  M
B  I  T  L  L  Y  M  X  F  T  M  U  O  Z  O
D  D  T  N  I  L  R  I  U  I  H  S  B  L  N
I  E  H  S  E  B  U  R  T  E  X  R  O  I  O
R  O  B  T  I  M  A  F  E  S  Q  P  U  N  L
H  U  W  N  T  L  E  D  N  B  P  A  L  G  O
T  S  Z  H  L  S  A  L  N  I  K  R  E  S  G
N  L  A  Y  P  A  E  B  P  E  A  C  V  O  U
Z  Y  C  E  C  H  U  N  I  M  P  P  A  E  E
K  O  S  P  L  A  Y  S  I  N  O  E  R  L  D
L  F  B  T  N  A  R  R  A  A  N  C  D  E  B
P  E  R  T  A  I  N  E  D  C  L  A  S  Q  E
E  S  C  A  R  P  M  E  N  T  S  P  C  Z  Z
```

ARRANT	DEITIES	PERTAINED
BLACKBERRYING	DEPENDABILITY	PLAINEST
BOULEVARDS	DIARY	REMITS
CANNIBALISTIC	ESCARPMENTS	SPLAYS
CASUAL	HIDEOUSLY	WRATH
COMPLEMENT	LEASH	
CRIMSON	MONOLOGUED	
DAZZLINGS	PAINFULLER	

Assorted Words 19

```
Z  T  S  R  E  G  N  I  R  R  E  D  G  D  X
B  B  U  S  H  W  H  A  C  K  E  R  Q  K  P
E  T  O  O  K  W  S  T  R  I  F  L  E  D  D
N  H  R  A  S  E  D  M  S  L  T  F  O  L  A
N  I  L  O  U  E  C  R  R  I  H  C  D  B  T
A  N  F  L  T  Y  H  I  A  I  M  H  R  U  T
W  N  Y  E  Y  A  L  C  R  O  F  S  D  A  R
D  E  B  B  A  R  C  E  R  P  B  N  O  F  I
T  S  B  V  G  G  S  I  S  A  A  P  O  J  B
B  T  L  S  E  P  R  L  L  N  E  C  U  C  U
S  D  N  A  L  T  E  W  I  P  E  S  M  C  T
U  F  A  S  R  S  X  R  O  P  P  M  E  M  A
V  A  R  S  I  T  I  E  S  C  P  A  M  R  B
U  E  X  E  G  E  S  E  S  T  A  E  I  I  L
J  D  U  P  L  I  C  A  T  I  N  G  D  W  E
```

ALOFT	CONFIRMS	SLIPPED
APPLICATOR	CRABBED	THINNEST
ARCTIC	CUPBOARD	TRIFLED
ASTRAL	DERRINGERS	VARSITIES
ATTRIBUTABLE	DUPLICATING	WETLANDS
BUSHWHACKER	EXEGESES	
CAPRICE	IMMENSELY	
CLAYEY	RESEARCHES	

Assorted Words 20

```
E  L  B  A  T  C  U  L  E  N  I  A  N  Y  L
G  M  C  E  N  S  D  G  M  O  H  A  I  R  E
K  P  M  P  M  Y  V  E  N  J  B  Y  N  A  V
L  S  S  E  C  O  R  P  D  I  R  E  U  H  I
E  A  E  B  Y  S  S  N  G  I  L  A  U  L  T
P  Z  V  C  F  R  A  R  O  T  A  D  G  G  A
T  T  C  O  L  O  S  S  U  S  J  N  W  L  T
O  F  M  N  C  D  J  A  T  O  M  V  A  A  E
M  A  A  T  B  A  Z  R  E  F  F  E  D  R  D
A  D  B  R  I  Z  T  E  C  A  F  Y  T  E  X
N  G  P  A  D  Z  C  I  F  B  U  Z  V  S  M
I  Z  P  V  Y  L  S  U  O  L  O  V  I  R  F
A  J  C  E  L  E  N  C  O  N  V  E  R  T  P
H  K  Z  N  S  N  A  K  I  E  S  T  K  W  M
Z  E  S  E  Z  I  R  A  T  I  L  I  M  E  D
```

AIDED
ALIGN
AVOCATIONS
COLOSSUS
CONTRAVENE
CONVERT
DAWDLING
DAZZLE

DEMILITARIZES
DRAFT
FACET
FOURSOME
FRIVOLOUSLY
GLARES
INELUCTABLE
KLEPTOMANIA

LEVITATED
MOHAIR
PROCESS
REFFED
SNAKIEST

Assorted Words 21

```
T  S  A  S  G  B  M  R  M  W  H  G  Y  L  Q
I  X  C  D  E  L  T  K  E  C  A  F  H  R  B
D  D  M  I  Q  M  O  S  A  F  Y  F  V  E  L
S  I  B  M  T  J  I  W  E  O  I  M  S  X  A
W  E  S  W  A  E  S  T  W  G  N  E  M  T  S
E  F  R  I  A  R  H  E  N  O  G  O  H  E  P
T  O  Y  T  N  T  A  T  L  E  R  I  I  R  H
L  O  S  C  I  T  O  U  S  D  T  M  B  M  E
A  T  Z  Z  M  O  E  M  D  E  O  F  S  I  M
N  W  A  J  X  O  G  G  I  S  A  O  O  N  O
D  E  D  D  I  R  G  D  R  Z  G  N  G  A  U
P  A  T  C  H  I  N  G  U  A  E  F  A  T  S
L  R  S  E  I  L  R  E  V  O  T  R  C  O  L
M  A  L  F  U  N  C  T  I  O  N  E  S  R  Y
Y  V  S  E  I  L  O  P  O  N  O  M  S  A  F
```

ANAESTHETICS
ATOMIZERS
BIGGEST
BLASPHEMOUSLY
DIMWIT
DISINTEGRATES
EXTERMINATOR
FOOTWEAR

GLOWWORMS
GOITRES
GRIDDED
HAYING
HEIFER
MALFUNCTION
MARAUDS
MONOPOLIES

OFTENTIMES
OODLES
OVERLIES
PATCHING
WETLAND

Assorted Words 22

```
Y  H  S  A  L  F  M  A  I  L  B  O  X  C  F
X  S  Y  F  R  Y  I  A  U  N  Z  I  P  H  L
J  D  C  A  J  T  L  N  E  M  C  E  G  U  U
A  W  N  I  N  G  S  L  G  A  U  P  R  F  C
P  I  S  A  T  E  H  Y  A  E  R  G  N  R  T
R  T  X  E  L  C  S  H  H  C  R  T  C  U  U
E  G  A  R  I  Y  E  O  U  T  I  I  H  U  A
F  I  C  E  D  F  R  L  O  C  E  L  N  P  T
E  R  V  C  B  E  I  I  C  N  S  M  C  G  E
C  D  T  A  P  D  T  T  A  E  R  J  A  Y  D
T  L  E  P  A  O  A  E  S  F  U  U  H  C  C
U  E  X  P  G  X  U  E  P  U  R  Q  B  C  H
R  S  E  E  N  Z  L  D  D  R  J  W  U  G  L
E  E  W  D  I  E  L  O  N  G  A  T  I  N  G
T  N  L  G  N  I  L  L  I  M  W  C  X  B  E
```

AMETHYST	ECLECTICS	MAILBOX
AWNINGS	ELONGATING	MILLING
BURNOOSE	FAIRYLAND	PREFECTURE
CARPETED	FINGERING	RECAPPED
CURRIES	FLASHY	UNZIP
CYCLICALLY	FLUCTUATED	
DEADBEAT	GIRDLES	
EARTH	JUSTIFIES	

Assorted Words 23

```
U  G  B  S  E  I  R  A  L  O  T  S  I  P  E
K  S  R  O  N  J  Z  E  K  A  I  L  U  U  F
S  T  E  A  D  I  E  R  I  W  Z  R  G  N  V
E  R  O  M  R  E  H  T  R  U  F  I  S  D  N
E  D  E  M  R  A  H  C  H  N  C  I  E  I  E
M  S  H  V  F  T  R  I  P  O  D  Q  X  S  L
L  N  I  C  A  Q  H  E  P  C  E  G  R  G  T
T  V  E  A  A  E  N  T  M  R  O  M  A  U  L
D  U  F  K  I  H  L  V  C  A  C  E  P  I  A
S  B  T  A  V  L  T  C  O  B  C  C  T  S  Y
D  E  T  E  G  D  U  B  N  B  B  O  U  E  O
F  P  N  B  G  N  I  D  D  I  R  G  R  D  F
V  R  W  G  T  R  X  B  G  L  U  U  E  Z  F
L  Q  O  B  T  Q  A  C  P  Y  T  H  O  N  M
R  K  Y  D  N  U  O  B  H  T  U  O  S  F  M
```

BARGE	FURTHERMORE	SOUTHBOUND
BUDGETED	IPECAC	STEADIER
CAMERA	LAYOFF	TRIPOD
CHARMED	LAZIEST	UNDISGUISED
CHINS	LIAISE	
CLEAVERS	PYTHON	
CRABBILY	RAPTURE	
EPISTOLARIES	RIDDING	

Puzzle #24

Assorted Words 24

```
I E P Z S I E L I T N A F N I
Q G P O D E N O I T U L O V E
F D S X V E V B O R J T G U P
E R C E E C F A O D E Y E B O
Q I T E T X R O E A G K Z S U
C B F S N A P E R L R N C R J
E B N P U T L E T M Y D S I N
H L B O L O E U R I S L S Q W
T I Z S I L R R T I N D F C U
M N D Z L T E T F S M O L C A
H G A D A W O P A O O E U A G
W S Z T H D A M S L L P N S B
S O Q Y U B E H O S O D X T K
B S D Y L M Q B S R I D P E M
U D J W T Y T I N U P M I Y F
```

BALDS
BEDAZZLE
CASTE
CENTERFOLD
CRETINOUS
DEFORMS
DRIBBLING
EVOLUTION

EXPERIMENT
EXPOSTULATES
FLYLEAVES
IDOLATROUS
IMPUNITY
INBOARDS
INFANTILE
MISSPELL

MUTANT
OBEYED
PROMOTION
SHAWLS
WICKER

Assorted Words 25

```
J  R  S  E  D  I  R  O  L  H  C  D  F  M  U
D  P  E  J  R  E  A  E  H  C  A  R  T  U  L
U  F  D  Z  F  T  D  E  P  O  L  S  D  S  R
E  A  A  E  O  Z  C  U  H  S  D  C  E  I  P
E  H  L  U  C  D  G  A  L  F  R  S  K  C  P
G  T  P  G  Z  N  L  N  R  C  O  J  V  O  H
T  N  A  O  N  R  A  L  I  E  N  A  B  L  E
G  S  I  R  R  I  E  H  U  D  V  O  Z  O  R
M  F  E  R  E  T  R  S  N  B  N  O  C  G  T
X  Y  X  I  U  D  S  E  N  E  I  E  X  Y  Y
X  Q  V  M  T  T  E  A  D  E  D  I  T  E  B
I  P  I  R  T  S  S  F  T  N  C  Z  F  T  W
I  M  P  I  S  H  A  E  N  A  A  C  S  T  A
R  E  T  L  I  U  Q  P  G  O  C  P  X  W  B
H  F  D  I  E  R  E  S  I  S  C  G  F  O  L
```

ALIENABLE	CONCLUDE	PANDERING
ATTENDING	CONFEDERATE	PASTIEST
BETIDED	DIERESIS	QUILTER
BULLDOZER	ENHANCED	SLOPED
CALDRON	GESTURING	TRACHEAE
CATASTROPHE	IMPISH	
CENSER	MUSICOLOGY	
CHLORIDES	OVERACT	

Assorted Words 26

```
O  Q  S  E  N  O  T  S  M  E  G  F  A  M  V
Z  Y  K  B  I  C  A  P  T  I  O  U  S  T  Y
S  N  G  I  S  E  O  L  F  I  S  T  A  O  G
W  A  Q  U  I  E  C  L  Q  Y  L  J  G  M  P
B  U  N  G  I  N  G  W  L  Z  U  F  G  G  A
W  I  S  H  E  D  E  M  R  O  F  N  O  C  H
X  S  G  N  I  F  F  I  T  R  Q  Q  G  N  F
L  T  S  A  M  P  O  T  F  O  R  U  M  C  J
L  A  N  O  I  T  C  U  R  T  S  N  I  I  R
D  E  R  E  D  N  U  A  M  S  B  A  B  E  K
F  Z  N  K  F  L  L  I  B  E  R  A  T  E  S
Q  J  Q  K  S  Z  S  A  D  N  E  G  A  R  Q
M  R  M  E  R  I  T  O  R  I  O  U  S  L  Y
H  B  M  X  P  R  A  C  T  I  C  A  B  L  Y
C  T  N  E  I  C  I  F  F  U  S  N  I  K  V
```

AGENDAS	GEMSTONES	MERITORIOUSLY
BUNGING	GOATS	PRACTICABLY
CAPTIOUS	INSTRUCTIONAL	SIGNS
COLLOQUIES	INSUFFICIENT	TIFFING
CONFORMED	KEBABS	TOPMAST
FLITS	LARKS	WISHED
FLOES	LIBERATES	
FORUM	MAUNDERED	

Assorted Words 27

```
S  C  P  R  I  S  S  I  E  S  T  T  R  F  T
U  E  O  F  D  P  D  A  N  D  I  E  S  T  A
P  Y  I  N  S  E  A  S  H  I  E  R  E  S  S
R  B  F  R  S  S  N  T  D  C  S  T  Z  I  F
O  E  U  I  O  T  E  O  E  E  N  E  L  S  C
V  E  B  N  S  T  R  N  I  R  O  E  L  O  L
I  M  V  M  D  N  R  U  S  T  N  C  L  X  B
S  A  B  I  U  L  E  E  C  U  I  I  P  C  P
I  W  X  H  T  L  I  T  F  T  O  D  T  L  B
O  K  K  G  N  O  P  N  N  F  S  I  U  Y  Q
N  I  F  G  A  H  M  Y  G  I  O  E  V  A  C
E  S  D  A  E  H  T  O  H  H  F  H  R  B  C
D  H  D  Y  S  P  E  P  T  I  C  S  P  Y  O
V  S  L  I  T  T  E  R  H  U  D  Q  P  Y  P
I  I  J  A  N  O  I  T  A  V  A  C  X  E  A
```

ASHIER	DANDIEST	PATERNITY
AUDITIONED	DYSPEPTICS	PLUMBER
AUTOMOTIVE	EXCAVATION	PRISSIEST
BOLTED	HOTHEADS	PROVISIONED
BUNDLING	INTENSIFY	PYRES
CLENCH	MAWKISH	SLITTER
COEDS	OBVIOUSNESS	
CONSTRUCTS	OFFERTORIES	

Assorted Words 28

```
L  Y  S  E  T  N  E  M  G  D  U  J  C  D  G
D  D  N  N  P  R  E  P  P  I  E  S  T  E  S
T  E  E  N  O  B  D  E  T  A  D  E  S  A  X
B  N  T  W  U  I  I  L  O  Q  J  I  N  C  C
S  Y  A  A  O  F  T  C  B  D  M  D  K  O  O
A  M  R  S  T  R  L  A  Y  U  S  S  N  N  A
H  N  O  A  A  I  R  C  T  C  G  P  P  E  S
L  R  O  O  T  E  P  O  S  I  L  G  I  S  T
S  E  O  I  R  N  L  A  B  O  M  I  I  S  A
M  P  N  D  N  K  E  P  C  M  Q  I  S  E  L
K  I  B  A  N  T  A  M  W  E  I  G  H  T  S
Z  A  X  L  P  O  I  O  E  A  D  M  Q  O  S
G  T  Z  B  V  U  C  N  L  L  B  I  P  V  K
A  R  V  J  Q  Y  V  E  G  C  E  H  U  K  S
P  T  R  O  L  L  S  H  A  Z  I  E  S  T  M
```

ANOINTING
BANTAMWEIGHTS
BICYCLISTS
BORROWED
BUGGIES
CLOAKROOMS
COASTAL
CONDOR

DEACONESS
DECAPITATED
ELEMENTARY
FUNNY
HAZIEST
IMITATIONS
JUDGMENT
PANEL

PLEASANT
PREPPIEST
SEDATED
TROLLS

Assorted Words 29

```
O  W  G  N  I  T  A  I  R  U  F  N  I  P  T
V  Y  H  C  H  O  R  S  E  Z  I  M  E  T  I
E  S  B  A  E  S  E  E  N  J  O  W  L  S  R
T  S  G  N  X  H  S  Q  H  B  S  C  E  L  E
E  Q  U  N  H  B  U  G  B  R  F  E  C  V  S
R  U  N  I  I  T  M  Z  A  I  R  T  T  V  I
A  I  F  B  L  L  E  O  D  S  B  Z  R  O  G
N  C  I  A  A  X  B  N  M  T  M  Z  O  A  N
S  K  N  L  R  I  Z  M  O  L  E  F  N  K  A
T  E  I  I  A  I  L  A  U  Y  E  Z  S  L  T
A  R  S  S  T  D  R  K  T  B  A  N  P  K  I
S  E  H  T  E  E  S  M  H  K  V  B  I  R  O
S  R  E  I  C  O  M  E  S  U  V  B  E  P  N
E  Z  D  C  R  A  E  N  O  H  P  O  X  A  S
L  D  B  J  D  E  L  L  E  B  I  L  E  W  Y
```

BADMOUTHS	INFURIATING	SAXOPHONE
BAYONET	ITEMIZES	SEETHES
BRISTLY	JOWLS	SPINE
BUMBLINGS	LIBELLED	TASSEL
CANNIBALISTIC	NOTES	UNFINISHED
COMES	QUICKER	VETERANS
ELECTRONS	RESIGNATIONS	
EXHILARATE	RESUME	

Assorted Words 30

```
P  L  N  N  H  I  S  T  O  G  R  A  M  T  V
G  A  P  E  O  O  N  N  G  S  N  K  J  V  G
L  N  L  Y  R  I  D  R  O  N  R  I  H  C  B
A  A  O  L  L  D  T  E  E  I  I  E  V  O  C
M  Y  N  L  I  H  L  A  N  T  T  T  B  I  Q
E  V  Q  E  E  R  S  I  C  O  T  O  N  O  H
N  R  S  J  S  B  R  I  H  I  O  I  M  E  S
T  A  C  E  H  T  Y  E  T  C  F  T  B  E  R
A  P  L  S  R  O  H  F  U  U  D  I  R  N  D
T  A  U  W  G  I  M  E  B  G  R  N  D  A  H
I  C  E  S  Q  X  M  I  T  T  R  B  A  O  C
O  I  I  J  T  K  O  R  E  I  L  F  U  R  C
N  O  N  G  C  A  D  T  Y  R  C  M  O  A  G
S  U  G  Z  E  N  C  O  D  E  R  S  H  C  B
U  S  W  K  G  N  I  R  E  D  D  A  L  W  N
```

ANESTHETICS	DEMOTIONS	LADDERING
BELONG	ENCODER	LAMENTATIONS
BITTERN	FLIER	MIRES
BRUTISHLY	GRANDCHILDREN	RAPACIOUS
CARTOONED	GUERRILLA	RENTING
CATSUP	HISTOGRAM	SOBERS
CLUEING	HIVING	
CODIFICATION	HOMIER	

Assorted Words 31

```
V  N  E  T  T  I  R  W  D  N  A  H  W  Q  A
D  B  G  E  S  Y  S  L  A  B  E  L  I  N  G
P  E  H  N  I  E  G  T  J  H  F  I  F  Q  Z
A  H  H  D  I  L  S  N  D  J  X  A  I  I  N
R  D  C  C  E  T  E  S  I  L  W  I  R  N  B
T  S  E  R  N  R  U  B  A  L  E  F  E  B  P
I  C  Y  R  V  U  I  C  L  R  W  V  B  O  E
T  S  A  Y  E  M  A  V  O  U  R  E  O  U  R
I  P  J  L  X  D  F  H  E  R  L  A  M  N  F
O  I  V  T  C  M  N  R  D  S  T  D  B  D  U
N  N  T  E  I  I  U  E  O  E  W  C  S  M  M
S  N  H  G  S  O  U  L  G  T  B  A  E  M  E
T  E  S  N  I  E  K  M  U  N  H  M  L  L  S
P  R  S  T  O  G  I  P  S  G  E  Y  O  F  E
B  S  J  J  N  J  F  A  C  E  L  I  F  T  S
```

BELIE	FIREBOMBS	MEWLING
CALCIUM	FLAWS	PARTITIONS
DERIVES	FROTHY	PERFUMES
ELECTROCUTING	HANDWRITTEN	SPIGOTS
EMBARRASSES	HAUNCHED	SPINNERS
ENGENDERED	INBOUND	TOMBED
EXCISION	INSET	VELDTS
FACELIFTS	LABELING	

Assorted Words 32

```
R  U  C  V  P  R  I  O  R  S  S  W  L  F  R
H  M  S  V  R  O  Z  M  D  R  E  K  A  U  Q
W  E  E  T  A  I  T  I  P  O  R  P  N  J  D
H  K  I  S  N  C  Z  C  X  E  J  M  I  O  B
H  S  U  G  B  E  E  O  C  S  L  Y  E  M  R
K  L  S  F  H  U  I  A  N  I  H  L  G  B  E
G  O  O  E  T  T  R  R  G  O  R  G  E  U  D
A  S  R  A  N  Y  S  S  O  Y  T  C  N  D  U
D  H  T  P  K  N  D  E  T  S  E  V  O  S  C
U  E  E  Q  M  O  A  N  L  I  X  V  M  M  T
E  S  R  F  I  L  L  E  R  A  N  F  E  E  I
L  I  A  T  E  V  O  D  M  Q  N  G  T  N  O
S  R  E  N  N  A  L  P  Q  I  X  M  Z  G  N
F  F  A  S  T  I  D  I  O  U  S  L  Y  H  S
P  H  E  N  O  M  E  N  O  N  S  D  L  H  E
```

BURSTING	HEIGHTS	PRIORS
COARSENED	HYMNAL	PROPITIATE
DOVETAIL	IMPELLED	QUAKE
DUELS	MEANNESS	REDUCTIONS
FASTIDIOUSLY	OMBUDSMEN	SLOSHES
FILLER	ORIENTS	SORTER
GENOME	PHENOMENONS	VESTED
GORGE	PLANNERS	

Assorted Words 33

```
E  A  T  A  B  L  E  S  S  S  C  L  M  H  U
N  W  O  R  D  S  T  J  T  N  H  A  K  D  B
S  Y  D  K  B  I  E  A  J  E  A  T  E  U  W
U  Z  W  V  S  R  G  S  X  B  N  L  A  F  M
B  H  U  F  F  I  E  R  I  I  T  O  P  P  R
M  R  D  P  Q  U  E  U  E  M  I  P  R  M  M
E  B  E  D  U  T  E  O  U  S  E  N  M  O  W
R  K  S  L  L  S  Y  Q  T  R  S  D  G  V  C
G  N  I  H  G  I  E  W  T  U  O  U  Y  Q  I
E  N  E  T  O  G  B  D  U  D  G  E  O  N  M
D  Y  I  H  I  J  A  C  K  I  N  G  S  P  A
M  Z  U  X  M  K  L  H  W  J  O  X  O  T  E
O  B  I  C  E  Q  L  D  E  T  R  O  P  E  R
G  N  I  D  A  V  N  I  U  O  Z  F  D  I  M
I  X  W  Y  L  T  H  G  I  N  T  R  O  F  D
```

CHANTIES	EYEBALL	PLANS
CORONETS	FORTNIGHTLY	QUEUE
DEMISES	HAGGLER	REPORTED
DIGRESS	HIJACKINGS	SUBMERGED
DROWN	HUFFIER	TAXIING
DUDGEON	INVADING	VEXING
DUTEOUS	OUTWEIGHING	
EATABLES	PATHS	

Assorted Words 34

```
S  T  A  U  Q  S  S  I  S  O  M  S  O  R  H
T  I  E  X  U  B  E  R  A  N  T  L  Y  X  D
X  W  O  L  I  B  R  E  T  T  O  Y  U  L  C
R  N  I  C  K  I  N  G  E  K  V  H  E  J  O
S  E  D  R  T  N  I  M  A  N  L  I  E  R  R
P  E  C  M  M  L  A  Y  V  O  J  X  T  B  R
O  T  T  T  Z  R  R  B  E  Z  T  Z  O  O  E
N  O  N  A  U  C  E  N  S  E  R  S  P  M  L
T  A  L  A  U  M  Z  T  D  O  S  E  C  B  A
O  Y  R  K  V  N  S  V  R  Z  L  S  O  A  T
O  E  N  O  D  R  E  V  O  A  D  U  A  R  I
N  A  N  P  X  O  E  T  P  K  C  Z  T  D  O
I  J  Y  O  U  T  H  S  X  W  S  I  S  E  N
N  F  O  R  T  R  E  S  S  E  D  Y  N  D  S
G  S  Q  S  O  P  E  R  A  T  I  V  E  G  I
```

ABSOLUTES	FORTRESSED	RECTUMS
ANKLET	LIBRETTO	RETRACING
BOMBARDED	MANLIER	SERVANT
CENSERS	NICKING	SQUATS
CORRELATIONS	OPERATIVE	TOPCOATS
EAVESDROP	OSMOSIS	YOUTHS
EXTENUATES	OVERDONE	
EXUBERANTLY	PONTOONING	

Assorted Words 35

```
A  H  O  A  A  G  O  O  D  W  I  L  L  C  X
K  E  X  P  W  M  I  S  L  E  A  D  S  Y  N
Z  S  Z  H  G  N  I  F  F  I  M  B  S  I  I
S  N  O  I  T  A  N  G  I  S  E  D  V  J  L
H  L  C  D  L  G  L  I  S  S  A  N  D  I  X
I  C  F  E  J  A  N  S  S  Y  G  D  U  M  S
F  J  P  S  T  T  U  I  N  E  O  A  L  P  O
T  L  M  P  M  A  F  T  T  I  I  N  L  G  B
E  D  A  E  R  P  I  L  P  A  O  D  Z  P  R
D  C  N  T  A  O  C  L  M  E  N  L  L  E  I
H  B  I  W  F  C  E  M  I  Q  C  I  U  O  E
R  T  C  V  M  O  S  T  E  C  H  N  M  M  T
F  K  S  D  O  W  N  T  U  R  N  G  O  O  Y
F  O  O  T  B  A  L  L  E  R  E  O  J  C  D
F  K  R  E  D  H  E  A  D  S  M  D  C  K  R
```

APHIDES	FOOTBALLER	MISLEADS
CONCEPTUALIZE	GLISSANDI	OLDIES
CONCILIATE	GOODWILL	REDHEADS
DANDLING	LIPREAD	SHIFTED
DESIGNATIONS	LOINS	SMUDGY
DOMINATING	MANICS	SOBRIETY
DOWNTURN	MERED	
FICES	MIFFING	

Assorted Words 36

```
H  P  X  P  N  D  S  H  M  H  N  B  M  C  P
E  U  O  J  E  M  I  S  S  I  O  N  S  G  M
A  C  S  W  T  Y  D  A  E  I  Z  U  M  J  W
D  H  U  G  E  S  Q  E  G  L  L  Z  P  C  X
S  A  R  M  O  R  E  D  D  R  T  U  E  C  F
T  S  M  A  D  T  L  G  A  N  A  F  O  N  W
O  T  I  A  Q  G  S  J  N  J  E  M  I  H  S
N  E  S  L  R  C  H  E  M  I  S  T  I  H  G
E  R  E  Q  L  A  O  A  F  X  M  Z  E  N  S
S  K  W  R  Z  U  B  B  W  A  J  R  I  R  G
P  E  Y  O  O  Q  K  O  B  Q  E  A  A  I  P
P  V  C  S  V  C  C  S  U  L  R  D  G  H  N
A  F  J  C  Z  G  N  I  T  S  E  G  N  O  C
C  N  Z  R  E  M  A  E  R  T  S  D  P  T  N
T  N  E  M  E  R  U  G  I  F  S  I  D  Z  S
```

ARMORED	DISFIGUREMENT	PRETENDED
CHARMINGEST	EMISSIONS	SHIFTLESS
CHASTER	ENCORE	SKULL
CHEMIST	GHOULISH	STREAMER
COBBLED	HEADSTONES	SURMISE
CONGESTING	MARABOUS	
DEAFEST	MIZZENS	
DIAGRAMING	POWER	

Assorted Words 37

```
T  S  I  N  O  O  T  R  A  C  N  O  F  S  R
K  H  H  Q  D  Y  W  S  W  A  G  X  E  Z  S
D  E  T  T  E  V  A  C  O  G  B  M  L  G  M
K  A  Q  T  A  M  D  L  A  I  M  U  I  S  D
T  R  N  D  R  Y  R  T  P  L  G  L  C  X  F
S  T  C  M  T  T  A  I  H  Y  W  T  I  S  P
D  L  R  O  H  F  C  B  U  E  B  I  T  M  E
P  A  A  I  M  I  H  W  N  Q  B  P  O  O  R
R  N  U  Q  Q  B  M  S  G  H  S  L  U  D  T
E  D  C  O  N  V  A  L  E  S  C  E  S  E  E
P  N  O  S  E  Y  S  T  R  L  K  X  K  R  S
A  M  U  D  I  V  E  S  T  I  N  G  O  N  T
R  J  S  B  P  A  D  A  R  E  D  E  V  I  L
E  C  L  D  U  M  F  O  U  N  D  S  F  S  A
D  A  Y  K  F  A  T  H  O  M  I  N  G  M  X
```

BYPLAY	DRACHMAS	NOSEY
CAGILY	DUMFOUNDS	PERTEST
CARTOONIST	FATHOMING	PREPARED
COMBATTED	FELICITOUS	RAUCOUSLY
CONVALESCES	HEARTLAND	SQUIRM
DAREDEVIL	HUNGER	VETTED
DEARTH	MODERNISM	
DIVESTING	MULTIPLEX	

Assorted Words 38

```
J  S  R  O  T  A  V  I  T  L  U  C  D  U  M
G  H  F  D  A  F  L  N  O  I  T  C  E  R  E
Q  N  D  H  A  R  V  E  S  T  S  T  T  D  C
A  E  I  O  D  E  S  P  O  T  I  S  M  I  Q
W  C  S  T  O  S  O  U  N  D  E  D  N  P  F
C  R  O  L  E  H  C  A  B  W  C  F  B  S  L
V  H  C  L  A  P  T  F  Z  X  U  U  A  O  U
D  S  A  O  O  C  R  L  E  G  B  M  B  M  O
S  E  R  G  M  S  I  A  U  E  I  I  S  A  R
N  Y  C  E  R  P  S  M  C  D  C  G  T  N  E
I  H  Y  A  L  I  E  U  E  M  A  A  I  I  S
P  M  C  F  D  G  N  T  S  H  L  T  N  A  C
I  C  Y  I  Y  E  G  I  E  E  C  I  E  H  I
N  F  A  G  Q  X  N  I  N  D  S  O  N  R  N
G  W  X  H  U  F  E  T  G  G  P  N  T  U  G
```

ABSTINENT	COMPETED	FUMIGATION
ADULTHOOD	CUBICAL	GIGGLERS
AFRESH	CULTIVATORS	HARVESTS
BACHELOR	DECADENT	SNIPING
CARPETING	DESPOTISM	SOUNDED
CHAGRINING	DIPSOMANIA	
CHEMICALS	ERECTION	
COLOSSUSES	FLUORESCING	

Assorted Words 39

```
I A A D S E S P A L G H B X I
N G M V U P G G N I B B I J G
A R N Z D C O M E D I E S P F
R A F I L N C H O J R A O Y C
T M N X Z E U R S K L A T S U
I M H S J I N O I R U T N E C
C A E D G I H Y R T E K X L K
U R D K V O A C X G I B B T O
L I E N G O R G E S Y Q R C L
A A M E Z X C H P T L A U A D
T N S T O P P I N G A I L E B
E R E I N F O R C E S C V P S
Y K V C I N O I R T S I H E Q
Q E X P E R I M E N T I N G E
T N S S E N L U F T E G R O F
```

APSES

BARBERSHOPS

CATECHIZING

CENTURION

COMEDIES

CRITIQUES

CUCKOLD

ENGORGES

EVILS

EXPERIMENTING

FORGETFULNESS

GRAMMARIAN

HISTRIONIC

INARTICULATE

JIBBING

PLAYGROUND

REINFORCES

STALKS

STOPPING

Assorted Words 40

```
M  I  S  L  A  Y  S  C  B  V  C  Y  S  P  I
S  S  Z  I  C  S  L  E  I  A  S  U  L  R  K
N  I  F  A  J  X  P  L  C  K  D  A  L  O  K
O  E  A  P  P  R  A  I  S  I  N  G  E  P  P
R  M  E  G  X  V  E  B  H  H  V  G  E  O  H
K  Q  D  D  N  I  S  U  O  C  B  E  F  S  K
E  I  C  E  B  U  N  G  E  D  M  Y  D  A  L
L  G  N  I  T  S  U  A  H  X  E  D  P  L  U
I  E  V  G  U  S  K  F  O  R  A  G  E  D  T
N  I  Z  T  E  J  A  Z  Y  Y  T  S  A  H  Z
G  O  U  A  S  S  L  L  T  F  N  Z  L  G  I
Q  P  V  L  H  J  T  R  I  G  G  I  N  G  E
C  R  I  S  S  C  R  O  S  S  I  N  G  P  R
E  Q  Z  U  D  E  Z  I  L  A  R  T  U  E  N
R  D  G  F  O  R  B  E  A  R  A  N  C  E  I
```

APPRAISING	EXHAUSTING	MISLAYS
BADGE	FORAGED	NEUTRALIZED
BODEGA	FORBEARANCE	PROPOSAL
BUNGED	HASTY	RIGGING
CHIPS	HAZEL	SNORKELING
COUSIN	INGEST	
CRISSCROSSING	KLUTZIER	
DEVICE	LASTED	

Assorted Words 41

```
E  W  J  O  V  I  A  L  I  T  Y  A  B  R  G
H  R  D  J  P  H  C  L  A  M  I  X  A  M  I
Y  E  G  E  B  A  F  I  L  L  I  P  S  K  G
A  D  C  O  L  E  E  E  T  S  Q  K  F  B  A
C  E  V  R  N  L  L  Y  W  O  O  D  E  D  B
I  E  Q  L  U  O  E  O  E  H  X  S  K  C  Y
N  M  C  V  Q  M  M  N  N  K  I  E  S  H  T
T  E  C  L  A  S  P  I  N  G  C  G  S  O  E
H  R  X  P  X  C  Y  L  C  E  I  U  P  W  U
D  S  E  S  R  O  D  N  E  S  K  N  B  D  M
X  G  N  I  N  U  R  P  Z  C  A  D  G  E  S
S  E  T  A  R  O  T  C  E  P  X  E  M  R  X
V  H  U  R  R  V  C  O  I  N  C  I  D  E  R
C  A  Z  K  Q  C  O  H  E  R  I  N  G  D  H
G  Q  P  T  D  K  C  H  O  P  P  I  E  S  T
```

BELONGING	CRUMPLE	JOVIALITY
BUCKEYE	ENDORSES	KENNELLED
CADGES	ERGONOMICS	MAXIMAL
CHOPPIEST	EXOTIC	PRUNING
CHOWDERED	EXPECTORATES	REDEEMERS
CLASPING	FILLIPS	WOODED
COHERING	GIGABYTE	
COINCIDE	HYACINTH	

Assorted Words 42

```
X  V  S  S  E  N  I  S  A  E  U  Q  E  L  Y
M  U  D  X  Y  K  C  A  J  H  G  I  H  H  Q
W  H  M  E  A  L  F  I  S  D  E  N  R  U  T
N  O  B  X  T  B  T  A  S  E  I  N  N  E  P
R  M  L  I  R  S  X  N  L  B  S  C  L  E  C
I  O  C  E  N  T  I  M  E  S  T  I  V  P  R
F  P  T  R  G  D  F  L  V  G  I  O  S  Z  E
L  H  G  S  A  N  R  L  K  E  I  T  N  A  P
E  O  E  K  T  N  I  A  A  C  R  L  Y  A  R
D  B  R  U  I  N  S  V  O  G  A  M  I  D  I
H  I  M  W  Q  S  C  A  A  B  G  L  L  D  S
B  C  F  Y  D  O  P  I  E  R  P  I  B  O  I
S  L  E  U  Q  E  R  P  R  N  K  I  N  J  N
L  H  O  O  L  I  G  A  N  I  S  M  L  G  G
E  V  L  T  P  O  T  A  B  L  E  N  Z  C  D
```

BAROQUE	FLAGGING	QUEASINESS
BLACKLISTED	HIGHJACK	RAVING
BRUINS	HOMOPHOBIC	REPRISING
CENTIMES	HOOLIGANISM	RIFLED
CLIPBOARD	PANTIE	SISES
DILIGENTLY	PENNIES	TURNED
DOPIER	POTABLE	
FALSITY	PREQUELS	

Assorted Words 43

```
X  R  G  N  A  S  A  L  I  Z  E  D  B  C  B
Y  T  I  L  U  D  E  R  C  V  Q  W  F  U  L
C  R  B  R  U  B  A  P  T  I  Z  E  K  R  B
M  A  E  C  O  U  N  T  E  R  F  E  I  T  E
P  A  X  T  R  C  O  Z  P  U  H  T  N  A  R
S  H  B  J  U  E  D  A  B  A  T  E  E  I  A
E  E  Q  O  K  R  Y  P  M  O  H  F  T  N  D
C  W  I  U  L  V  N  D  R  E  B  K  I  B  I
U  P  S  R  I  I  E  I  E  E  B  F  C  T  C
R  S  T  Z  A  C  S  M  N  K  P  A  S  G  A
E  Q  M  O  A  E  K  H  R  G  C  P  D  S  T
S  J  C  B  V  S  R  I  E  Q  Y  A  E  W  E
T  W  H  E  E  L  E  D  N  S  F  T  P  D  D
K  D  B  F  Y  Y  F  R  E  C  K  L  I  N  G
R  L  A  C  I  M  O  N  O  R  T  S  A  G  U
```

ABATE	CURTAIN	QUICK
ABOLISHES	DREARIES	RETURNING
AMEBA	ERADICATED	SECUREST
ANODYNES	FRECKLING	UNPACKED
BAPTIZE	GASTRONOMICAL	WHEELED
CERVICES	KINETICS	
COUNTERFEIT	NASALIZED	
CREDULITY	PREPPED	

Assorted Words 44

```
U  K  J  J  S  P  I  H  C  O  R  C  I  M  Z
S  L  I  G  H  T  B  H  D  E  K  O  O  R  E
Q  E  S  C  H  U  M  O  N  G  O  U  S  B  C
W  X  I  G  O  C  M  T  N  E  I  C  N  A  Q
H  I  J  C  N  L  O  B  U  F  F  I  N  G  U
Y  E  N  T  N  I  E  M  G  N  I  K  I  L  I
C  C  R  F  E  E  N  S  E  N  S  R  D  S  N
A  T  N  I  L  L  B  R  L  L  Q  J  E  F  T
V  E  S  E  T  U  N  M  O  A  Y  O  Y  S  E
Y  Q  Y  C  D  A  E  I  U  C  W  S  E  O  S
W  I  S  Y  A  N  G  N  I  C  X  Y  L  B  S
J  Y  L  I  R  E  E  E  Z  L  N  L  I  B  E
E  C  N  A  M  O  R  P  Q  A  R  I  D  I  N
O  I  D  I  S  I  N  H  E  R  I  T  S  N  C
H  M  O  L  L  I  F  I  E  D  L  M  I  G  E
```

ANCIENT	EERILY	MICROCHIPS
BONFIRES	EYELID	MOLLIFIED
BUFFING	HERITAGE	QUINTESSENCE
COLESLAW	HUMONGOUS	ROMANCE
COMELY	INCUMBENCIES	ROOKED
CORNING	INFLUENZA	SLIGHT
DEPENDENCY	INLET	SOBBING
DISINHERITS	LIKING	

Assorted Words 45

```
I  D  U  C  O  N  S  T  R  U  C  T  O  R  N
C  M  E  I  O  G  D  Y  S  E  G  T  W  I  Y
L  S  E  L  Y  N  N  E  O  E  I  X  F  E  U
I  C  O  R  I  V  G  I  R  B  I  K  K  U  H
N  Q  S  W  O  A  H  E  P  E  Y  K  U  Z  A
G  T  I  Q  H  F  V  C  N  P  T  A  C  L  L
E  M  T  T  U  F  E  E  L  I  I  T  L  U  F
R  F  S  W  U  I  T  B  R  A  A  S  A  P  L
I  P  R  F  E  L  T  H  E  P  R  L  S  L  E
N  K  V  O  J  I  U  S  F  J  E  I  I  O  F
G  D  D  W  N  A  B  S  C  E  S  S  M  T  G
L  M  S  R  O  T  A  G  I  T  S  N  I  D  Y
Y  D  P  Y  R  E  P  O  L  E  V  E  D  J  A
N  A  E  B  Y  L  L  E  J  S  K  E  W  E  D
O  D  E  G  G  O  R  F  P  A  E  L  H  I  I
```

ABSCESS	FLUKIER	PLAYBOYS
ADMIRAL	FRONT	PREVAILED
AFFILIATE	GOSSIPPING	QUITS
BEFORE	INSTIGATORS	SKEWED
CONGENIALITY	JELLYBEAN	
CONSTRUCTOR	LEAPFROGGED	
DEVELOPER	LINGERINGLY	
FLATTERED	LUCKIEST	

Assorted Words 46

```
D N P S N A E B Y L L E J E B
N E T R A E H F G E P A J I M
O F B D I R E S L O S O R E A
V X B B E N A S E U B A Q Q L
E V I M O K T C I S X S B N A
R C S S S B C A S M A E E A D
A E N D N T S O B A E L S P J
C O D A E O S T T L M H T M U
H I G N N B I I I S E H C A S
I X W D I E M T S F E M V N T
E D S H L K T E C N L R D U M
V S A V R N N N S E O E F M E
E N W M S V O U I O F C S I N
X T G N I N O T N A W N F T T
V R E O D G N O R W M U I U E
```

ABASE

AEROSOLS

ATLASES

BOBBED

CHEMISE

CONSISTS

EMBEDS

FLUXES

HEARTEN

INFECTIONS

JELLYBEANS

MAINTENANCE

MALADJUSTMENT

MANUMIT

MASCARAS

OVERACHIEVE

PRINTABLE

RESTOCKED

STIFLES

UNKINDER

WANTONING

WRONGDOER

Assorted Words 47

```
S E S U S I M L B Y Z P K P O
Z G M A C H I N I S T S O O E
O F N I P S E H T O L C S P H
E N O I T A Z I N A M U H U L
S F D P R O V I D E D L E L C
B G E C R E O C S T R T R A L
R Y N X H D H L G U C U S T I
E N W I C H I T I N G R R E Q
S W E O R Q D S O G R A N D U
U N K M R E K E L R A L R W E
B Y K E E D M S T O B R U J F
M X N F K E I M Q N C D C R I
I D P P I P R L A S A A X H E
T S E V I A N F S H O L T Q D
S A S E T A L E R R O C S E I
```

BROTHERING
BYWORD
CHITIN
CLOTHESPIN
COERCE
CORRELATES
CULTURAL
DISLOCATE

FREEMEN
HAMMERINGS
HUMANIZATION
KOSHERS
LIQUEFIED
MACHINISTS
MISUSES
NAIVEST

OLIGARCH
POPULATED
PROVIDED
RESUBMITS
SLANTED
SUGAR

Assorted Words 48

```
S  E  V  I  T  A  C  I  D  N  I  L  P  W  S
M  H  C  S  X  D  W  J  M  D  J  S  L  F  P
U  A  J  W  F  R  I  N  U  A  E  E  A  X  U
I  D  S  G  E  X  X  S  H  S  S  K  C  V  M
R  Y  Q  S  C  S  B  K  M  B  C  T  K  V  O
E  S  P  R  E  S  I  C  N  O  C  W  E  M  N
M  F  I  S  S  D  P  S  K  L  U  H  T  R  I
A  G  O  B  B  L  E  D  Q  K  T  N  S  Y  S
R  P  N  R  L  A  P  F  I  D  G  E  T  E  D
K  F  E  F  C  H  D  E  K  O  O  R  B  E  D
A  J  E  E  N  I  W  O  L  F  E  B  Z  G  D
B  K  R  G  Z  T  B  O  O  G  D  M  H  L  R
L  X  E  U  N  G  Q  L  M  L  A  Y  P  U  B
Y  U  D  C  A  E  R  Q  Y  U  F  E  F  L  L
K  C  G  R  A  C  E  F  U  L  L  E  R  E  H
```

BROOKED	GOBBLED	REMARKABLY
CONCISER	GRACEFULLER	SPUMONI
DISMOUNTED	HULKS	
EAGLE	INDICATIVES	
FECES	MASSED	
FIDGETED	MASTERS	
FLOOD	PIONEERED	
FORCIBLY	PLACKETS	

Assorted Words 49

```
B  H  X  S  E  T  A  G  I  T  I  L  G  J  F
R  T  D  I  S  C  O  U  R  T  E  S  I  E  S
I  M  P  U  R  E  Q  B  D  U  M  D  H  Y  U
P  A  C  E  R  T  I  F  Y  E  N  U  S  I  W
T  Y  C  A  U  Q  E  D  A  V  W  G  S  N  C
R  L  S  C  M  W  C  S  O  Y  V  E  I  F  Q
O  B  U  R  O  E  P  F  N  B  W  K  P  E  J
T  A  P  C  E  M  S  R  M  A  M  M  A  S  R
U  F  E  Z  I  L  P  S  O  M  E  O  A  T  K
N  T  R  I  Y  F  L  L  I  C  J  L  G  S  O
D  R  E  Z  M  K  F  I  I  E  I  N  C  L  E
A  L  D  W  E  L  B  I  T  S  U  B  M  O  C
S  O  R  B  I  T  A  L  D  S  H  R  X  U  M
D  E  H  C  A  E  L  R  J  G  I  E  S  H  D
J  O  B  L  E  S  S  N  E  S  S  D  D  E  U
```

ACCOMPLISHED	DISTILLERS	MESSIEURS
ADEQUACY	GRUNGIER	ORBITAL
BODIES	IMPURE	ROTUNDAS
CERTIFY	INFESTS	SPEWED
CLEANSE	JOBLESSNESS	SUPERED
COMBUSTIBLE	LEACHED	
DIFFICULT	LITIGATES	
DISCOURTESIES	MAMMAS	

Assorted Words 50

```
Y  O  S  E  C  N  E  R  E  F  F  I  D  J  C
G  S  D  L  A  E  R  I  O  T  O  U  S  N  M
L  A  C  O  V  S  C  B  E  G  G  A  R  X  I
O  G  A  W  A  P  H  A  A  G  H  B  N  D  R
O  U  D  I  L  I  V  N  F  Z  S  O  Z  I  A
K  S  G  N  I  R  B  J  L  D  T  P  W  L  C
O  S  I  G  E  E  P  O  A  U  L  C  Q  E  L
U  E  N  D  R  S  Y  I  M  E  E  O  E  T  E
T  T  G  U  O  H  U  S  P  B  V  T  B  T  S
S  S  R  R  J  C  E  T  R  V  E  I  B  A  U
P  R  I  O  R  I  T  Y  E  R  L  R  S  N  E
R  E  L  A  B  E  L  O  Y  X  E  C  M  T  E
F  X  N  A  I  F  F  U  R  C  S  Z  L  I  R
Z  S  R  E  D  N  U  A  L  E  T  D  A  S  M
E  G  R  A  H  C  R  E  V  O  D  X  Q  M  P
```

BANJOIST	DILETTANTISM	MIRACLES
BEGGAR	DOCTORED	OVERCHARGE
BOLDFACE	GUSSETS	PRIORITY
BOMBER	LAMPREY	RELABEL
BRINGS	LAUNDERS	RIOTOUS
CADGING	LEVELEST	RUFFIAN
CAVALIER	LOOKOUTS	SPIRES
DIFFERENCES	LOWING	

Puzzle # 1
ASSORTED WORDS 1

```
Y C A R I P S N O C
  R T   L   S G I
  I E H   E   E E N M
O N I E   T   G L N I M
V K S R   T   N B T D U
E W S E   U   I A R U N
R E U B U C O L I C S C U E E
P L E Y O E       W U C F
L L D E V O U T N E S S O D
A S P I R A T I O N     D E
Y P   M A G N E T I Z I N G
    P       D
    D E L L E N N A H C
      N O I T A N I M A X E
      S E D U T I T L U M
```

Puzzle # 2
ASSORTED WORDS 2

```
G Y           D
S O R D E P O L E V E D
  R U E E E M B A L M I N G
    E G D F     L   L
      T I U R   W       O
R       F N R A A G       T
U         I G P Y R N       X
D           R   S S O I       E
D         F I N D S     T O W
E F L A S H I E S T     A M A
R M I R T H L E S S       O E S
S M O O R H C N U L E V E L D
          P O L I S H E R     F
R A T T R A P R E P U S
R E S P E C T F U L L Y
```

Puzzle # 3
ASSORTED WORDS 3

```
H O U S E P L A N T       R H
R   E A R T H I N E S S C E O
D E Z I T E H T S E A N A E U
E E W   G   T S         V N S
V R V O   N E T C       E L E
O O E A L Y I T O I     A I B
L   F F E F L T I L T   T S R
U     F R R D I N S B P T T E
T       I A E E R E A   E   A
I         C I B R A U R D S K
O B A S E L I N E U T Q A   I
N           A S     T E E P N
S R E R E T S A L P   S N R G
  I N A U G U R A L S   A O F
  S K O O B S S A P     P M
```

Puzzle # 4
ASSORTED WORDS 4

```
          C L E A N S E D L
E C N A V E I R G V     D U O
  G N I Z I L A C O L   I N D
    G N I M I R G C     S C G
G     L   G N I C N A H C L O I
G E   I B E R E F T     O R N
D R N   B       S   I   D K G
  E U E   R       T O   G S S
    R E R   E B E N E F I C E
H A R E S A F T N S A     N
      P O T I T A     M G
      M M I X I M     R
      A E O E S O     O
  Q U I N T E T L N R T E   D
E L G G A R T S   Y S S S Y
```

Puzzle # 5
ASSORTED WORDS 5

			S	S	U	O	I	D	I	S	N	I	
	H			S	W	E	R	B				W	
S	A	T		D	T	D	H	O				A	
Q	T		W		E	E	E	C	O			N	
U	T	N		I	K	P	K	W	A	L		N	T
I	E	M	E		N	R	P	N	O	T	F	E	A
N	R		O	M	P	E	O	A	A	R	E	S	R
T	S			O	Y	A	A	W	C	L	R	D	T
E				R	A	R	M	H	I	B	A		N
R	E	H	T	E	T	G	P	T	P	C	D		F
R	E	G	E	N	T	S	E	N	S	E	T	N	S
H	E	F	T	I	E	S	T	D	O	N	R	A	A
G	N	I	K	C	I	S	U	M	I	N	I	A	P
P	A	N	O	P	L	I	E	S		R		H	G
E	N	T	I	R	E	T	Y			B		C	E

Puzzle # 6
ASSORTED WORDS 6

	Y	L	E	T	A	I	D	E	M	M	I		S
T	H	G	I	E	W	R	E	T	N	U	O	C	C
		N	O		S	T	L	I	U	Q	P		R
	S	G	N	I	L	F					O		A
			H	L		P				R	R		T
A			P		C	E		U		T	U		C
T	S	K	A	R	O	N	A	H		F		R	B
T	W	K			L		O			F	A	B	I
U	Y	A	E			E		R			I	L	N
N		O	Y	W			V		B		T	E	G
E	Y		B	L		M	U	E	S	L	I	S	R
D		T		H	A		F	O	N	D	E	S	T
		N		G	Y			P	O	S	T	S	
S	E	I	F	I	D	I	M	U	H			S	
			M		H	S	N	A	R	L	E	D	

Puzzle # 7
ASSORTED WORDS 7

	C	H	I	L	L	I	N	E	S	S		L	
				Z		A				O			
L	L	I	R	H	T		Z		G			O	
		M	A	L	A	R	I	A	O		S	F	
P	A	N	T	H	E	I	S	T	R		H	E	A
D	G				F	A	T	E	F	U	L	L	Y
	E	N	C	H	A	N	T	R	E	S	S	Y	T
		H	I		D	I	S	T	R	A	C	T	E
		C	T		S	I	G	N	B	O	A	R	D
			N	I	E	X	H	U	M	E	S	I	
			U	M			S	T	O	N	K		
S	E	X	O	B	L	L	I	P				G	
	G	N	I	H	C	R	U	L	R	E	K	E	E
M	O	I	S	T	U	R	I	Z	E				
	S	N	O	I	T	I	R	A	P	P	A		

Puzzle # 8
ASSORTED WORDS 8

			H		F	I	S	H	T	A	I	L	S
N	O	T	P	Y	R	K		V	O	L	L	E	Y
	R		S	G			G	W	O	E	F	U	L
	E	H	H	I				N					
N	A	A	E		D	O	R	M	I	T	O	R	Y
H	U	R	M	N		S	T	E	E	R	T	S	
A	M	D	E	I	G					T			
R	B	C	F	C	E	N	T	R	A	L	I	Z	E
B	E	O	A	S	Y	F	I	N	U	E	R	J	B
O	R	V	C	P	S	H	A	R	P	E	D	O	O
R	E	E	E		P			I			H		S
I	D	R	D		L			F		N		S	
N	A	M	I	N	G	D	I	N	G	I	E	S	I
G					S	N	E	D	D	E	R		N
S	T	N	E	M	T	S	U	J	D	A			G

Puzzle # 9
ASSORTED WORDS 9

```
.  S  .  D  .  S  S  S  .  .  .  .  .
I  K  E  .  D  E  F  E  A  T  I  S  M
N  N  .  V  V  E  S  S  S  N  O  .  .
S  I  .  .  A  E  C  S  M  R  D  H  .
T  G  .  .  P  T  I  A  A  O  B  S  .
I  H  H  .  .  I  O  P  G  W  D  A  P
G  T  R  E  T  T  O  H  E  H  .  G  N  N  U
A  L  .  F  .  .  S  S  E  .  I  E  K
T  Y  C  O  N  T  O  R  T  E  D  R  .  W
E  .  .  .  S  .  D  I  L  .  I
D  .  .  B  A  S  E  R  V  T  .  N
.  G  N  I  N  G  I  S  E  R  A  A  T  .  G
I  N  F  U  R  I  A  T  I  N  G  T  D  A
.  .  .  E  Z  I  C  R  O  X  E  .  B
.  Y  L  L  A  C  O  V  I  U  Q  E  R
```

Puzzle # 10
ASSORTED WORDS 10

```
.  .  .  B  .  .  I  N  T  E  R  S  E  C  T
E  .  M  C  L  U  T  C  H  I  N  G  .  .  P
M  I  I  G  A  R  R  U  L  I  T  Y  .  .  R
B  L  N  C  O  M  M  A  N  D  I  N  G  O
R  I  J  O  R  D  E  N  W  A  P  S  .  .  T
O  N  T  U  S  I  E  .  L  B  .  .  U  R  E
I  O  I  R  M  E  T  T  .  E  .  .  G  A  C
D  R  A  I  E  I  X  A  T  C  S  .  L  S  T
E  M  M  E  .  D  S  I  L  A  .  S  I  H  I
R  A  E  S  I  .  W  C  S  L  H  .  E  N  O
I  L  N  .  .  T  .  E  U  M  E  .  D  E  N
E  C  .  .  .  O  .  L  E  .  P  .  S  S
S  Y  T  I  L  A  R  O  M  D  .  .  P  S
.  .  B  I  D  I  R  E  C  T  I  O  N  A  L
.  .  C  R  E  D  I  B  I  L  I  T  Y
```

Puzzle # 11
ASSORTED WORDS 11

```
.  I  N  T  E  N  S  I  V  E  L  Y
.  .  S  .  P  R  O  F  U  S  I  O  N
S  .  C  B  .  .  F  .  .  R  E  A  D  E  R
.  D  E  C  A  M  P  I  E  R  E  K  N  A  L
.  S  N  .  .  Z  B  G  N  I  T  E  E  L  S
.  T  E  .  L  O  O  .  C  .  .  .  M
P  .  S  A  P  S  A  O  T  .  H  .  .  C  I
E  E  E  L  R  P  K  T  K  H  .  E  .  O  S
.  G  D  I  A  C  A  I  A  E  .  S  M  C
.  D  I  Z  I  H  .  U  B  S  R  .  M  A
.  O  G  O  D  Y  .  M  R  .  E  O  R
.  .  L  R  O  .  .  .  H  O  .  D  R
D  I  V  E  R  S  E  L  Y  .  .  C  .  E  I
.  .  I  E  F  .  .  .  S  S  E
S  T  I  P  P  L  E  D  D  .  .  .  S
```

Puzzle # 12
ASSORTED WORDS 12

```
R  T  .  .  P  E  T  T  I  N  E  S  S  R
P  E  E  S  R  E  T  T  I  S  Y  B  A  B  E
R  P  R  T  .  D  L  R  E  T  T  A  T  .  C
E  I  .  E  A  D  E  T  .  .  T  .  O
P  D  .  D  G  E  P  I  S  .  I  .  V
O  F  H  .  F  N  D  Y  P  T  L  .  T  .  E
N  .  O  .  O  .  U  O  E  O  N  A  U  .  R
D  .  R  R  R  .  S  A  O  B  R  E  D  .  S
E  .  S  E  E  .  G  L  L  O  P  I  E
R  .  E  A  T  H  .  N  .  F  S  N  .  M
A  .  W  C  A  .  E  Q  U  I  P  P  I  N  G
N  .  H  T  S  .  A  .  D  .  Z  D
C  .  I  O  T  .  D  .  .  L  E
E  .  P  R  E  .  H  O  I  S  T  E  D
M  A  S  S  E  U  S  E  .  .  .  G
```

Puzzle # 13
ASSORTED WORDS 13

S	D				H	F	S	I	N	N	E	R	S
L	E	O	C	I	R	O	T	S	I	H	E	R	P
O		D	W			O	M						C
V		P	A	N	S	T	N	E	G	A	E	R	Y
C	E		O	N	L	S			W				B
O	N			S	E	O	C			O			E
S	L			H	R	A	O			R			R
M	I			G	E	G	D	N			K	P	
O	E			E	N	S		I	S				U
S	S	R	O	T	A	I	T	I	N	I	N	U	N
E	T					A	Y			G	L	K	
S	T	S	I	V	I	T	C	A	N	T	H	E	M	S
	D	N	U	O	B	E	R			O	P		
S	E	C	N	E	R	E	F	E	R	P	D	M	
	M	E	T	A	T	A	R	S	A	L		E	

Puzzle # 14
ASSORTED WORDS 14

			Y		G	N	I	P	Y	T	E	R	F
F	D	Y	L	T	N	E	I	D	E	B	O	S	I	D
S	A	E			I	V	Q					D	P
	D	I	N			L	E		U			G	A
	I	R	T	O	G	N	I	G	N	I	R	C	E	R
	S	Y	A	H	M			B	A		E		T	T
	P	E	L	O	L	I		Y	I	N		T	S	I
	O	E	G	B	B	E	N		E	D	S		T
	R	R	L	A	A	K	S	A	Q	V	U		I
E	T		O	P	T	R	C	S	T	U	R	A		O
	S			T	M	N	O	U	L	I	O	U		N
		N			U	I	O	N	B	Y	N	T	P	I
			I			N	P	R	O			G	H	N
S	F	F	U	R	C	S	D		F	H				G
					K	C	A	S	P	A	N	K

Puzzle # 15
ASSORTED WORDS 15

				R	E	D	W	O	P	N	U	G
		S	T	S	I	G	O	L	O	Y	R	B	M	E
	S	E	E	G	A	G	T	R	O	M	
F				Y		P	A	V	I	L	I	O	N
A		O	V	E	R	S	U	P	P	L	I	E	S
L	C		C	M	A	L	A	D	R	O	I	T
S		C	U			T	H	E	S	I	S
I		E	T		G	G	I	W	I	R	E	P
F			L	T		L		D
I	S	W	I	P	E	M	P	L	O	Y	E
E			R	R			B		R
D			S	R	A	B	E	D	E		E
	E	X	P	E	N	D	I	T	U	R	E	S		H
	O	R	A	N	G	E	A	D	E	S
G	N	I	Z	I	L	A	T	I	P	S	O	H

Puzzle # 16
ASSORTED WORDS 16

T	F	A	C	E	L	I	F	T				
N	E	X	O	R	B	I	T	A	N	T	
	E			M	T	R	A	N	S	M	U	T	E
L	I	F	D		R	P	R			Y	L	W	E	N
A	N	L		N		E	O	O	R	E	P	P	U	S
B	C	A	M	I	E	D	I	S	P	E	R	S	A	L
U	A	M		U	D	P		H	T	A
R	R	M	E	T	R	E	E		C	S	E
N	C	A		L	R	K	O	D		T	M	S
U	E	B		P	I	I	L	O		A	L
M	R	I		M	M	E	O	C		R	A
S	A	L			E	S	R	G			C	B
	T	I		H	A	B	I	T	A	T	I	O	N	S
D	E	T	A	R	T	S	U	L	L	I		E
	Y		M	I	R	A	C	U	L	O	U	S

Puzzle # 17
ASSORTED WORDS 17

```
. . . O H E G A T R O P E R
. . . R I N T N E L O I V
. D D . . T D O
. E . E . . H E T P
S A T G . I C S O A S E
U L R . E D N H W D W E E
B . A T . S E N E A O A M L
S . C T . T C A R B N Y I S
E R T . N S I A S N O B T S L
C . E . . E T . T E . O E I
T . D T . D E V I L S T D A
I . T U R N S I S . O A . S
O . . . A . . C . . N O
N . . . . G . . C . . . C
. P L A N N I N G S A
```

Puzzle # 18
ASSORTED WORDS 18

```
Y . G . . W C . D . . . D
. T R N R . . R R E . . A
C H I E I E Y R A I D . . Z M
. I T L L Y M . . T M . . Z O
. D T N I L R I . I H S B L N
. E . S E B U R T E . . O I O
. O . I M A F E S . . U N L
H U . T L E D N B . . L G O
. S . L S A L N I K . E S G
. L A . A E B P E A C V . U
. Y . E . U N I M P P A . E
. S P L A Y S I N O E R L D
. T N A R R A A N C D . B
P E R T A I N E D C L A S
E S C A R P M E N T S P C
```

Puzzle # 19
ASSORTED WORDS 19

```
. S R E G N I R R E D
. B U S H W H A C K E R
. T . . . S T R I F L E D
. H R . S E D M . . T F O L A
. I . O . E C R R . C . . T
. N . . T Y H I A I . R . T
. N Y E Y A L C R O F . A R
D E B B A R C E R P B N . . I
. S . . . S I S A A P O . B
. T L . . L L N E C U C U
S D N A L T E W I P E S . C T
. . R . . . P P M E . A
V A R S I T I E S . P A M R B
. E X E G E S E S . E I L
. D U P L I C A T I N G D . E
```

Puzzle # 20
ASSORTED WORDS 20

```
E L B A T C U L E N I . . L
. . E . D G M O H A I R E . E
K . . M . E N . . . . . V
L S S E C O R P D I . . . I
E A . . S N G I L A . . T
P . V C . R . A D . G A
T . C O L O S S U S . W L T
O F . N C D . . O . . A E
M . A T A . R E F F E D R D
A . R . Z T E C A F . E
N . A D Z . I . . . S
I . V Y L S U O L O V I R F
A . E . E C O N V E R T
. N S N A K I E S T
. S E Z I R A T I L I M E D
```

Puzzle # 21
ASSORTED WORDS 21

	S		S	G			R			H				
		C	D	E	L	T		E		A				B
D			I		M	O	S		F	Y			E	L
S	I		M	T		I	W	E		I			X	A
W	E	S	W	A	E	S	T	W	G	N	E		T	S
E	F	R	I	A	R	H	E	N	O	G		H	E	P
T	O		T	N	T	A	T	L	E	R	I		R	H
L	O			I	T	O	U	S	D	T	M	B	M	E
A	T				O	E	M	D	E	O	F	S	I	M
N	W				G	G	I	S	A	O	O	N	O	
D	E	D	D	I	R	G		R	Z		N		A	U
P	A	T	C	H	I	N	G		A	E		A	T	S
	R	S	E	I	L	R	E	V	O	T	R		O	L
M	A	L	F	U	N	C	T	I	O	N	E	S	R	Y
	S	E	I	L	O	P	O	N	O	M	S			

Puzzle # 22
ASSORTED WORDS 22

Y	H	S	A	L	F	M	A	I	L	B	O	X		F
	S				Y	I		U	N	Z	I	P		L
	D	C			T	L	N	E		C				U
A	W	N	I	N	G	S	L	G	A	U				C
P		S	A	T	E		Y	A	E	R				T
R	T		E	L	C	S		H	C	R	T			U
E	G	A	R	I	Y	E	O		T	I	I	H		A
F	I		E	D	F	R	L	O		E	L	N		T
E	R		C	B	E	I	I	C	N	S	M	C	G	E
C	D		A		D	T	T	A	E	R		A	Y	D
T	L		P		A	E	S	F		U				C
U	E		P		E	P	U			B				
R	S		E			D	R	J						
E			D		E	L	O	N	G	A	T	I	N	G
		G	N	I	L	L	I	M		C				

Puzzle # 23
ASSORTED WORDS 23

			S	E	I	R	A	L	O	T	S	I	P	E
			N					A				U		
S	T	E	A	D	I	E	R			Z			N	
E	R	O	M	R	E	H	T	R	U	F	I		D	
E	D	E	M	R	A	H	C					E	I	
	S	V		T	R	I	P	O	D			S		
		I		A			E		C		R	G	T	
		A		E			M	R		A	U	L		
		I		L		C	A	C	E	P	I	A		
		L		C		B	C			T	S	Y		
D	E	T	E	G	D	U	B		B			U	E	O
		G	N	I	D	D	I	R			R	D	F	
		R				L				E		F		
		A		P	Y	T	H	O	N					
		D	N	U	O	B	H	T	U	O	S			

Puzzle # 24
ASSORTED WORDS 24

			S	I	E	L	I	T	N	A	F	N	I	
			D	E	N	O	I	T	U	L	O	V	E	
	D	S			E	V	B		R					
R	C	E	E	C	F	A	O	D	E	Y	E	B	O	
I		E	T	X	R	O	E	A		K				
B		S	N	A	P	E	R	L	R		C			
E	B	N		U	T	L	E	T	M	Y	D		I	
L		O	L	O	E	U	R	I	S	L	S		W	
T	I	Z	S	I	L	R	R	T	I	N	D	F		
N		Z	L	T	E	T	F	S	M	O	L	C		
G	A		A	W	O	P	A	O	O	E	U	A		
	T		D	A	M	S	L	L	P	N	S	B		
		U		E	H	O	S	O	D	X	T			
		M		B	S	R	I	D		E				
		Y	T	I	N	U	P	M	I					

Puzzle # 25
ASSORTED WORDS 25

```
R S E D I R O L H C . . M
. E . . E A E H C A R T U
. . D Z . T D E P O L S . S
E . . E O . C U . . D . I
E H . . C D G A L . R . C
G T P G . N L N R C O . O
T N A O N R A L I E N A B L E
. S I R R I E H U D V O . O
. . E R E T R S N B N O C G
. . . I U D S E N E . E . Y
. . . . T T E A D E D I T E B
. . . . S S F T N C . . T
I M P I S H A E N A A . . A
R E T L I U Q P G O C P
. D I E R E S I S C
```

Puzzle # 26
ASSORTED WORDS 26

```
. . S E N O T S M E G
. . . C A P T I O U S
S N G I S E O L F I S T A O G
. . . . L . . L
B U N G I N G . L . . F
W I S H E D E M R O F N O C
. . G N I F F I T . Q
L T S A M P O T F O R U M
L A N O I T C U R T S N I
D E R E D N U A M S B A B E K
. . K . . L I B E R A T E S
. . . S . S A D N E G A
. . M E R I T O R I O U S L Y
. . . P R A C T I C A B L Y
T N E I C I F F U S N I
```

Puzzle # 27
ASSORTED WORDS 27

```
S C P R I S S I E S T
. E O . D P D A N D I E S T
P Y I N S E A S H I E R
R B F R S S N T D C . T
O E U I O T E O E E N . L
V E B N S T R N I R O E . O
I M V M D N R U S T N C L . B
S A . I U L E E C U I I . C
I W . . T L I T F T O D T
O K . . O P N N F S I U Y
N I . . . M . G I O E V A
E S D A E H T O H . . R B
D H D Y S P E P T I C S . Y O
. S L I T T E R . U . . . P
. . N O I T A V A C X E
```

Puzzle # 28
ASSORTED WORDS 28

```
. Y S . T N E M G D U J . D
D D N N P R E P P I E S T E
T E E N O B D E T A D E S A
. N T W U I I . . . . C C
S Y A A O F T C B . . O O
A M R S T R . A Y U . . N A
N O A A I R . T C G . . E S
L R O O T E P O . I L G . S T
. E O I R N L A B . M I I S A
. N D N K E P C . . I S E L
. B A N T A M W E I G H T S
. . P O I O E . D . . . . S
. . . C N L L
. . . . G C E
T R O L L S H A Z I E S T
```

```
    G N I T A I R U F N I
V   C     R S E Z I M E T I
E S   A E   J O W L S R
T   G N X   S   B S   E   E
E Q U N H   U   B R   E C   S
R U N I I T M   A I     T   I
A I F B L L E   D S     R O G
N C I A A   B N M T     O   N
S K N L R     M O L     N   A
T E I I A     U Y E   S   T
A R S S T     T B A N     I
S E H T E E S H   B I   O
S   E I C O M E S     P N
E   D C     E N O H P O X A S
L       D E L L E B I L
```

```
    N N H I S T O G R A M
G A   E O   N N G S N
L N L Y R I D R O N R I
A A O L L D T E E I I E V
M   N L I H L A N T T T B I
E   E E R S I C O T O N O H
N R S   S B R I H I O I M E S
T A C E H T   E T C F T B E R
A P L   R O H   U U D I R   D
T A U   I M E   G R N D A
I C E S   M I T     B A O C
O I I   T   R E I L F   R C
N O N   A     R C       G
S U G   E N C O D E R S
  S     G N I R E D D A L
```

```
  N E T T I R W D N A H
D   G E S   S L A B E L I N G
P E   N I E G T     F
A   H D I L S N D     I I
R D   C E T E S I L     R N
T   E   N R U B A L E   E B P
I C   R   U I C   R W V B O E
T S A   E   A V O   R E O U R
I P   L X D F H E R   A M N F
O I     C   N R D S T   B D U
N N     I I   E O E W C S M M
S N     S   U   G T B A E   E
T E S N I   M   N H M L L S
  R S T O G I P S   E Y O F E
  S     N   F A C E L I F T S
```

```
        P R I O R S
H   S       M     E K A U Q
  E E T A I T I P O R P
    I   N     C   E       O
  S   G B E   O     L     M R
  L S   H U I A       L G B E
  O O E   T R R G O R G E U D
  S R   N   S S O       N D U
D H T     N D E T S E V O S C
U E E       A N L I     M M T
E S R F I L L E R A N     E E I
L I A T E V O D M   N G   N O N
S R E N N A L P     M       N
  F A S T I D I O U S L Y   S
P H E N O M E N O N S     H
```

Puzzle # 33
ASSORTED WORDS 33

E	A	T	A	B	L	E	S	S	S	C			
N	W	O	R	D	S	T		T	N	H			
S					I	E	A		E	A	T		
U				G	S	X		N	L	A			
B	H	U	F	F	I	E	R	I	I	T	O	P	P
M	R		Q	U	E	U	E	M	I		R		
E		E	D	U	T	E	O	U	S	E	N		O
R		L		Y				S	D	G		C	
G	N	I	H	G	I	E	W	T	U	O			
E	N		G	B	D	U	D	G	E	O	N		
D		I	H	I	J	A	C	K	I	N	G	S	
		X		L	H								
		E		L	D	E	T	R	O	P	E	R	
G	N	I	D	A	V	N	I						
		Y	L	T	H	G	I	N	T	R	O	F	

Puzzle # 34
ASSORTED WORDS 34

S	T	A	U	Q	S	S	I	S	O	M	S	O	
	E	X	U	B	E	R	A	N	T	L	Y		
			L	I	B	R	E	T	T	O			C
R	N	I	C	K	I	N	G	E					O
S	E				N		M	A	N	L	I	E	R	R
P	E	C			A		V				T	B	R
O	T	T		R		B	E				O	O	E
N	N	A	U	C	E	N	S	E	R	S	P	M	L
T		A	U	M		T	D	O			C	B	A
O		V	N	S		R		L		O	A	T	
O	E	N	O	D	R	E	V	O	A		U	A	R	I
N				E	T	P		C		T	D	O	
I	Y	O	U	T	H	S	X			I	S	E	N
N	F	O	R	T	R	E	S	S	E	D		N	D	S
G			O	P	E	R	A	T	I	V	E	G	

Puzzle # 35
ASSORTED WORDS 35

		A		G	O	O	D	W	I	L	L	
	E	P		M	I	S	L	E	A	D	S	
		Z	H	G	N	I	F	F	I	M		
S	N	O	I	T	A	N	G	I	S	E	D	
H			D	L	G	L	I	S	S	A	N	D	I
I			E	A	N	S	S	Y	G	D	U	M	S
F		S	T		U	I	N	E		A		O
T		M		A	F	T	T	I	I	N		B
E	D	A	E	R	P	I	L	P	A	O	D		R
D		N		C	L		E	N	L	L		I
		I		E	M	I		C	I		O	E
	C			S		E	C		N	M		T
	S	D	O	W	N	T	U	R	N	G	O	O	Y
F	O	O	T	B	A	L	L	E	R	E	O		C	D
	R	E	D	H	E	A	D	S			D	C

Puzzle # 36
ASSORTED WORDS 36

H	P			D	S	H	M	
E	O		E	M	I	S	S	I	O	N	S
A	C	S	W	T		D	A	E	I	Z
D	H	U		E	S		E	G	L	L	Z
S	A	R	M	O	R	E	D	D	R	T	U	E
T	S	M			T		G		N	A	F	O	N
O	T	I	A			S		N		E	M	I	H	S
N	E	S	L	R	C	H	E	M	I	S	T	I	H	G
E	R	E		L	A	O		F		M		E	N	S
S			R		U	B	B		A		R		R	G
		O		K	O	B		E		A	P
			C		S	U	L		D		H
		G	N	I	T	S	E	G	N	O	C
		R	E	M	A	E	R	T	S	D
T	N	E	M	E	R	U	G	I	F	S	I	D

Puzzle # 37
ASSORTED WORDS 37

```
T S I N O O T R A C     F
  H     D Y       A   E
D E T T E V A     G   M L
  A   A M D L   I   U I
  R   R   R   P L   L C
  T C   T   A I H Y   T I   P
  L R O H   C   U   B I T M E
P A A   M   H   N Q   P O O R
R N U     B M   G   S L U D T
E D C O N V A L E S C E S E E
P N O S E Y S T R     X   R S
A   U D I V E S T I N G   N T
R   S     D A R E D E V I L
E   L D U M F O U N D S   S
D   Y   F A T H O M I N G M
```

Puzzle # 38
ASSORTED WORDS 38

```
  S R O T A V I T L U C
G       F   N O I T C E R E
  N D H A R V E S T S   D
    I O D E S P O T I S M I
  C S T O S O U N D E D   P F
C R O L E H C A B   C F   S L
  H C L A P T   U U A O U
D S A O O C R L   B M B M O
S E R G M S I A U   I I S A R
N   C E R P S M C D C G T N E
I   A L I E U E   A A I I S
P   D G N T S H L T N A C
I   E G I E E C I E   I
N     N I N D S O N   N
G     T G G   N T   G
```

Puzzle # 39
ASSORTED WORDS 39

```
I     S E S P A
N G   P   G N I B B I J
A R N D C O M E D I E S
R A   I   N C H       C
T M   Z U R S K L A T S U
I M     I N O I R U T N E C
C A   H   R T E       K
U R   C G I B       O
L I E N G O R G E S Y Q R L
A A       T L A U A D
T N S T O P P I N G A I L E B
E R E I N F O R C E S C V P S
    C I N O I R T S I H E
  E X P E R I M E N T I N G
  S S E N L U F T E G R O F
```

Puzzle # 40
ASSORTED WORDS 40

```
M I S L A Y S   B       P
S         S E   A       R
N         P   C   D     O
O   A P P R A I S I N G   P
R         B H   V   E O
K   D   N I S U O C   E   S K
E I   E B U N G E D     D A L
L G N I T S U A H X E     L U
I E   G   S   F O R A G E D T
N   Z   E   A     Y T S A H Z
G   G   A   S   L       I
      H     T R I G G I N G E
C R I S S C R O S S I N G   R
      D E Z I L A R T U E N
    F O R B E A R A N C E
```

Puzzle # 41
ASSORTED WORDS 41

```
E   J O V I A L I T Y     G
H R D     C L A M I X A M I
Y E G E B   F I L L I P S   G
A D C O L E E   T       A
C E   R N L L Y W O O D E D B
I E   U O E O E   X     C Y
N M     M M N N K   E   H T
T E C L A S P I N G C     O E
H R       L C E I U   W
  S E S R O D N E S K N B D
  G N I N U R P   C A D G E S
S E T A R O T C E P X E   R
      C O I N C I D E
      C O H E R I N G D
      C H O P P I E S T
```

Puzzle # 42
ASSORTED WORDS 42

```
  S S E N I S A E U Q
    D   Y K C A J H G I H
  H E   L F   S D E N R U T
  O   T   T A S E I N N E P
R M     S   N L   S
I O C E N T I M E S   I     R
F P     G D F L   G I   S   E
L H     N R L K E I T N A P
E O E     I A A C   L Y   R
D B R U I N S V O G A   I   I
  I   Q       A B G L   D S
  C   D O P I E R P I B   I
S L E U Q E R P     I N   N
H O O L I G A N I S M L G G
    P O T A B L E     C
```

Puzzle # 43
ASSORTED WORDS 43

```
    N A S A L I Z E D   C
Y T I L U D E R C       U
  R   B A P T I Z E K R
    E C O U N T E R F E I T E
  A   T   C O       N A R
S   B U E D A B A T E E I A
E E Q O   R Y P M     T N D
C   I U L V N D R E   I   I
U   R I I E I E E B   C   C
R     A C S   N K P A S   A
E     E K H   G C P       T
S     S R   E     A E     E
T W H E E L E D   S     P D D
        F R E C K L I N G
  L A C I M O N O R T S A G U
```

Puzzle # 44
ASSORTED WORDS 44

```
    S P I H C O R C I M
S L I G H T B   D E K O O R
  E   C H U M O N G O U S
    I G O C   T N E I C N A Q
H I   C N L O B U F F I N G U
Y E N T N I E M G N I K I L I
  C R F E E N S E   R     N
    N I L L B R L L   E   T
    E T U N M O A Y   Y S E
      D A E I U C W   E O S
      N G N   C   L B S
  Y L I R E E E Z   N   I B E
E C N A M O R P   A   I D I N
    D I S I N H E R I T S N C
M O L L I F I E D     G E
```

Puzzle # 45
ASSORTED WORDS 45

```
    D   C O N S T R U C T O R
      E   O G D Y S E
  L   E L   N N E O E I
  I     R I   G I R B I K
  N     O A   E P E Y K U
  G     Q   F V   N P T A C L
  E       U F E E L I I T L U F
  R F       I   B R A A S A P L
  I   R     L T     P R L S L
  N     O   I   S       I I O F
  G         N A B S C E S S M T G
  L     S R O T A G I T S N I D Y
  Y       R E P O L E V E D     A
  N A E B Y L L E J S K E W E D
    D E G G O R F P A E L
```

Puzzle # 46
ASSORTED WORDS 46

```
  D   P S N A E B Y L L E J
  N E T R A E H F   E           M
  O   B D I R E S L O S O R E A
  V     B E N A S E U   A       L
  E       O K T C I S X   B     A
  R C S S S B C A S M A E   A D
  A E N D N T S O B A E L S     J
  C D A E O S T T L M H T M     U
  H   N N B I I I S E   C A S
  I     I E M T S F E       N T
  E       K T E C N L R     U M
  V         N N   E O E   M E
  E           U I   F C S I N
    G N I N O T N A W N     T T
    R E O D G N O R W M   I
```

Puzzle # 47
ASSORTED WORDS 47

```
  S E S U S I M             K P
    G M A C H I N I S T S O O
      N I P S E H T O L C S P
      N O I T A Z I N A M U H U
  S     P R O V I D E D L E L
  B G E C R E O C S     T R A L
  R Y N     D H L   U   U S T I
  E N W I C H I T I N G R   E Q
  S   E O R   D S O G   A   D U
  U     M R E   E L R A L R   E
  B       E D M   T O B R     F
  M         E   M   N C   C   I
  I           R   A   A A   H E
  T S E V I A N F   H   L T   D
  S   S E T A L E R R O C S E
```

Puzzle # 48
ASSORTED WORDS 48

```
  S E V I T A C I D N I   P   S
  M       D     M       L   P
    A     F   I     A   A   U
      S   E     S     S   C M
  R     S C     M       T K O
  E P R E S I C N O C     E   N
  M F I   S D   S K L U H T R I
  A G O B B L E D       N S   S
  R N R       F I D G E T E D
  K E   C   D E K O O R B E
  A E     I   O L             D
  B R     B   O G
  L E       L   L A
  Y D         Y   F E
    G R A C E F U L L E R
```

Puzzle # 49
ASSORTED WORDS 49

Puzzle # 50
ASSORTED WORDS 50

Puzzle # 49 — ASSORTED WORDS 49

```
      S E T A G I T I L
    D I S C O U R T E S I E S
I M P U R E     D U
  A C E R T I F Y E N       I
T Y C A U Q E D A   W G   N
R L S C M     S O     E I F
O   U R O E     N B       P E
T   P C E M S   M A M M A S R
U   E   I L P S     E       T
N   R   F L L I     L     S
D   E     F I I E     C
A   D   E L B I T S U B M O C
S O R B I T A L D S H R
D E H C A E L       I E S
J O B L E S S N E S S D D
```

Puzzle # 50 — ASSORTED WORDS 50

```
      S E C N E R E F F I D
    L A E R I O T O U S     M
L   C O V S C B E G G A R   I
O G A W A P   A         D R
O U D I L I   N F       I A
K S G N I R B J L D     L C
O S I G E E   O A   L   E L
U E N D R S   I M   E O   T E
T T G   O     S P B V   B T S
S S     C   T R   E     A
P R I O R I T Y E   L R   N
R E L A B E L O Y   E     T
    N A I F F U R   S     I
  S R E D N U A L E T     S
E G R A H C R E V O D     M
```

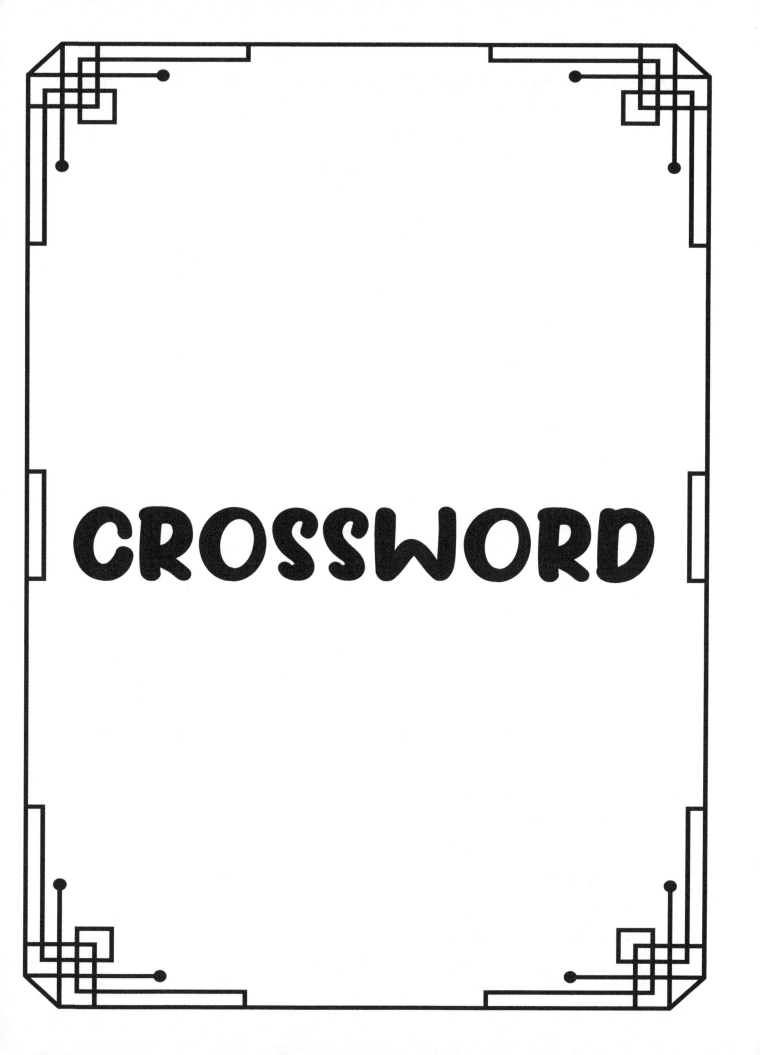

CROSSWORD

1. Using the Across and Down clues, write the correct words in the numbered grid below.

ACROSS

1. bowl-shaped vessel with many holes used to drain off water
3. excessively ornate swollen or bloated
4. able to use the left hand or the right equally well
7. production of a desired result
9. act of preaching
10. counterfeit
11. state of doubt or perplexity

DOWN

1. line made by crushing white line on the ground in cricket
2. agreeably pungent stimulating
5. join (two ends)
6. burst out suddenly/talk ardently
8. cowardly

2. Using the Across and Down clues, write the correct words in the numbered grid below.

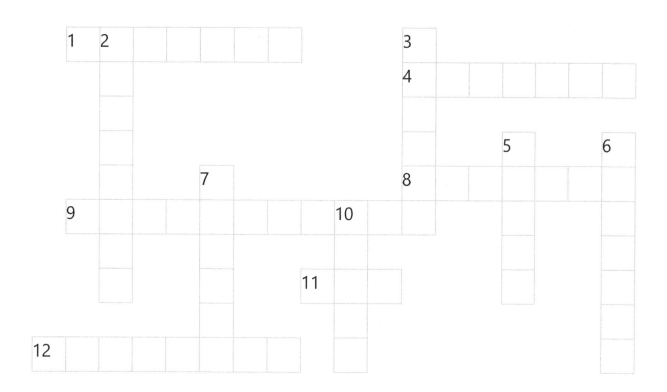

ACROSS

1. gruesome suggesting death
4. offensive disgusting (smell)
8. extreme astounding
9. incapable of being discovered or understood
11. try to win
12. dig up from the earth

DOWN

2. suspended action
3. put pour fill
5. sluggish dull not tight
6. trace or sign
7. piece of linen worn as a necktie
10. to tolerate endure

3. Using the Across and Down clues, write the correct words in the numbered grid below.

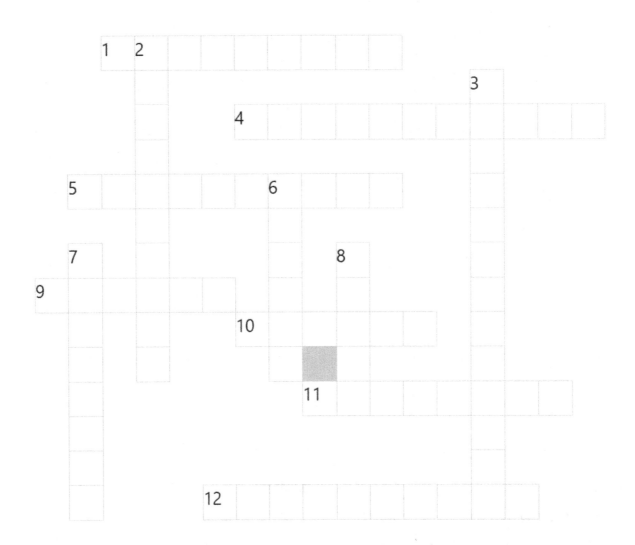

ACROSS
1. a beggar
4. of the present time only
5. person who has given help
9. slander say evil things
10. line made by crushing white line on the ground in cricket
11. bookish showing off learning

DOWN
2. calmness of temperament
3. surprise and fear dismay
6. disguised
7. member of a vigilance committee
8. angry

12. coming together and uniting
    into one substance

4. Using the Across and Down clues, write the correct words in the
   numbered grid below.

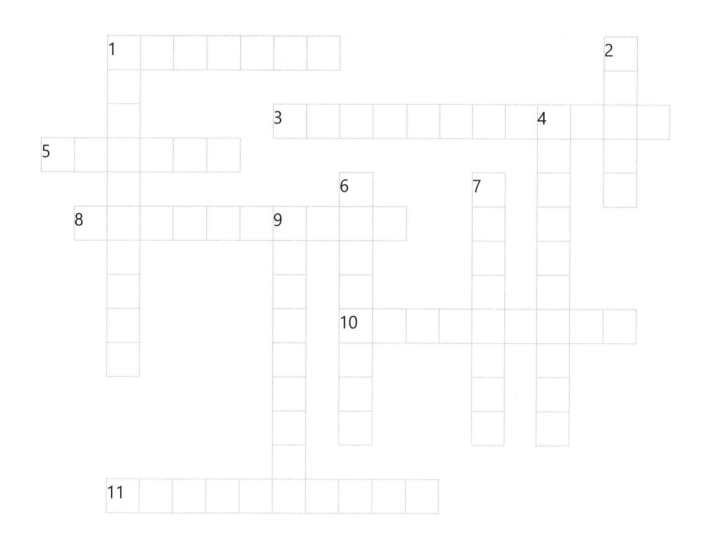

ACROSS

1. secret with a hidden meaning
3. attractive on the surface but of
   little value
5. induce by bribery or smth to
   commit perjury

DOWN

1. burdensome heavy and
   awkward to carry
2. pull the feathers off pick (e.g..
   flowers)
4. official duties

8. living in societies liking the company
10. witness/evidence
11. carved image on the prow of a ship

6. trifling/worthless
7. FALSE counterfeit
9. fill with fury or rage

5. Using the Across and Down clues, write the correct words in the numbered grid below.

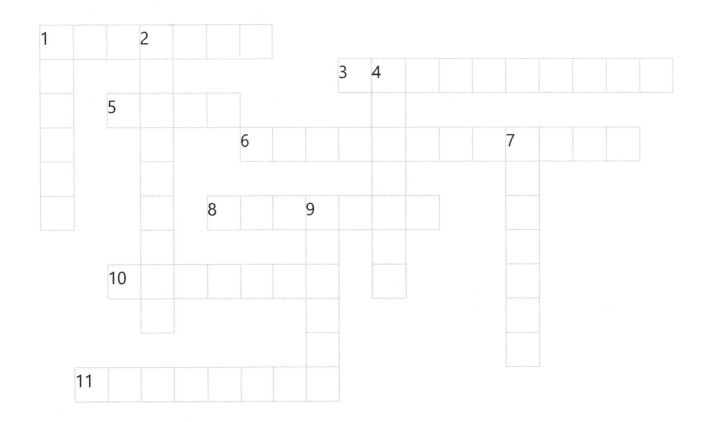

ACROSS

1. secret with a hidden meaning
3. mournful excessively sad
5. destructive thing or a person who is nuisance
6. becoming rotten

DOWN

1. disguised
2. common
4. discover and bring to light
7. form of a frog when it leaves the egg

8. quick hurried

9. porous rubber for washing live at once expense

10. hell

11. primitive unspoiled pure as in earlier times unadulterated

6. Using the Across and Down clues, write the correct words in the numbered grid below.

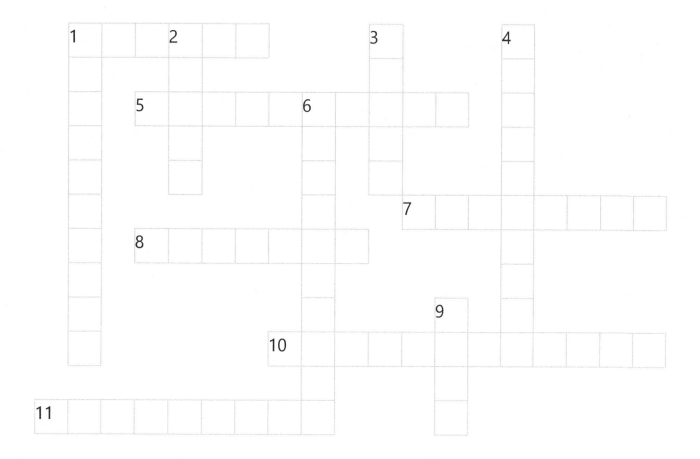

ACROSS

1. fit to be eaten/not poisonous
5. convincing firm belief
7. FALSE counterfeit
8. to be stained or discredited

DOWN

1. easy and painless death
2. to tolerate endure
3. to resist separation
4. mournful excessively sad

10. tending to comply obliging willingness to please

11. that cannot be changed

6. burdensome heavy and awkward to carry

9. scent waving movement carry lightly through

7. Using the Across and Down clues, write the correct words in the numbered grid below.

ACROSS

1. state or put forward as a necessary condition

DOWN

1. porous rubber for washing live at once expense

5. able to use the left hand or the right equally well

6. alarm excited state of mind

7. secret with a hidden meaning

9. easily gulled

10. becoming rotten

11. coming together and uniting into one substance

2. shameful dishonorable undignified disgraceful

3. discover and bring to light

4. person who has given help

8. agreeably pungent stimulating

8. Using the Across and Down clues, write the correct words in the numbered grid below.

ACROSS

1. easy and painless death

DOWN

2. abusive language curses

4. make rough

9. suddenly changeable

11. porous rubber for washing live at once expense

12. state of doubt or perplexity

3. narrow-mindedness isolated

5. soothe pacify calm

6. opening broken place breaking

7. show bodily or mental pain

8. fall back again

10. to be thrifty to set limits

9. **Using the Across and Down clues, write the correct words in the numbered grid below.**

ACROSS
1. becoming rotten
3. free giving generosity
5. daring foolishly bold impudent

7. think deeply mediate
8. person who has given help

DOWN
2. still in existence
4. upset the self-possession of
5. eager and cheerful readiness
6. dig up from the earth
7. burdensome heavy and awkward to carry

9. paint with dots

10. calmness of temperament

10. Using the Across and Down clues, write the correct words in the numbered grid below.

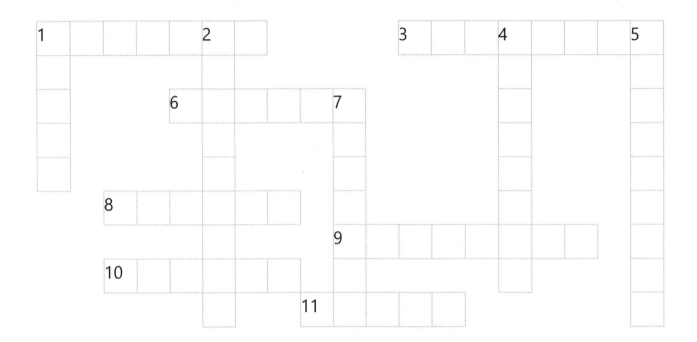

ACROSS
1. soothe pacify calm
3. dig up from the earth
6. talk excitedly utter rapidly
8. still in existence
9. bookish showing off learning
10. showing no emotion impassive
11. ready to do smth dishonest

DOWN
1. dried plum silly person
2. easily controlled or guided
4. not yet fully formed rudimentary elementary
5. greedy (esp for money)
7. fall back again

11. Using the Across and Down clues, write the correct words in the numbered grid below.

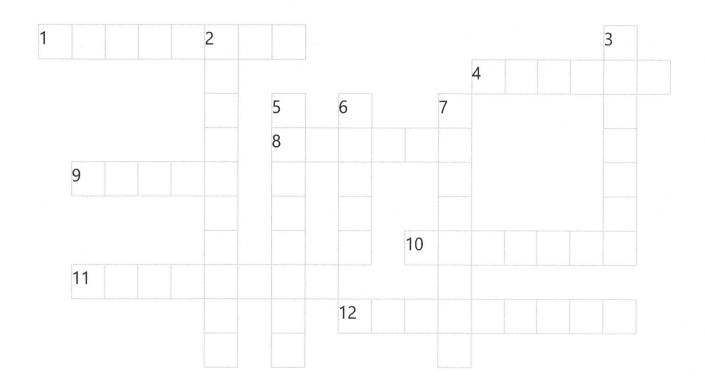

ACROSS

1. dig up from the earth
4. twisting force causing rotation
8. fit to be eaten/not poisonous
9. dried plum silly person
10. form of a frog when it leaves the egg
11. quality or condition of being sober
12. quick changeable in character fleeting

DOWN

2. suddenly changeable
3. worldly as opposed to spiritual commonplace everyday

5. bookish showing off learning
6. shy easily frightened
7. open disobedience or resistance

12. **Using the Across and Down clues, write the correct words in the numbered grid below.**

ACROSS

1. easily controlled or guided
5. strong dislike
6. make or become soft by soaking in water
8. agreeably pungent stimulating
9. act of preaching
11. moult lose hair feathers before new growing

DOWN

1. witness/evidence
2. person who has given help
3. suddenly changeable
4. feeling of regret for one's action
7. secret with a hidden meaning
10. sluggish dull not tight

13. **Using the Across and Down clues, write the correct words in the numbered grid below.**

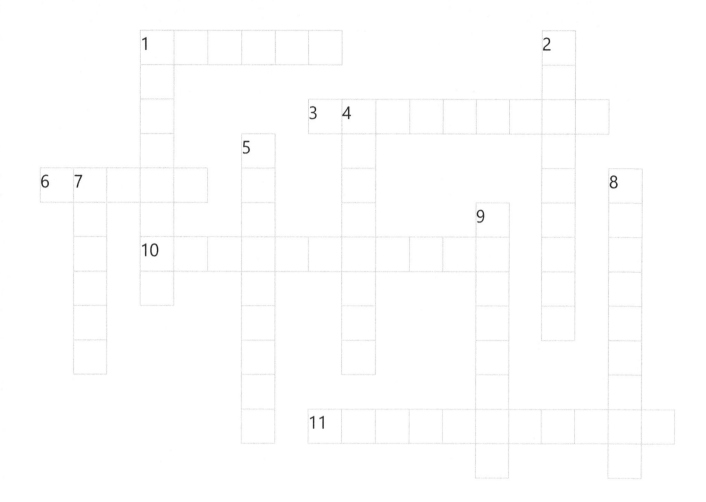

ACROSS

1. come to grips/settle conclusively
3. common
6. dried plum silly person
10. burden things that get on the way of
11. put smth on the top

DOWN

1. bowl-shaped vessel with many holes used to drain off water
2. a beggar
4. feeling or showing deep respect
5. fill with fury or rage
7. make rough
8. witness/evidence

9. bookish showing off learning

14. Using the Across and Down clues, write the correct words in the numbered grid below.

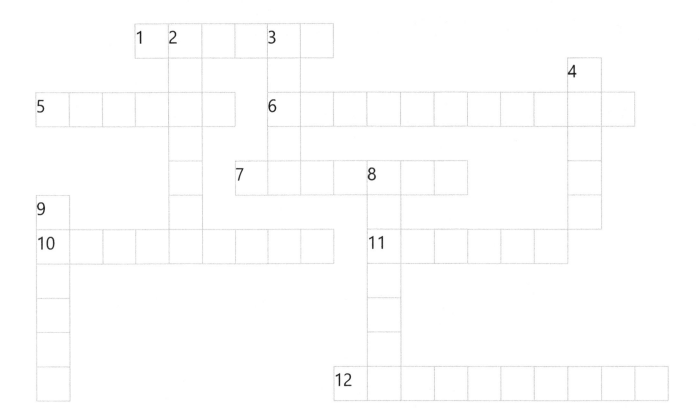

ACROSS

1. get back by payment compensate
5. induce by bribery or smth to commit perjury
6. alarm excited state of mind
7. fall plunge steeply
10. greedy (esp for money)
11. line made by crushing white line on the ground in cricket

DOWN

2. irregular in behaviour or opinion
3. praise highly
4. crouch shrink back
8. gruesome suggesting death
9. piece of linen worn as a necktie

12. pleasing in appearance
    attractive

15. Using the Across and Down clues, write the correct words in the numbered grid below.

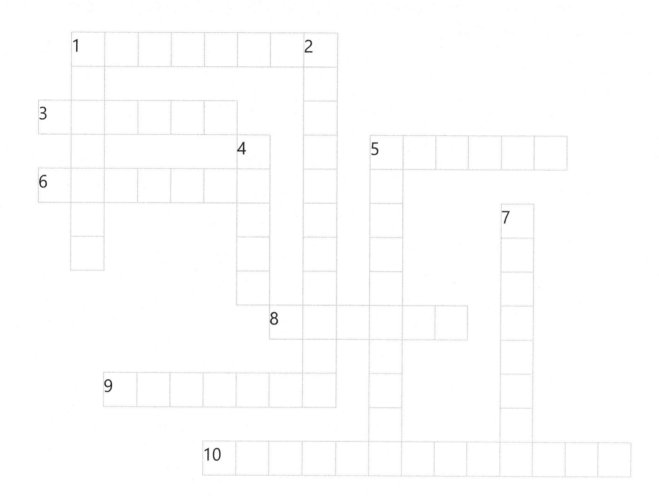

ACROSS

1. brave
3. bring into harmony
5. come to grips/settle conclusively
6. gruesome suggesting death

DOWN

1. lower the quality weaken the strength
2. put smth on the top
4. measure hoe heavy smth is
5. burdensome heavy and awkward to carry

8. compel to force to make obedient
9. soothe pacify calm
10. surprise and fear dismay

7. member of a vigilance committee

16. Using the Across and Down clues, write the correct words in the numbered grid below.

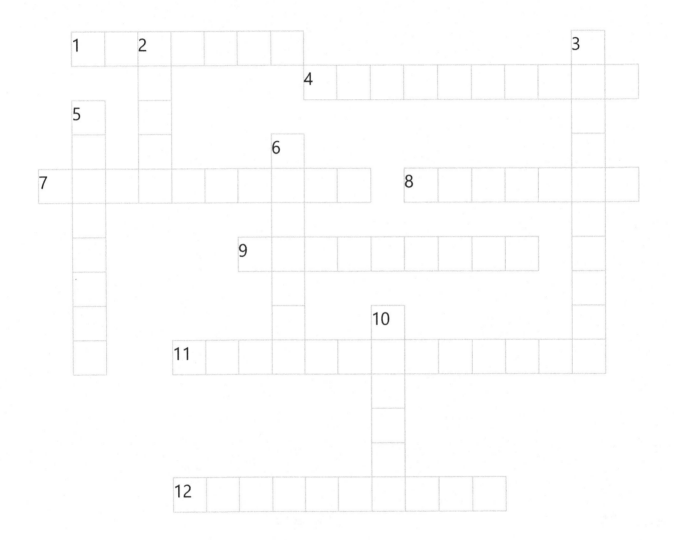

ACROSS
1. offensive disgusting (smell)
4. fond of in the habit of fighting
7. deep-rooted. long-established

DOWN
2. angry
3. burdensome heavy and awkward to carry

8. fall plunge steeply

9. greedy (esp for money)

11. calm not capable of being excited

12. act of preaching

5. increase in density strength make laconic

6. gruesome suggesting death

10. majestic venerable

17. Using the Across and Down clues, write the correct words in the numbered grid below.

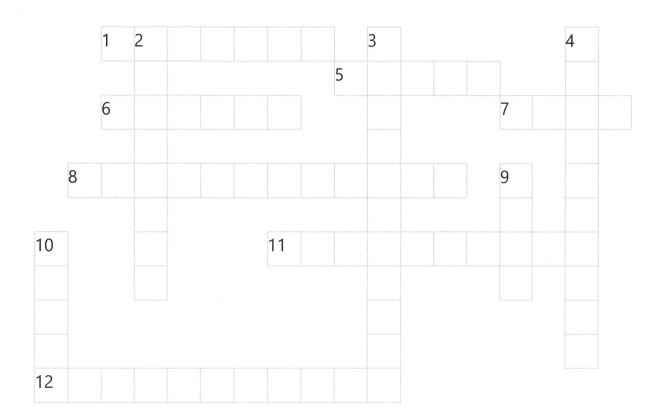

ACROSS

1. form of a frog when it leaves the egg

5. angry

6. compel to force to make obedient

DOWN

2. one who abandons long-held religious or political convictions

3. grow reproduce by rapid multification

7. burst out suddenly/talk ardently

8. becoming rotten

11. deep-rooted. long-established

12. burden things that get on the way of

4. untidy

9. waste away bite steadily

10. tool for cutting grooves in wood

18. Using the Across and Down clues, write the correct words in the numbered grid below.

ACROSS

1. disguised

6. tool for cutting grooves in wood

DOWN

1. increase in density strength make laconic

7. FALSE counterfeit

8. roughness harshness ill temper irritability

9. scent waving movement carry lightly through

10. attractive on the surface but of little value

2. to travel from place to place to peregrinate

3. incapable of being discovered or understood

4. hardened and unrepenting stubborn inflexible

5. ill-tempered unsocial

9. show bodily or mental pain

19. Using the Across and Down clues, write the correct words in the numbered grid below.

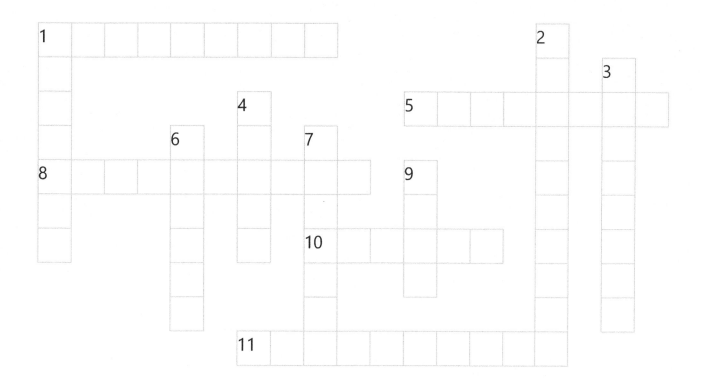

ACROSS

1. suggest unpleasantly make a way for smth gently

5. bookish showing off learning

DOWN

1. without taste or flavor

2. touching neighboring near

3. dig up from the earth

8. pleasing in appearance attractive
10. line made by crushing white line on the ground in cricket
11. living in societies liking the company

4. sluggish dull not tight
6. ill-tempered unsocial
7. soothe pacify calm
9. to turn away (from a habit)

20. Using the Across and Down clues, write the correct words in the numbered grid below.

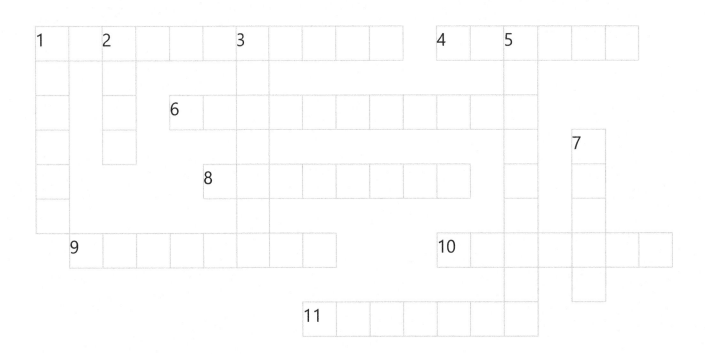

ACROSS
1. put smth on the top
4. draw move back wince
6. shameful dishonorable undignified disgraceful
8. make or become soft by soaking in water

DOWN
1. walk with long steps
2. neat formal
3. worldly as opposed to spiritual commonplace everyday
5. suggest unpleasantly make a way for smth gently
7. ready to do smth dishonest

9. quality or condition of being sober

10. soothe pacify calm

11. gruesome suggesting death

21. Using the Across and Down clues, write the correct words in the numbered grid below.

ACROSS

1. cowardly craven
4. sluggish dull not tight

DOWN

1. agreeably pungent stimulating
2. that cannot be rubbed out
3. to be stained or discredited

5. feeling or showing deep respect
9. becoming rotten
10. have more power than others

6. opening broken place breaking
7. that cannot be changed
8. one who abandons long-held religious or political convictions
9. dried plum silly person

22. Using the Across and Down clues, write the correct words in the numbered grid below.

ACROSS   **DOWN**

1. induce by bribery or smth to commit perjury
3. put pour fill
5. lower the quality weaken the strength
7. discover and bring to light
9. process of burning
10. able to use the left hand or the right equally well
11. low vulgar base tawdry

1. of the power of forming a solution
2. attractive on the surface but of little value
4. burdensome heavy and awkward to carry
6. touching neighboring near
8. oppose to alcohol

23. Using the Across and Down clues, write the correct words in the numbered grid below.

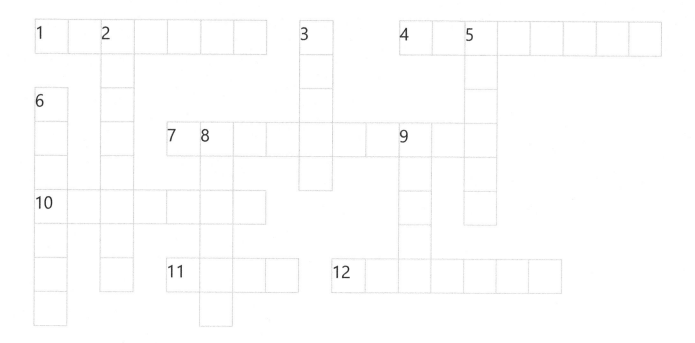

ACROSS
1. gruesome suggesting death
4. dig up from the earth
7. suddenly changeable

DOWN
2. think deeply mediate
3. crouch shrink back

10. soothe pacify calm

11. waste away bite steadily

12. discover and bring to light

5. showing no emotion impassive

6. form of a frog when it leaves the egg

8. bring into harmony

9. angry

24. Using the Across and Down clues, write the correct words in the numbered grid below.

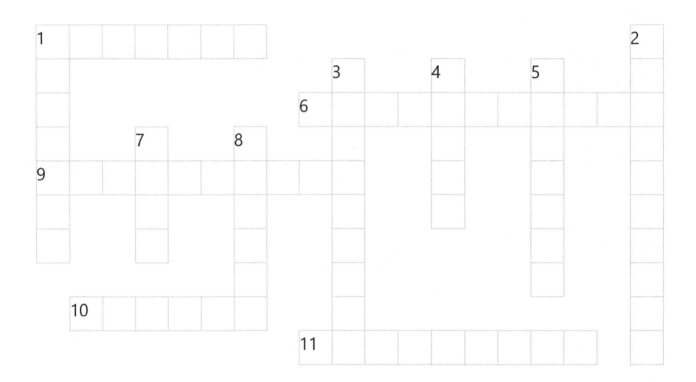

ACROSS

1. of the power of forming a solution

6. incapable of being discovered or understood

9. deep-rooted. long-established

10. disguised

DOWN

1. to be stained or discredited

2. living in societies liking the company

3. that cannot be rubbed out

4. angry

11. quick changeable in character fleeting

5. low vulgar base tawdry
7. to turn away (from a habit)
8. piece of linen worn as a necktie

25. Using the Across and Down clues, write the correct words in the numbered grid below.

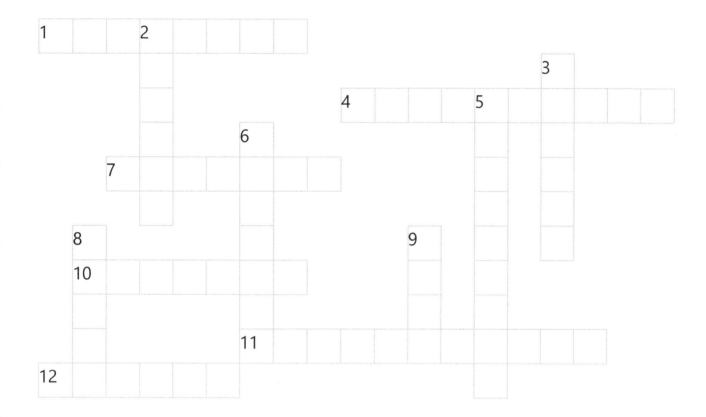

ACROSS

1. make or become soft by soaking in water
4. easy and painless death
7. hell
10. soothe pacify calm

DOWN

2. still in existence
3. talk excitedly utter rapidly
5. make (pain) easier to bear
6. secret with a hidden meaning
8. weapon with a metal point on a long shaft

11. feeling of regret for one's action

9. to turn away (from a habit)

12. opening broken place breaking

26. Using the Across and Down clues, write the correct words in the numbered grid below.

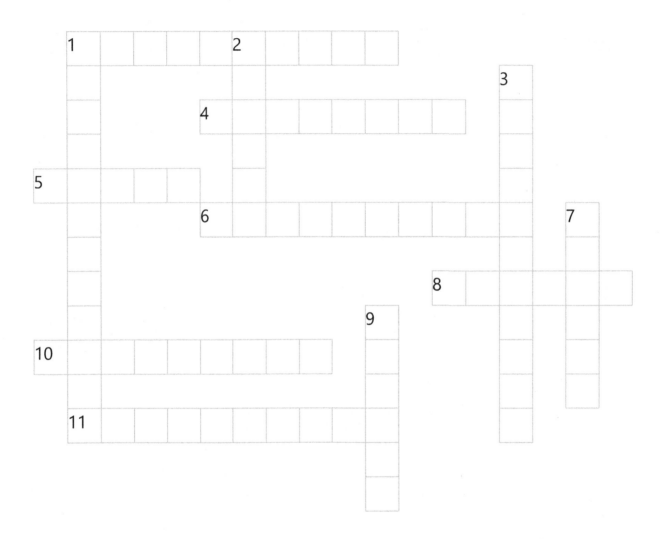

ACROSS

1. process of burning
4. causing grief or pain serious dire grave

DOWN

1. tending to comply obliging willingness to please
2. walk with long steps

5. pull the feathers off pick (e.g.. flowers)
6. person who has given help
8. make rough
10. suggest unpleasantly make a way for smth gently
11. easy and painless death

3. put smth on the top
7. slander say evil things
9. still in existence

27. Using the Across and Down clues, write the correct words in the numbered grid below.

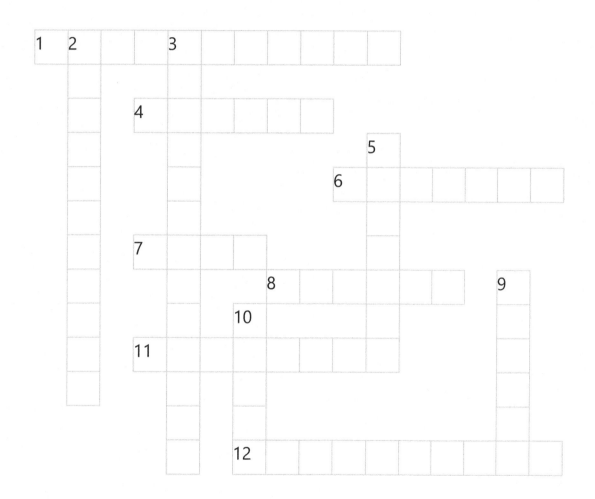

ACROSS
1. alarm excited state of mind

DOWN
2. to protest object

4. porous rubber for washing live at once expense
6. like a seed constituting a source originative
7. burst out suddenly/talk ardently
8. put pour fill
11. make or become soft by soaking in water
12. free giving generosity

3. calm not capable of being excited
5. person who lives alone and avoids people
9. piece of linen worn as a necktie
10. ready to do smth dishonest

28. Using the Across and Down clues, write the correct words in the numbered grid below.

ACROSS

1. put smth on the top
5. angry
8. a blindly devoted patriot
9. dig up from the earth
10. without taste or flavor
11. line made by crushing white line on the ground in cricket

DOWN

1. sensitiveness
2. production of a desired result
3. a beggar
4. calm not capable of being excited
6. try to avoid by sophistication
7. witness/evidence

29. Using the Across and Down clues, write the correct words in the numbered grid below.

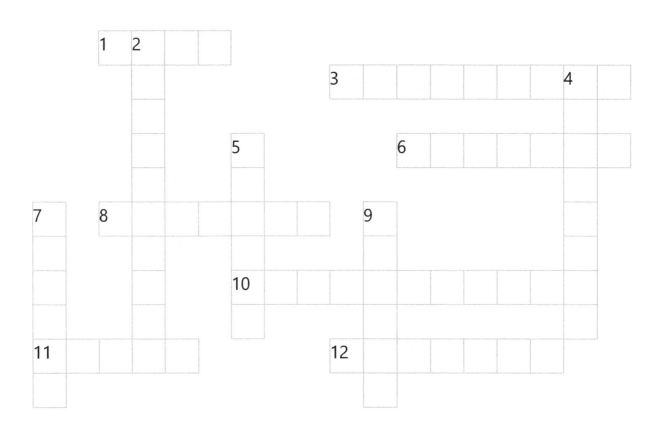

ACROSS

1. to turn away (from a habit)
3. weariness tiredness
6. fall back again
8. discover and bring to light
10. put smth on the top
11. weapon with a metal point on a long shaft
12. to be stained or discredited

DOWN

2. easy and painless death
4. dig up from the earth
5. threats to compel smb
7. ill-tempered unsocial
9. twisting force causing rotation

30. Using the Across and Down clues, write the correct words in the numbered grid below.

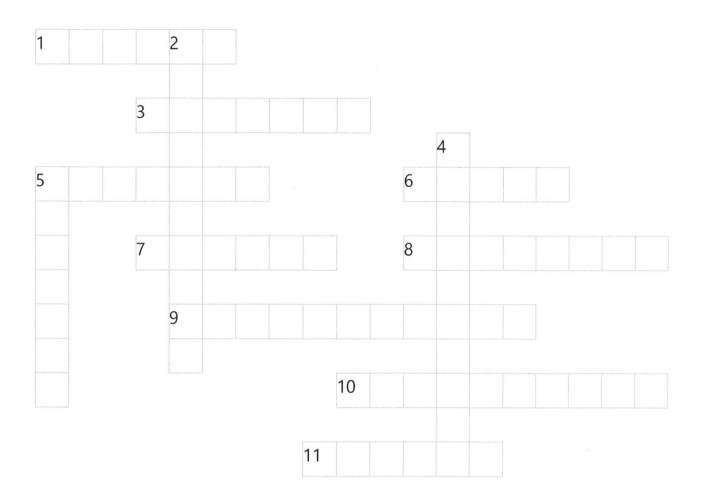

ACROSS

1. smth handed down from ancestors
3. gratify give way to satisfy allow oneself
5. to be stained or discredited
6. to tolerate endure
7. showing no emotion impassive

DOWN

2. convincing firm belief
4. hesitating undecided
5. of the power of forming a solution

8. lacking purpose or vitality
   ineffective careless
9. showing scorn or reproach
10. narrow-mindedness isolated
11. talk excitedly utter rapidly

31. Using the Across and Down clues, write the correct words in the numbered grid below.

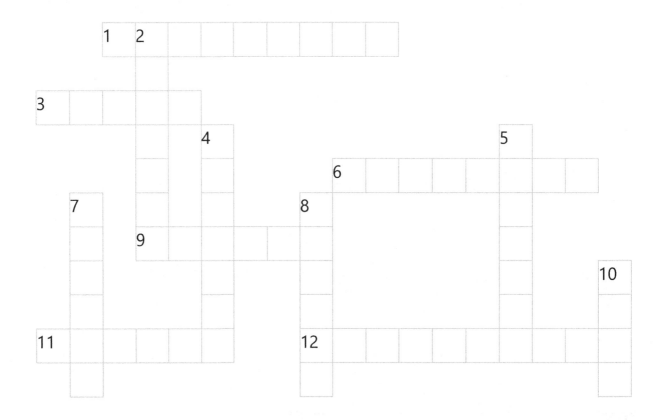

ACROSS
  1. that cannot be changed
  3. to be thrifty to set limits
  6. state of doubt or perplexity
  9. still in existence
  11. twisting force causing rotation

DOWN
  2. worldly as opposed to spiritual
     commonplace everyday

  4. trace or sign
  5. gruesome suggesting death

12. official duties

7. reproving a person for his faults

8. showing no emotion impassive

10. burst out suddenly/talk ardently

32. Using the Across and Down clues, write the correct words in the numbered grid below.

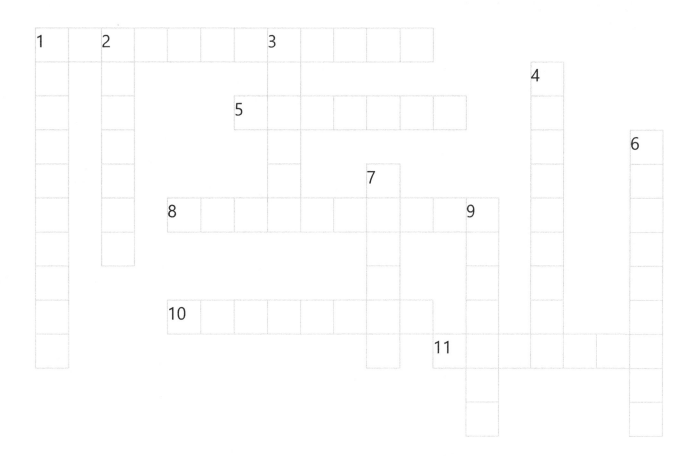

ACROSS

1. becoming rotten
5. low vulgar base tawdry
8. touching neighboring near

DOWN

1. fond of in the habit of fighting
2. form of a frog when it leaves the egg

10. lacking purpose or vitality ineffective careless

11. hell

3. piece of linen worn as a necktie

4. fill with fury or rage

6. greedy (esp for money)

7. majestic venerable

9. like a seed constituting a source originative

33. Using the Across and Down clues, write the correct words in the numbered grid below.

ACROSS

DOWN

1. shameful dishonorable undignified disgraceful
5. make rough
8. free giving generosity
9. fill with fury or rage
10. reserved indifferent
11. quality or condition of being sober

1. abusive language curses
2. narrow-mindedness isolated
3. calm not capable of being excited
4. coming together and uniting into one substance
6. attractive on the surface but of little value
7. primitive unspoiled pure as in earlier times unadulterated

34. **Using the Across and Down clues, write the correct words in the numbered grid below.**

ACROSS

1. witness/evidence
4. primitive unspoiled pure as in earlier times unadulterated
8. bowl-shaped vessel with many holes used to drain off water
10. narrow-mindedness isolated
11. that cannot be changed
12. a beggar

DOWN

2. fit to be eaten/not poisonous
3. FALSE counterfeit
5. not yet fully formed rudimentary elementary
6. have more power than others
7. easy and painless death
9. think deeply mediate

35. Using the Across and Down clues, write the correct words in the numbered grid below.

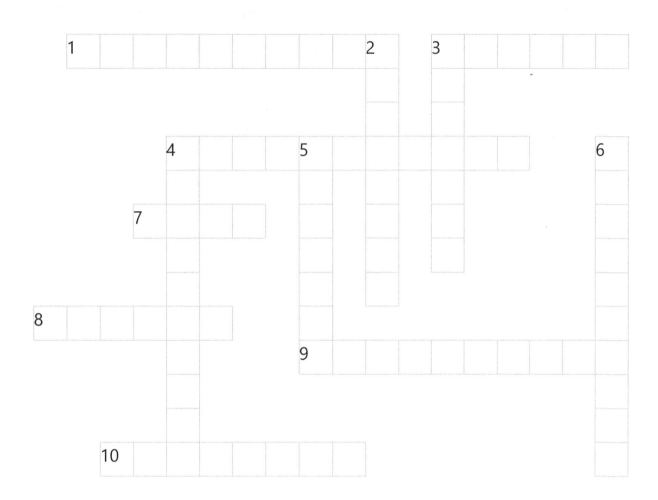

ACROSS

1. act of preaching
3. join (two ends)
4. feeling of regret for one's action
7. scent waving movement carry lightly through
8. put pour fill
9. act of preaching

DOWN

2. person who insists on importance of smth
3. like a seed constituting a source originative
4. coming together and uniting into one substance
5. discover and bring to light
6. burdensome heavy and awkward to carry

10. member of a vigilance
    committee

36. Using the Across and Down clues, write the correct words in the
    numbered grid below.

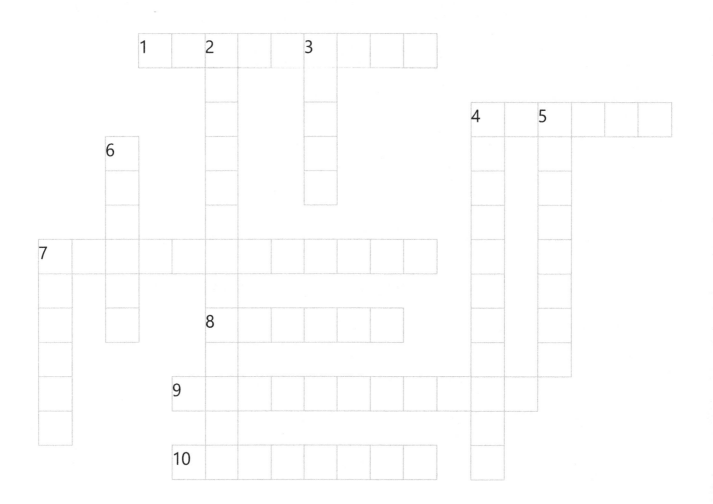

ACROSS
1. person hardened in sin one
   devoid of decency
4. person of great learning
7. tending to comply obliging
   willingness to please
8. put pour fill

DOWN
2. cowardly craven
3. to tolerate endure
4. put smth on the top
5. brave
6. reproving a person for his
   faults

9. feeling of regret for one's
   action
10. roughness harshness ill temper
    irritability

7. piece of linen worn as a
   necktie

37. Using the Across and Down clues, write the correct words in the
    numbered grid below.

ACROSS

1. that cannot be changed
7. piece of linen worn as a
   necktie
9. scent waving movement carry
   lightly through

DOWN

2. alarm excited state of mind
3. free giving generosity
4. becoming rotten
5. burdensome heavy and
   awkward to carry

10. quality or condition of being sober
11. state or put forward as a necessary condition
12. voracious devouring

6. line made by crushing white line on the ground in cricket
8. quick hurried

38. Using the Across and Down clues, write the correct words in the numbered grid below.

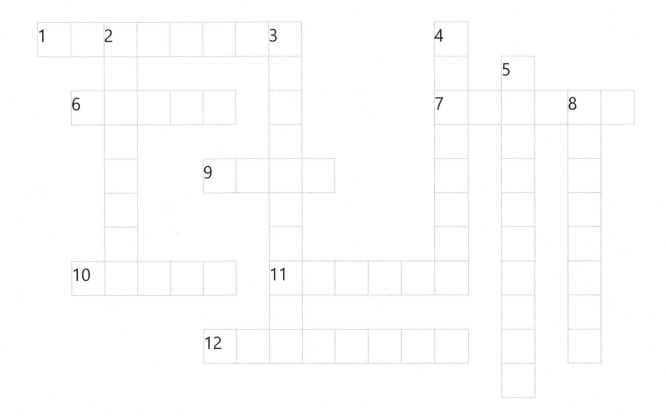

ACROSS

1. not yet fully formed rudimentary elementary
6. pull the feathers off pick (e.g.. flowers)
7. piece of linen worn as a necktie

DOWN

2. bowl-shaped vessel with many holes used to drain off water
3. easy and painless death
4. make or become soft by soaking in water

9. smth urging a person to action

10. to tolerate endure

11. join (two ends)

12. voracious devouring

5. suddenly changeable

8. one who abandons long-held religious or political convictions

39. Using the Across and Down clues, write the correct words in the numbered grid below.

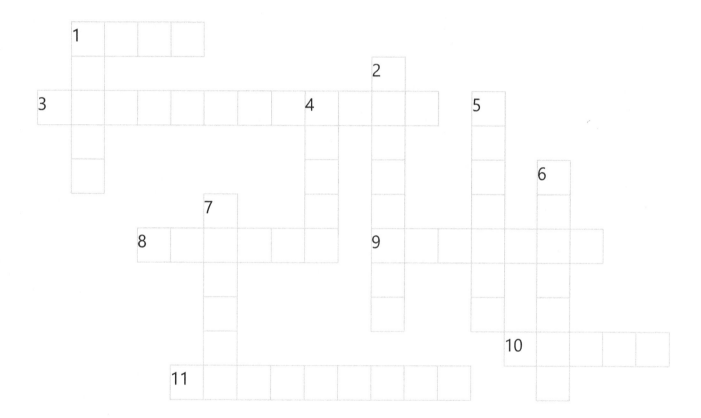

ACROSS

1. waste away bite steadily
3. becoming rotten
8. astute showing sound judgement

DOWN

1. tool for cutting grooves in wood
2. quality or condition of being sober
4. shy easily frightened

9. irregular in behaviour or opinion
10. to resist separation
11. witness/evidence

5. lower the quality weaken the strength
6. try to avoid by sophistication
7. line made by crushing white line on the ground in cricket

40. Using the Across and Down clues, write the correct words in the numbered grid below.

ACROSS
1. FALSE counterfeit
4. feeling of regret for one's action

DOWN
2. involving clever rogues or adventurers
3. fond of in the habit of fighting
5. oppose to alcohol

7. increase in density strength
   make laconic
8. act of preaching
10. that cannot be changed
11. soothe pacify calm
12. FALSE counterfeit

6. a beggar
9. lowest weakest point

41. Using the Across and Down clues, write the correct words in the numbered grid below.

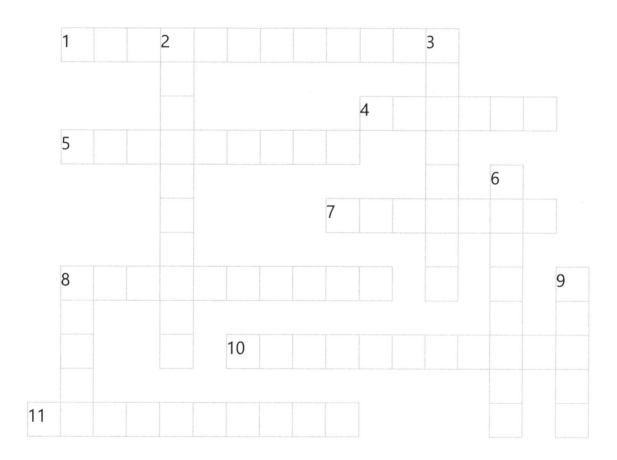

ACROSS

1. able to use the left hand or the right equally well
4. talk excitedly utter rapidly

DOWN

2. hesitating undecided
3. quality or condition of being sober

5. abusive language curses

6. not yet fully formed
   rudimentary elementary

7. hell

8. crouch shrink back

8. a blindly devoted patriot

9. weapon with a metal point on
   a long shaft

10. to protest object

11. living in societies liking the
    company

42. Using the Across and Down clues, write the correct words in the
    numbered grid below.

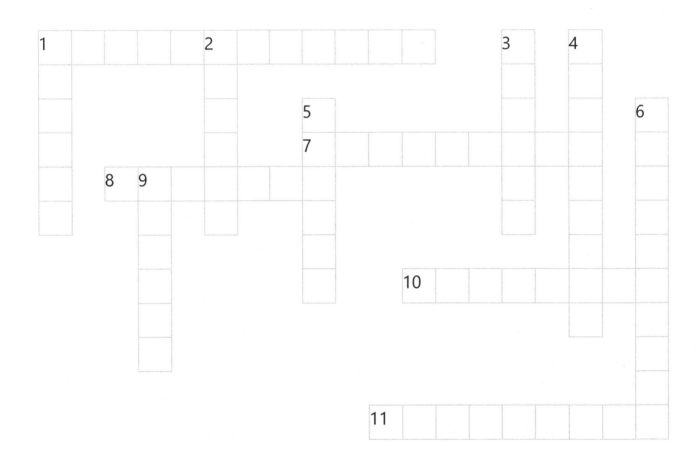

ACROSS

1. tending to comply obliging
   willingness to please

7. that cannot be changed

DOWN

1. disguised

2. majestic venerable

3. fit to be eaten/not poisonous

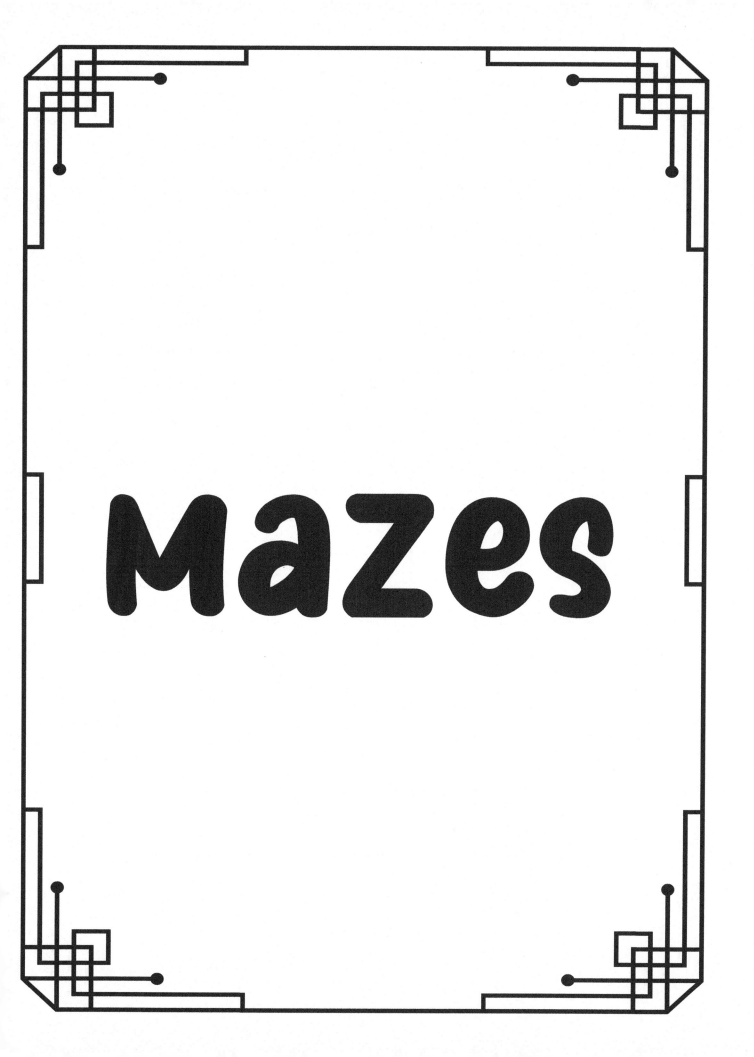

Mazes

Maze #1

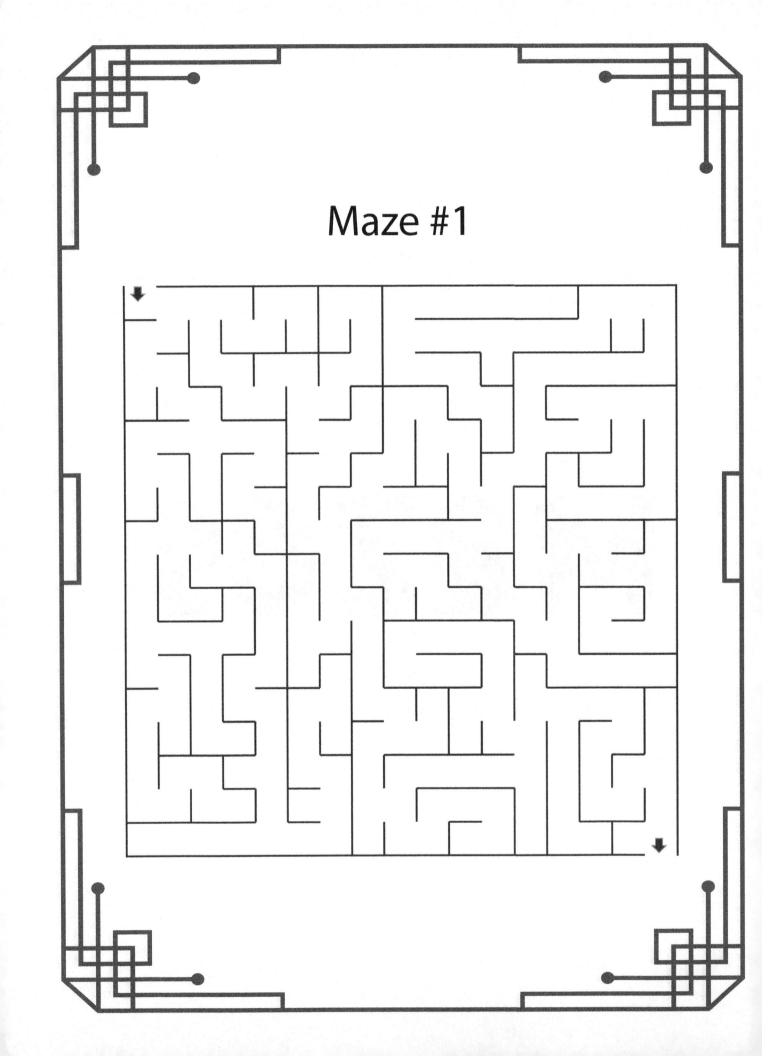

Maze #2

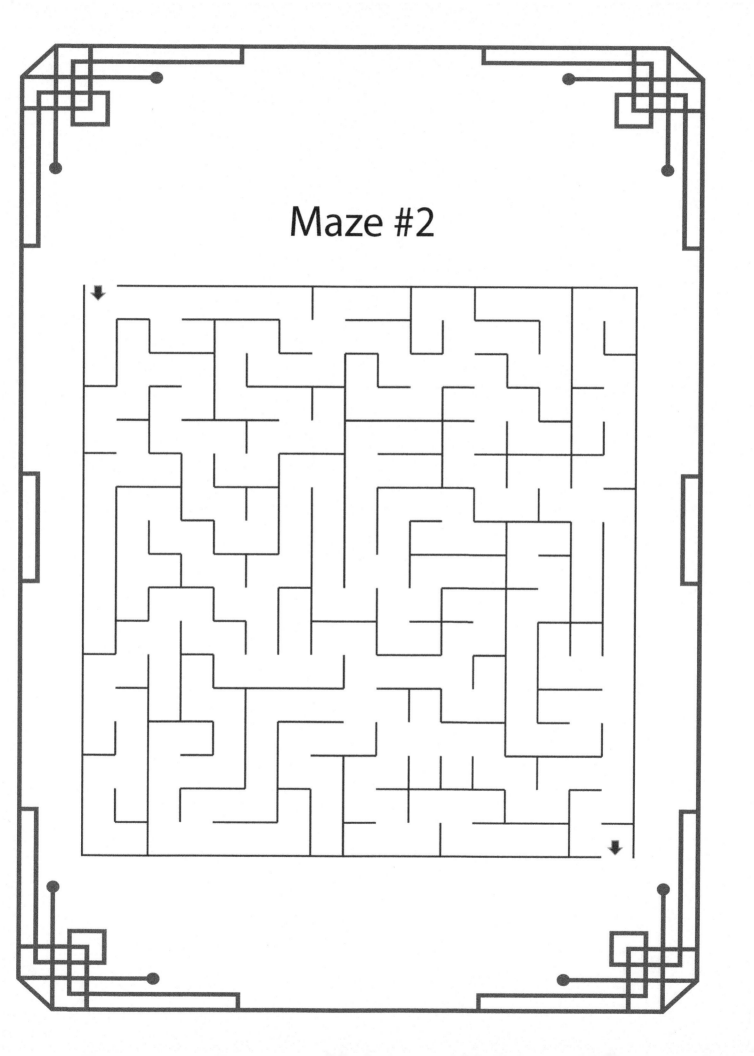

Maze #3

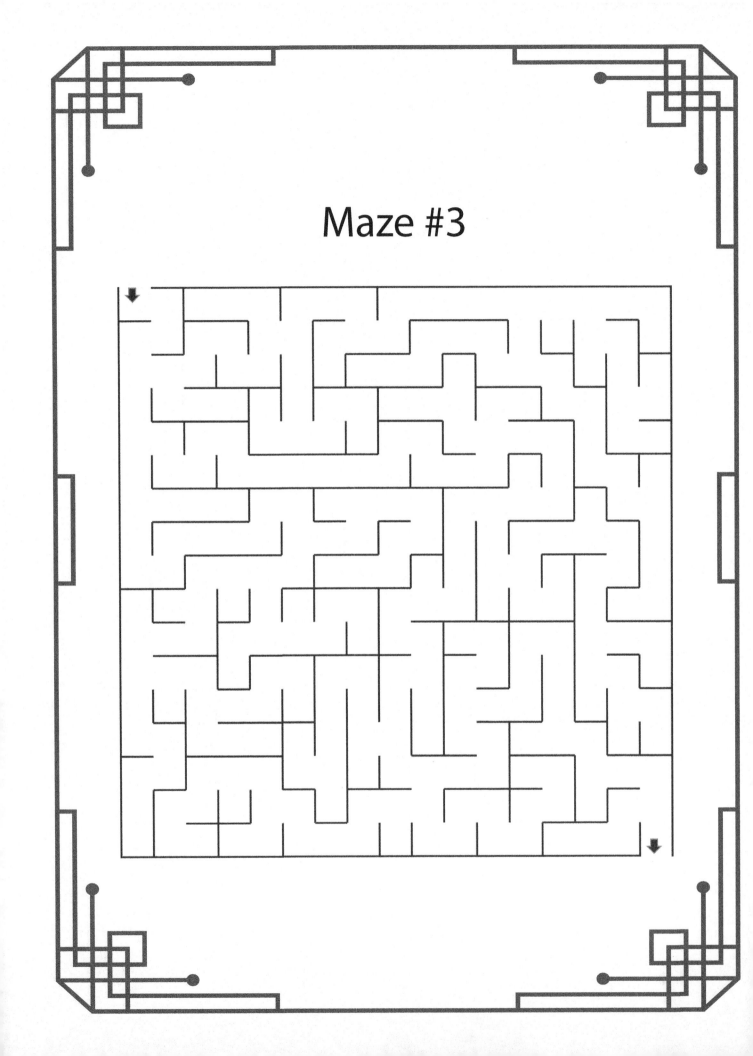

Maze #4

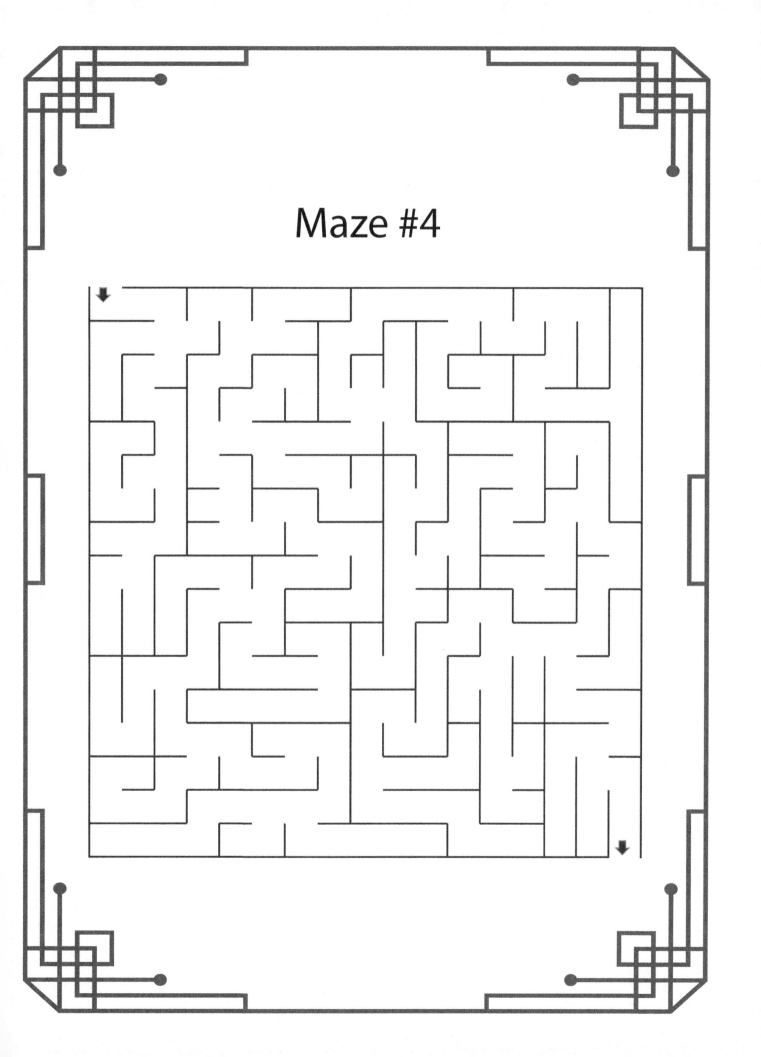

Maze #5

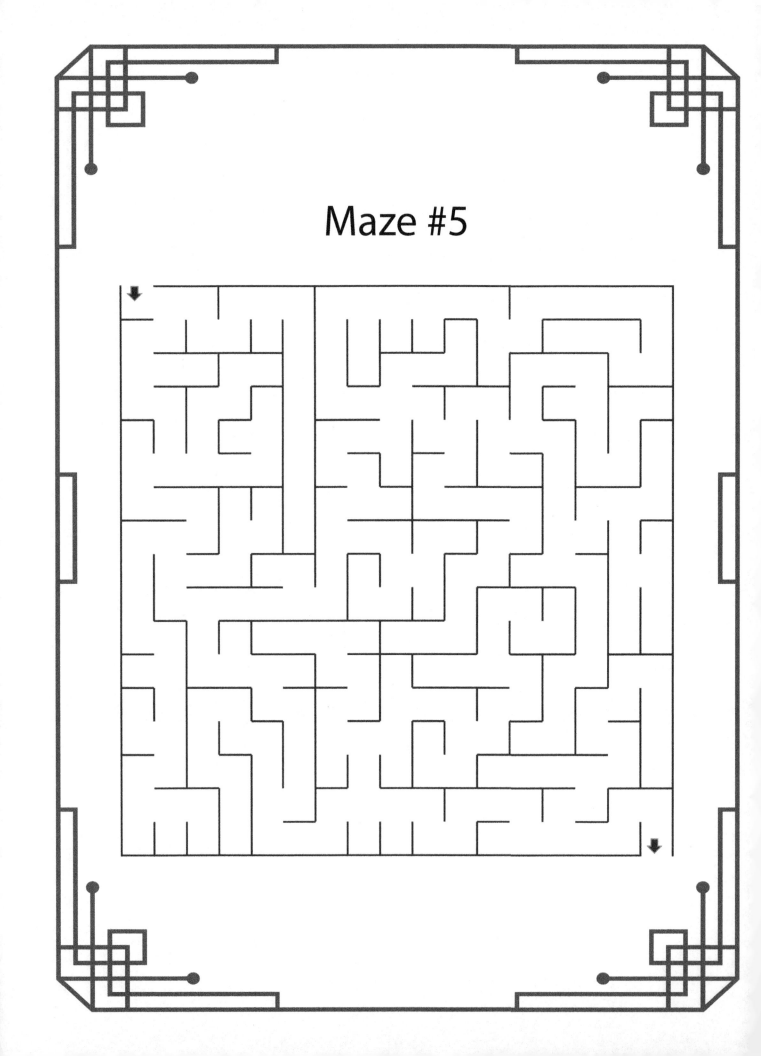

Maze #6

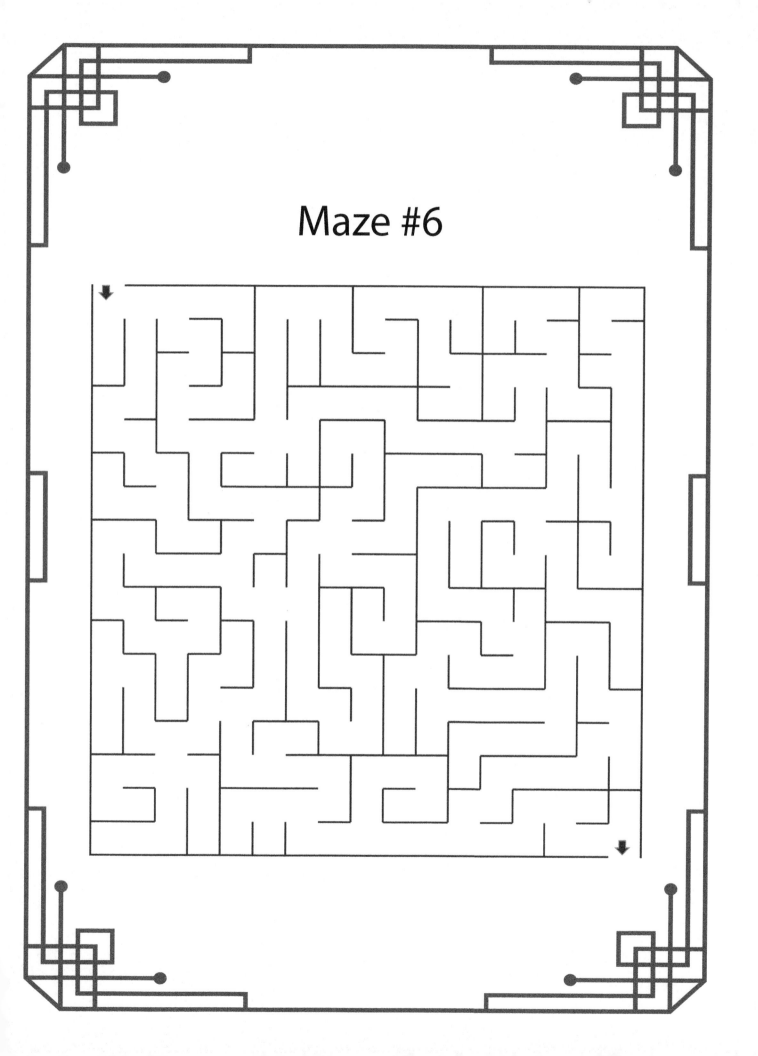

Maze #7

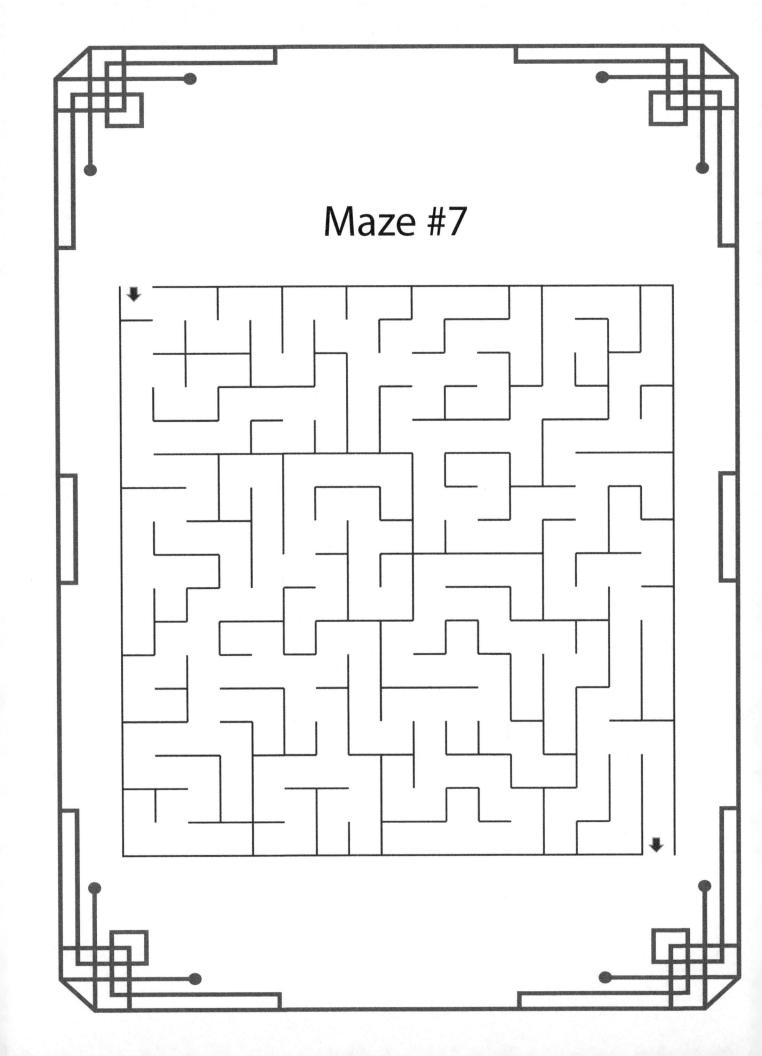

Maze #8

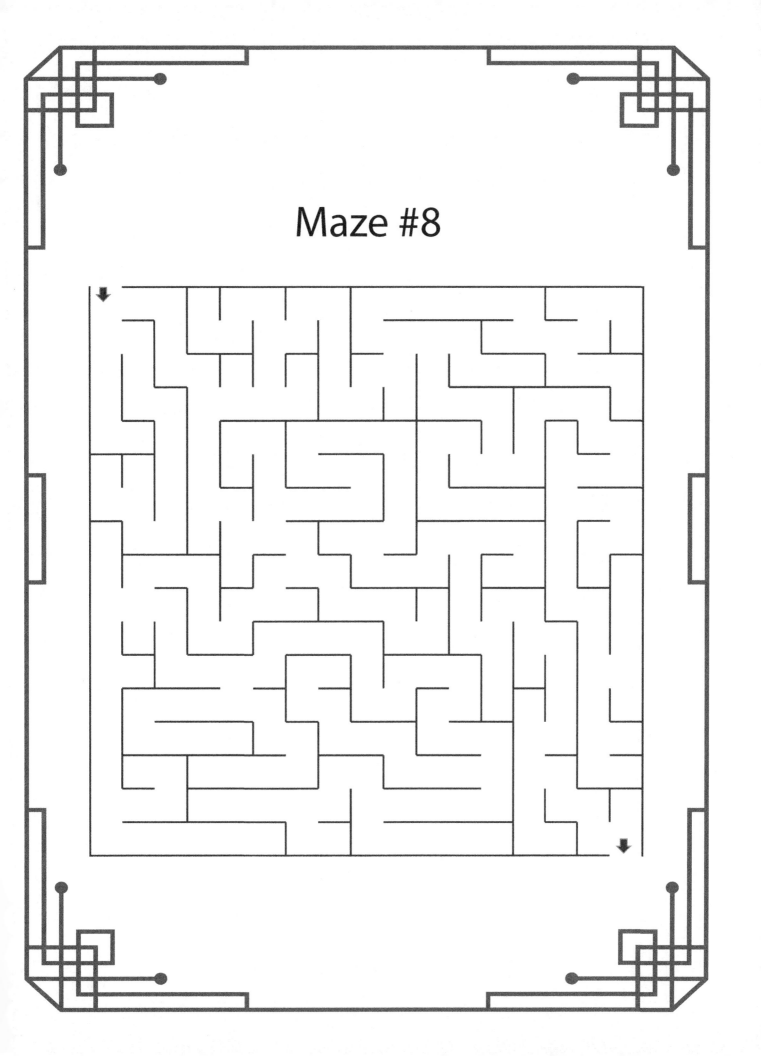

Maze #9

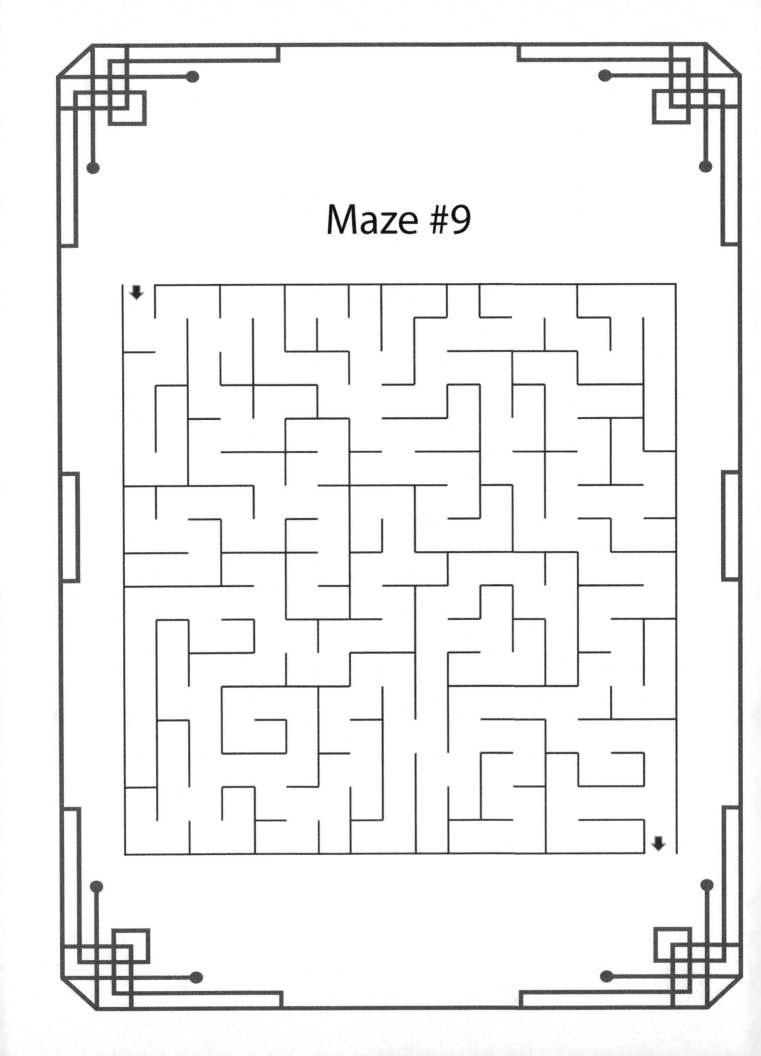

Maze #10

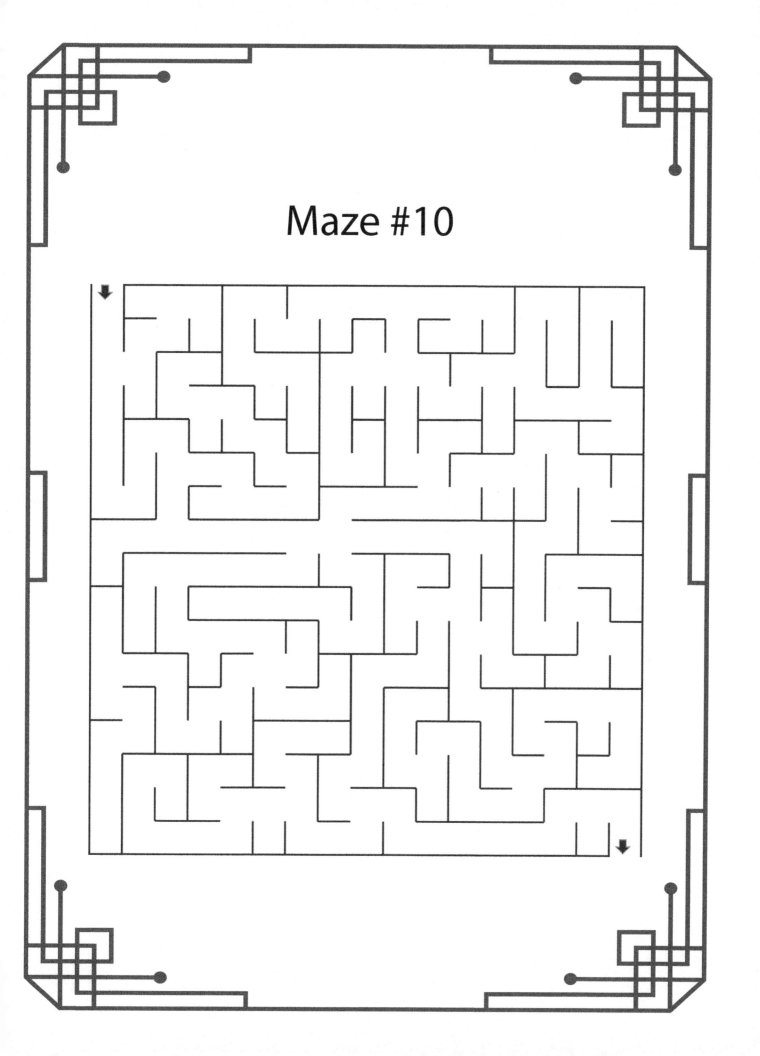

Maze #11

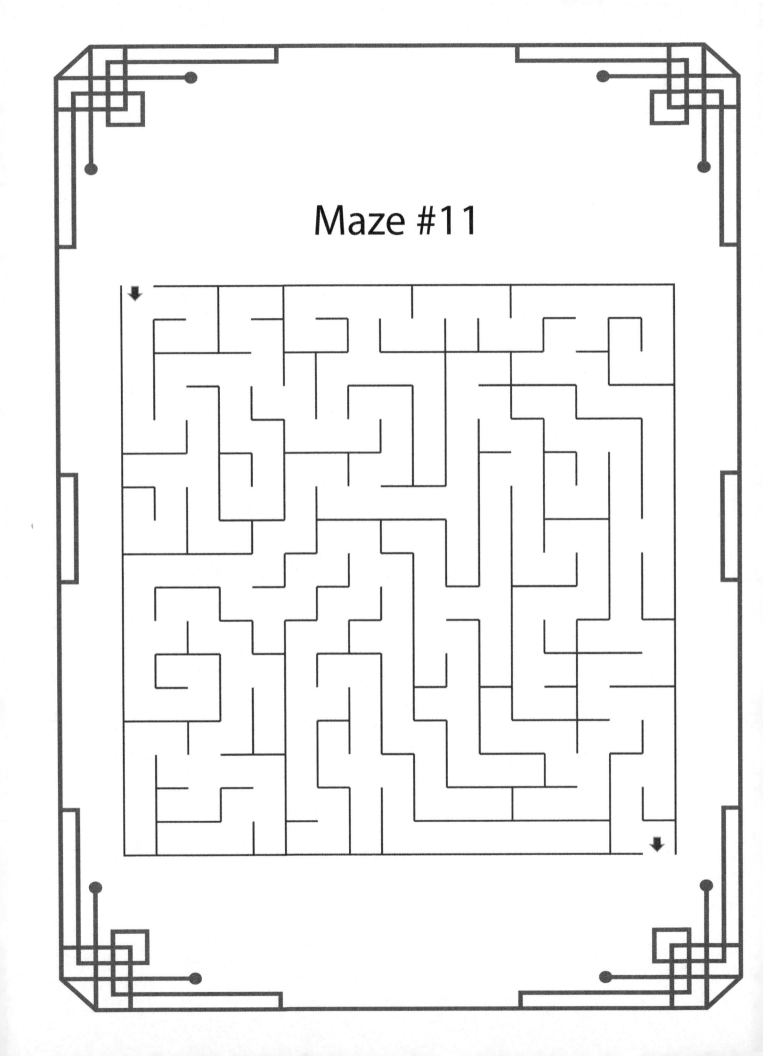

Maze #12

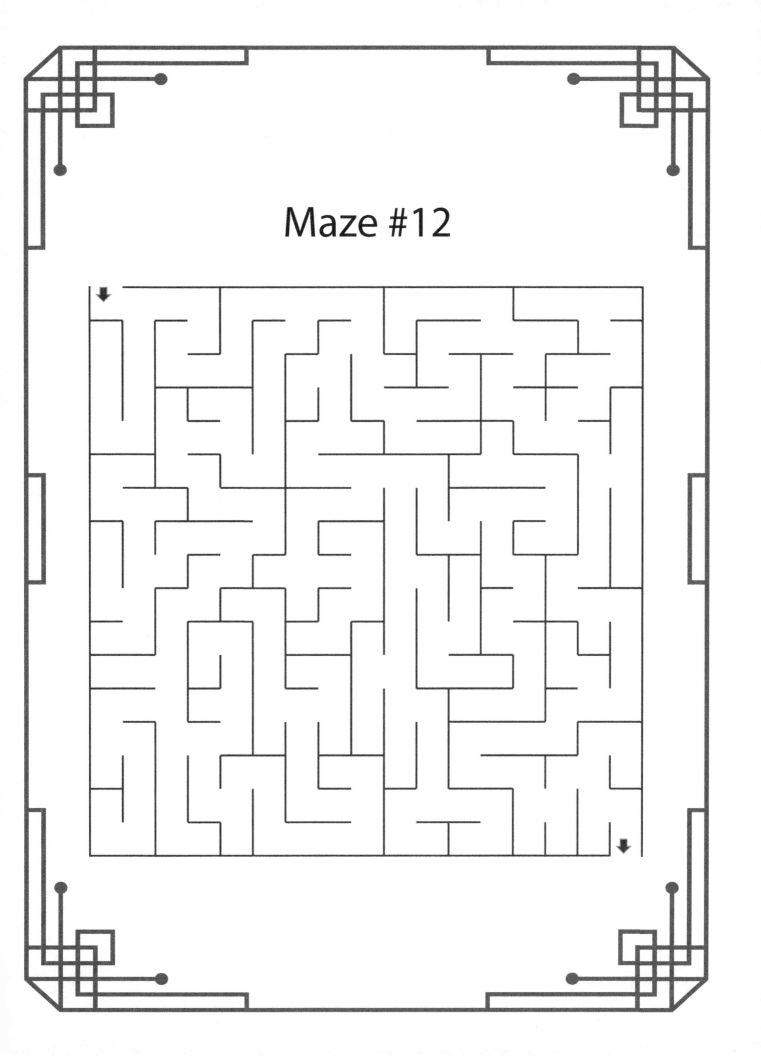

Maze #13

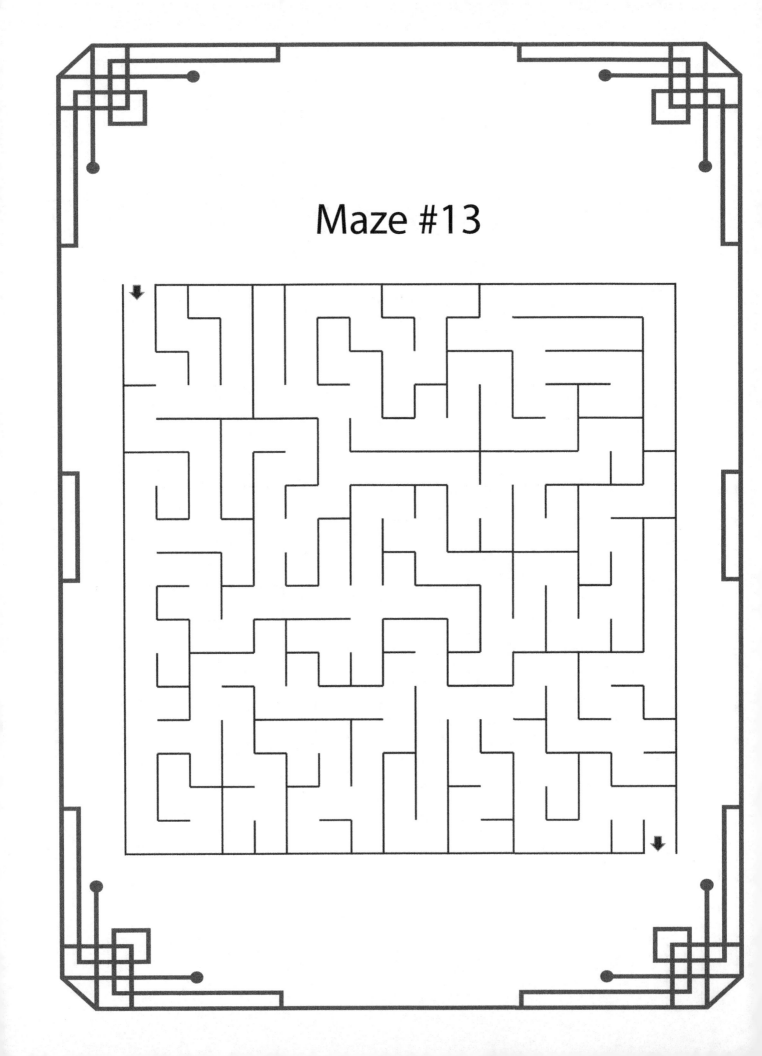

Maze #14

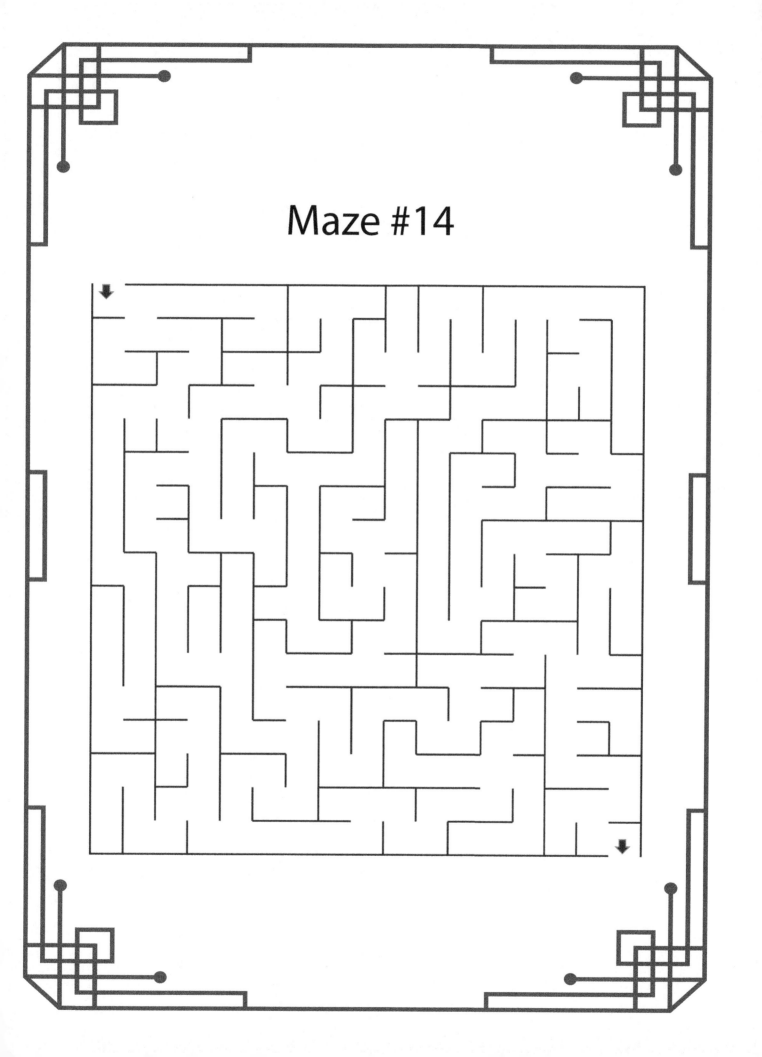

Maze #15

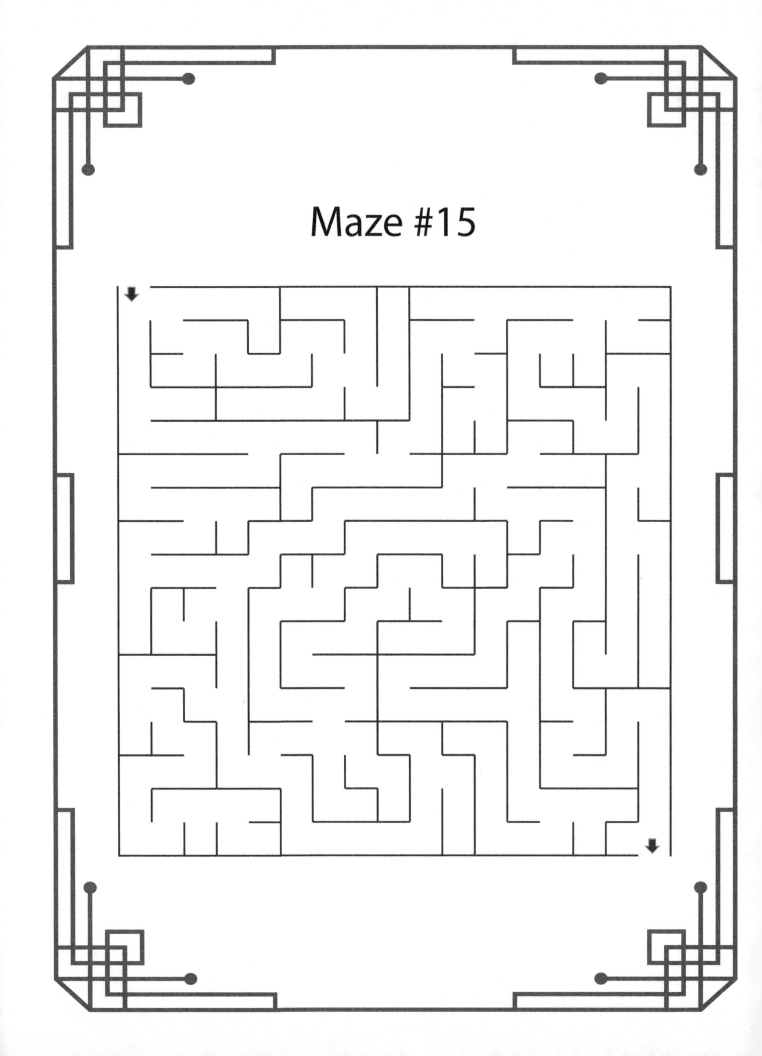

Maze #16

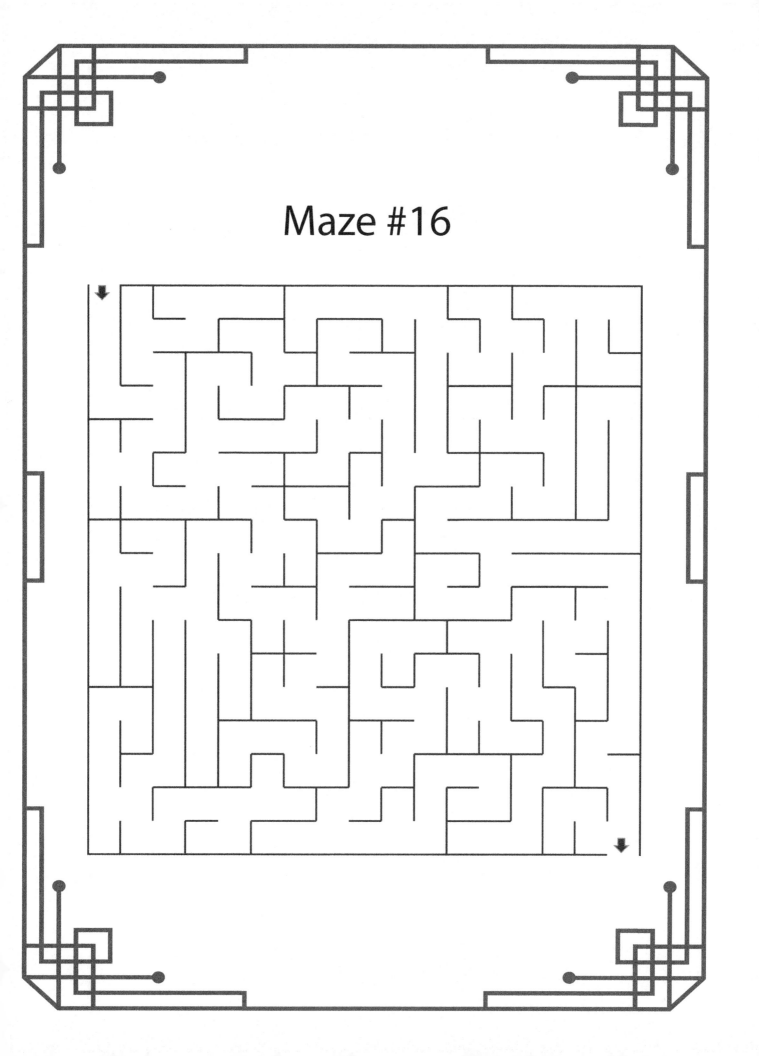

Maze #17

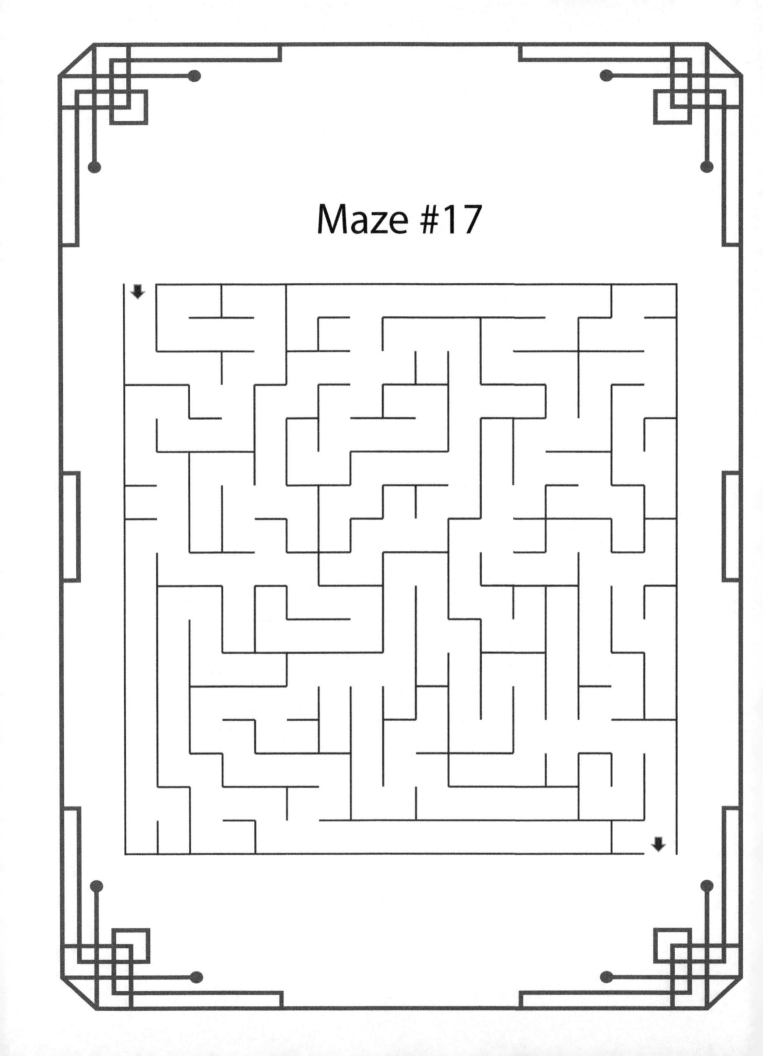

Maze #18

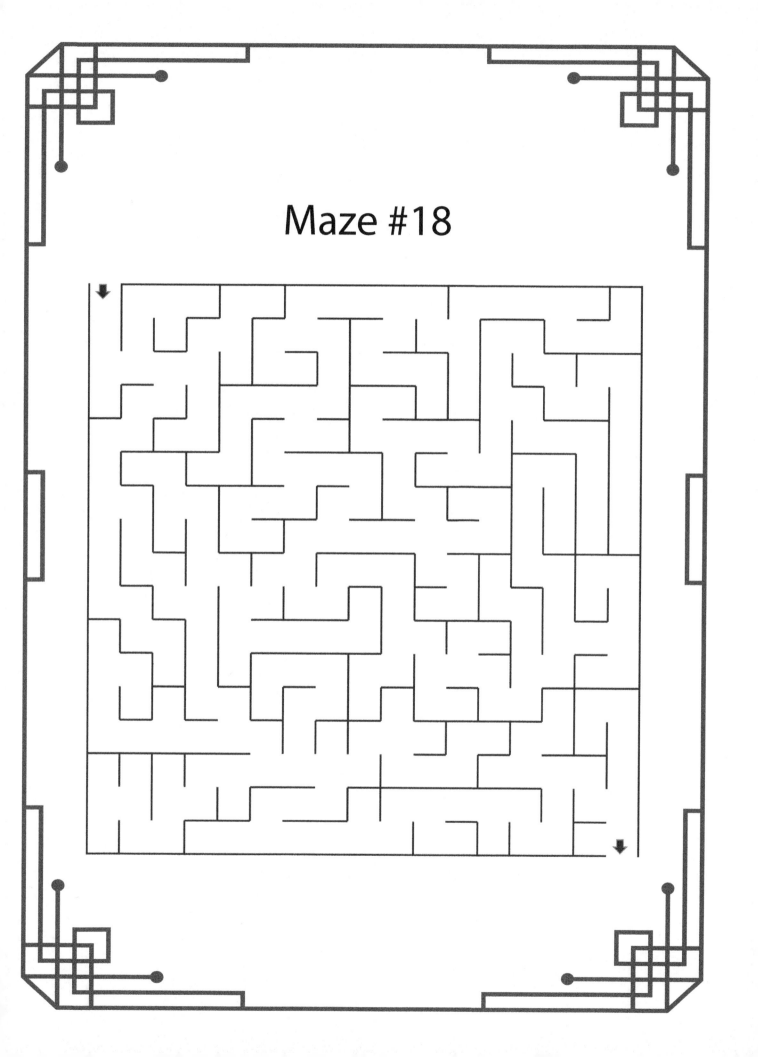

Maze #19

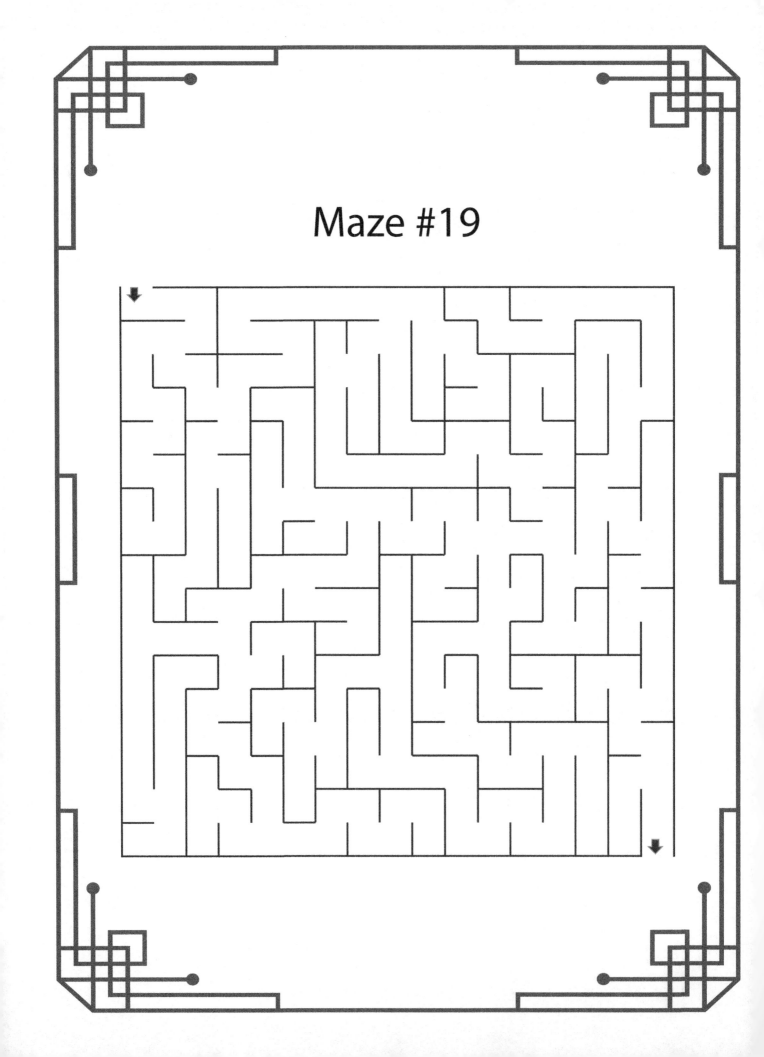

Maze #20

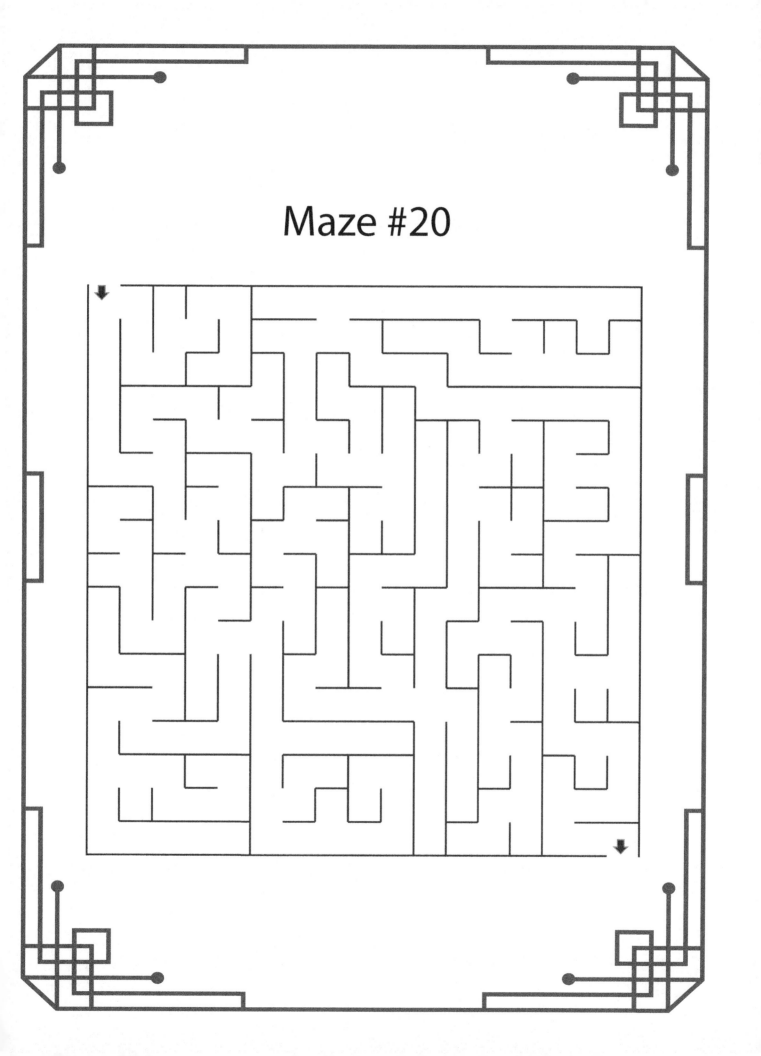

Maze #21

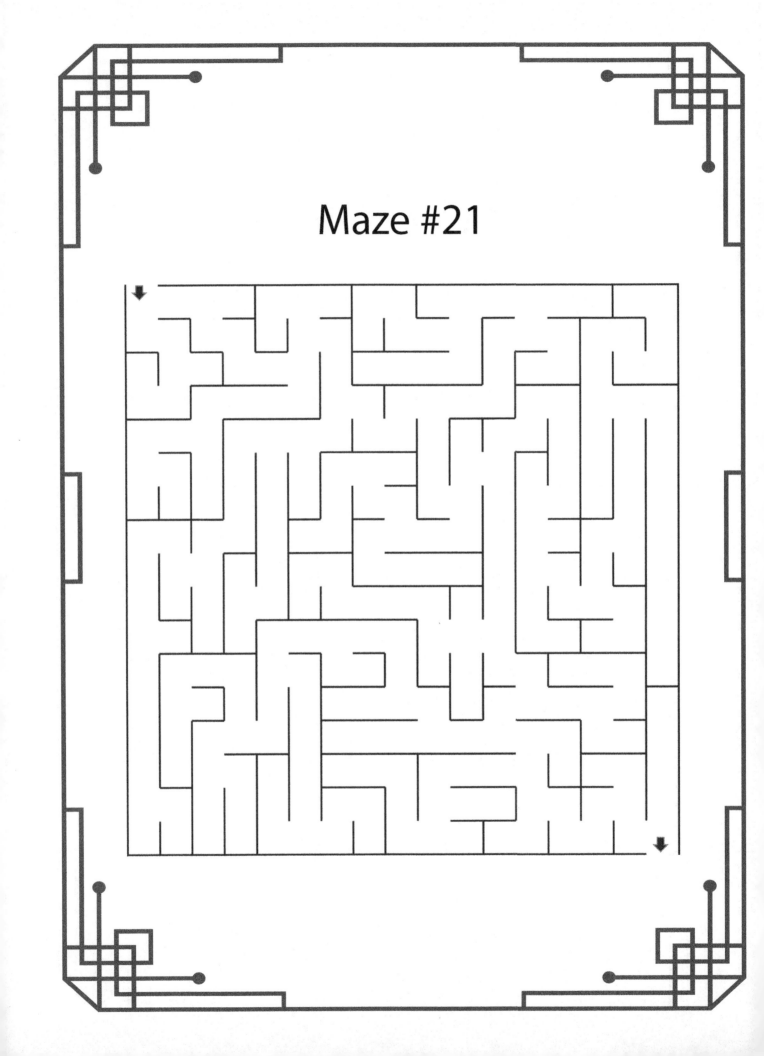

Maze #22

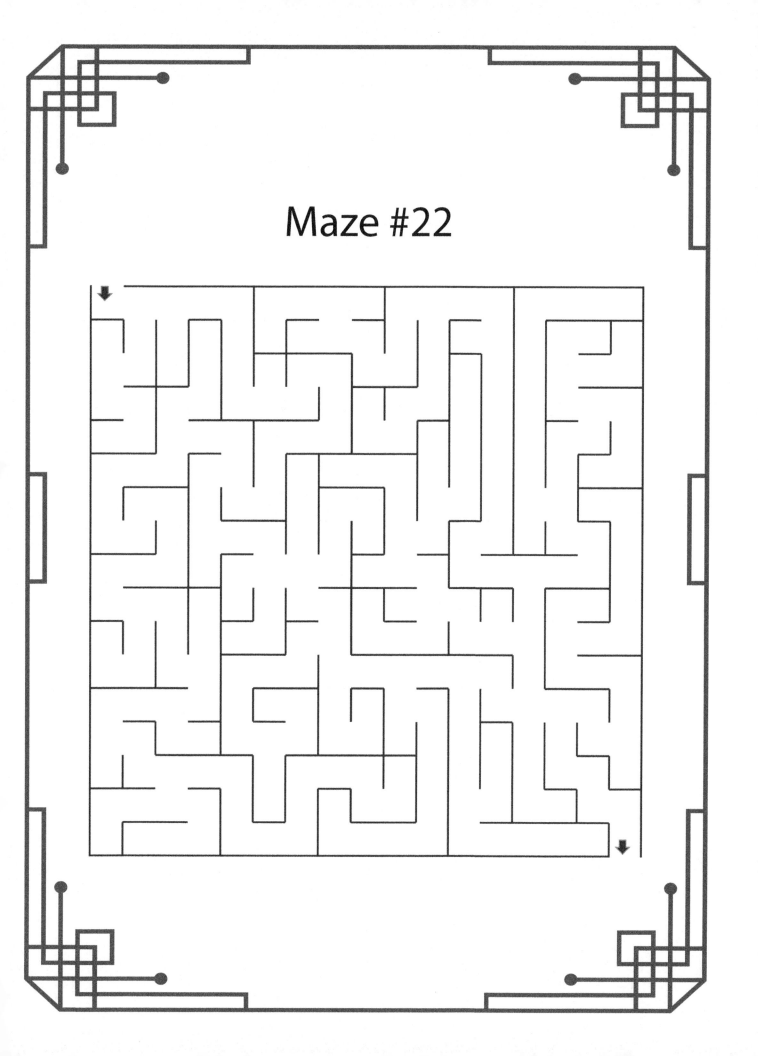

Maze #23

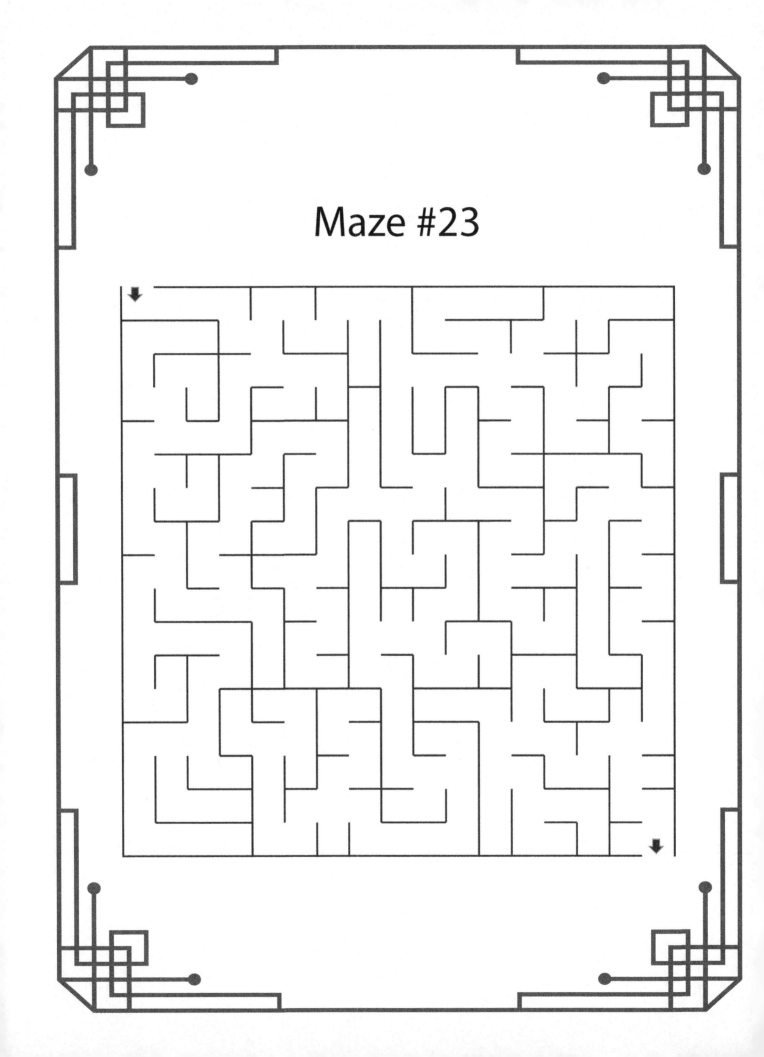

Maze #24

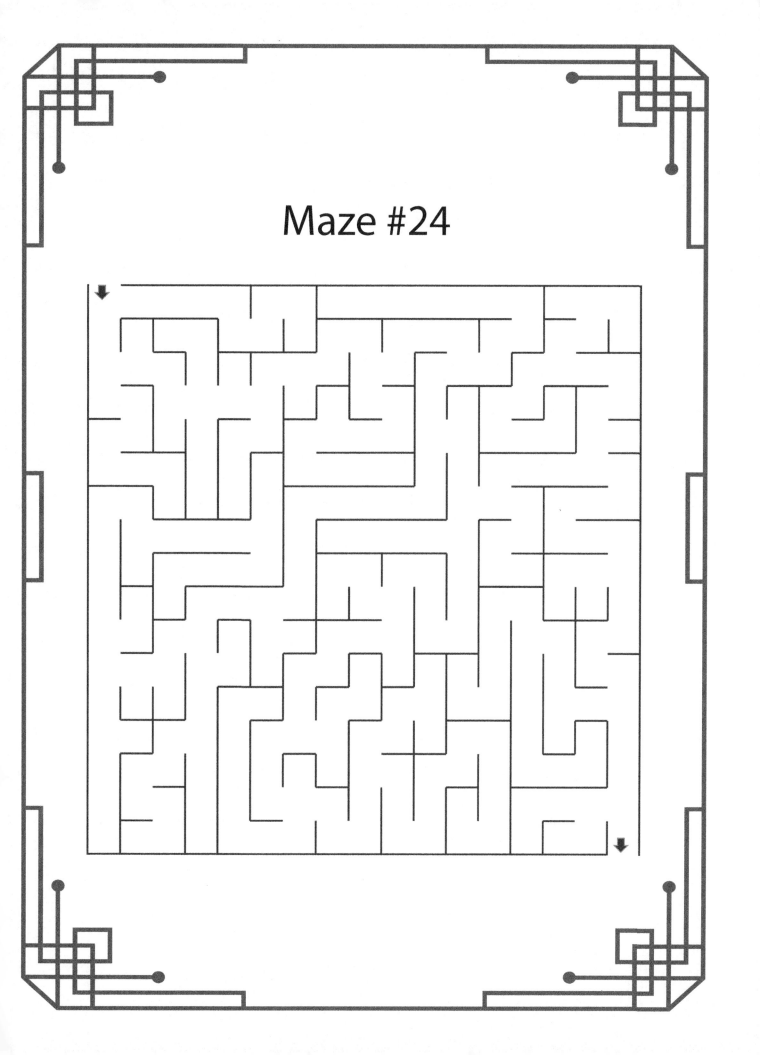

Maze #25

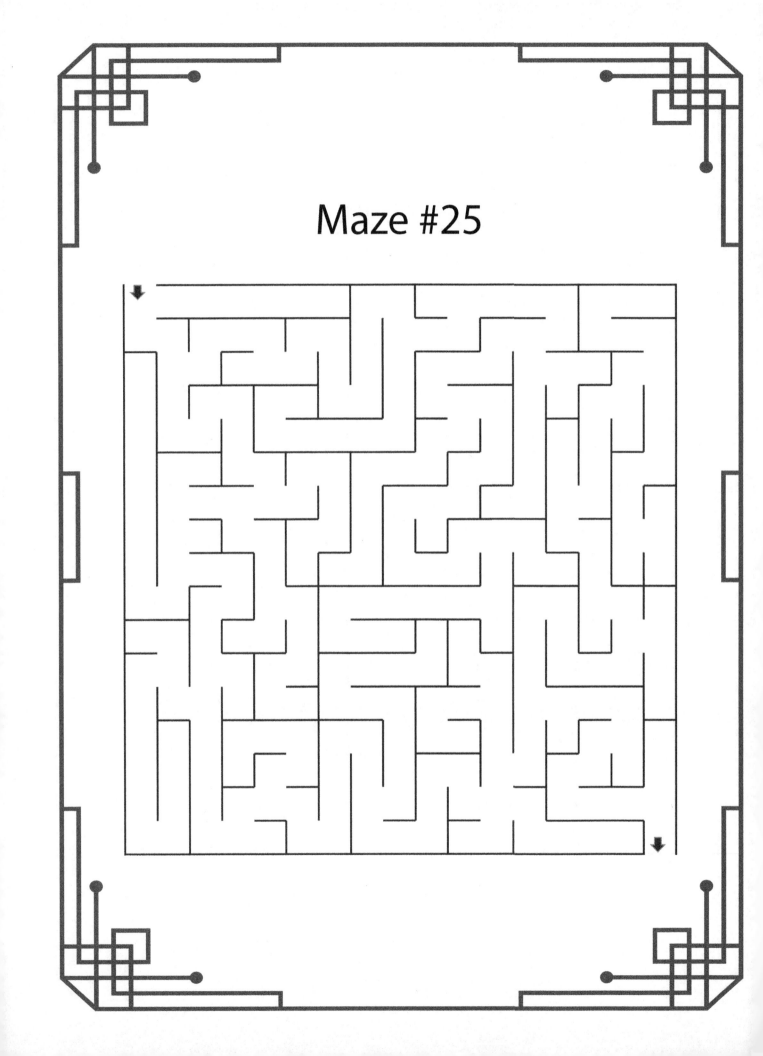

Maze #26

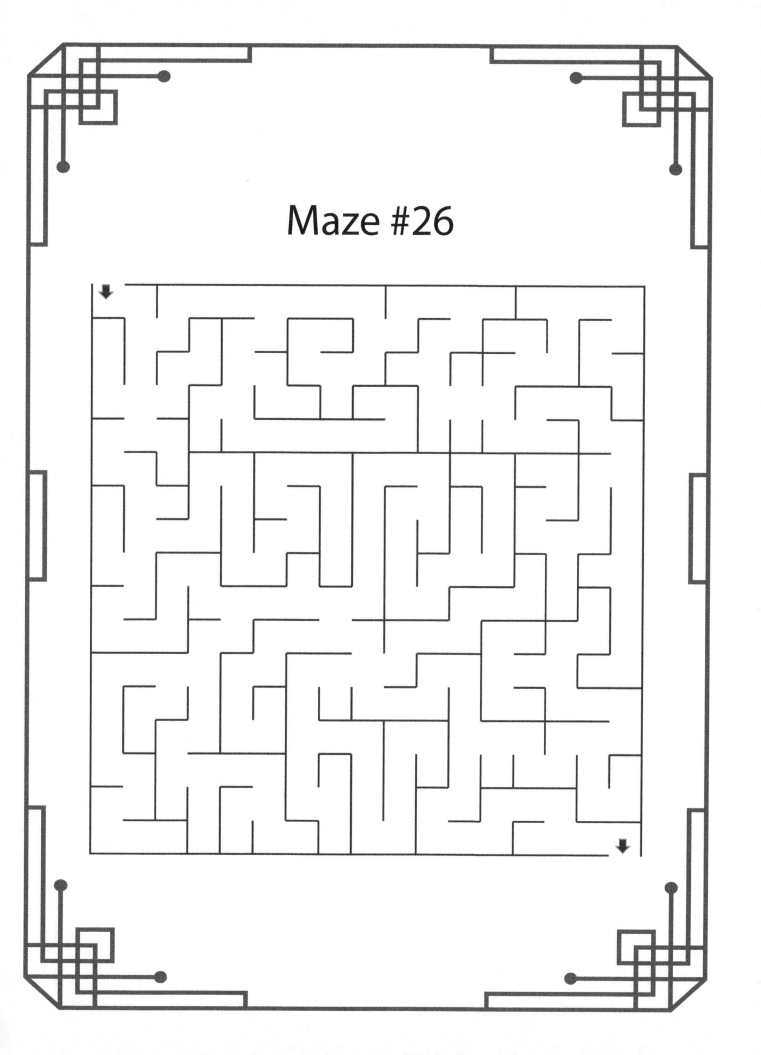

Maze #27

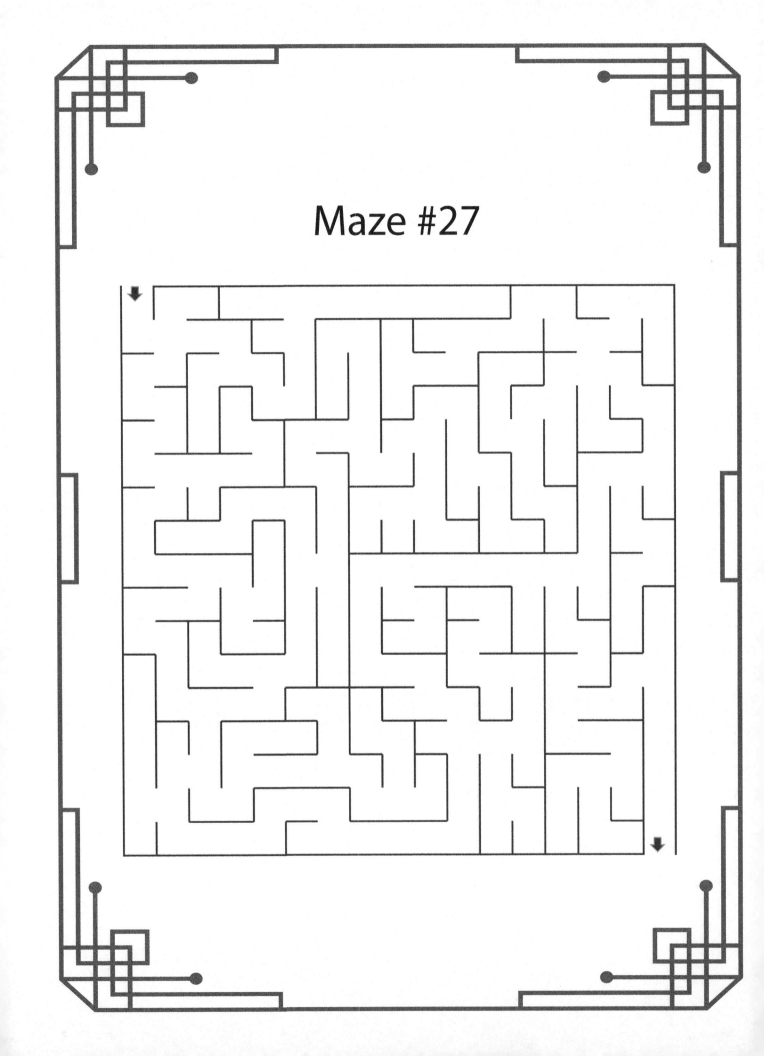

Maze #28

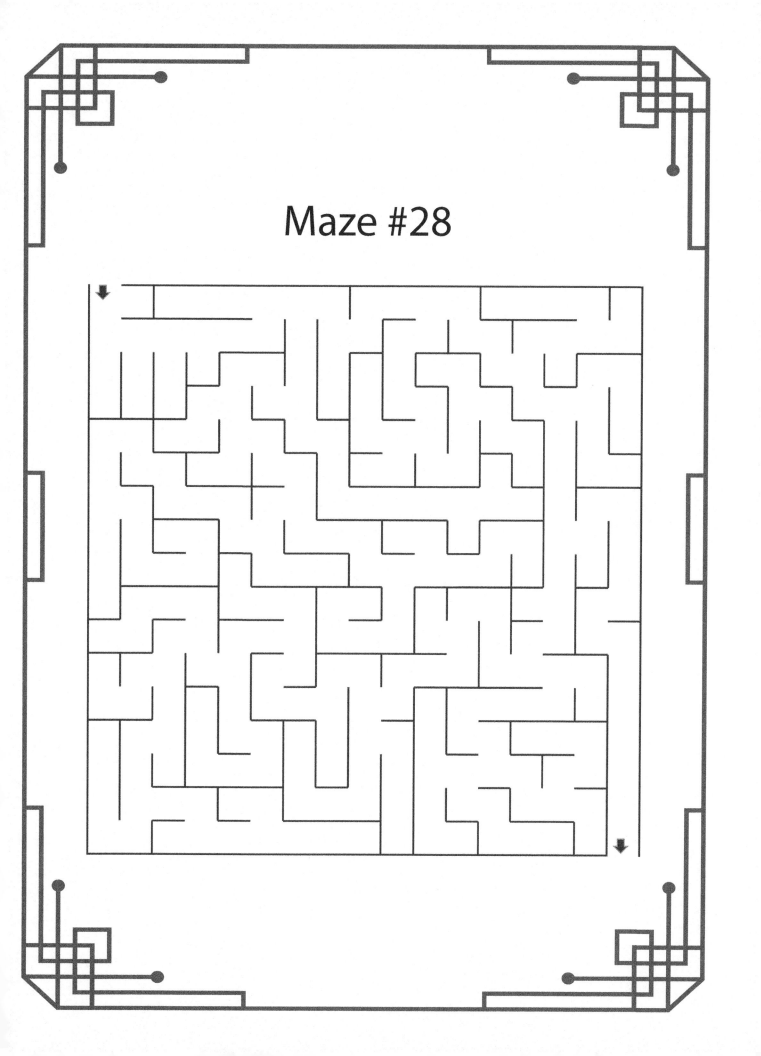

Maze #29

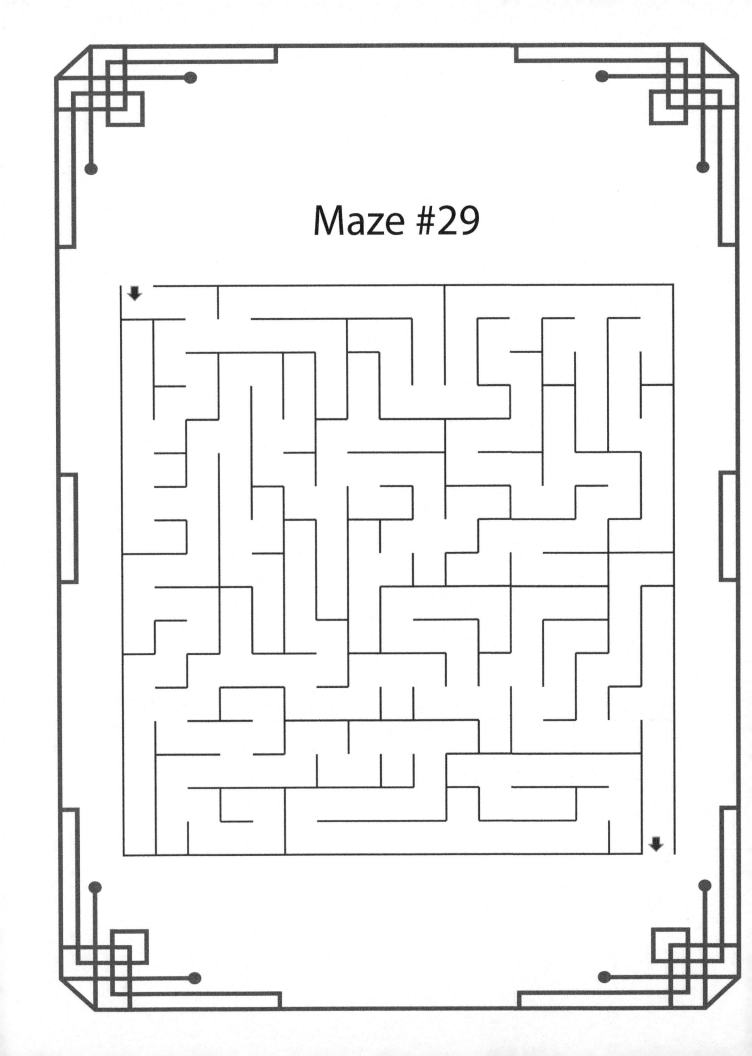

Maze #30

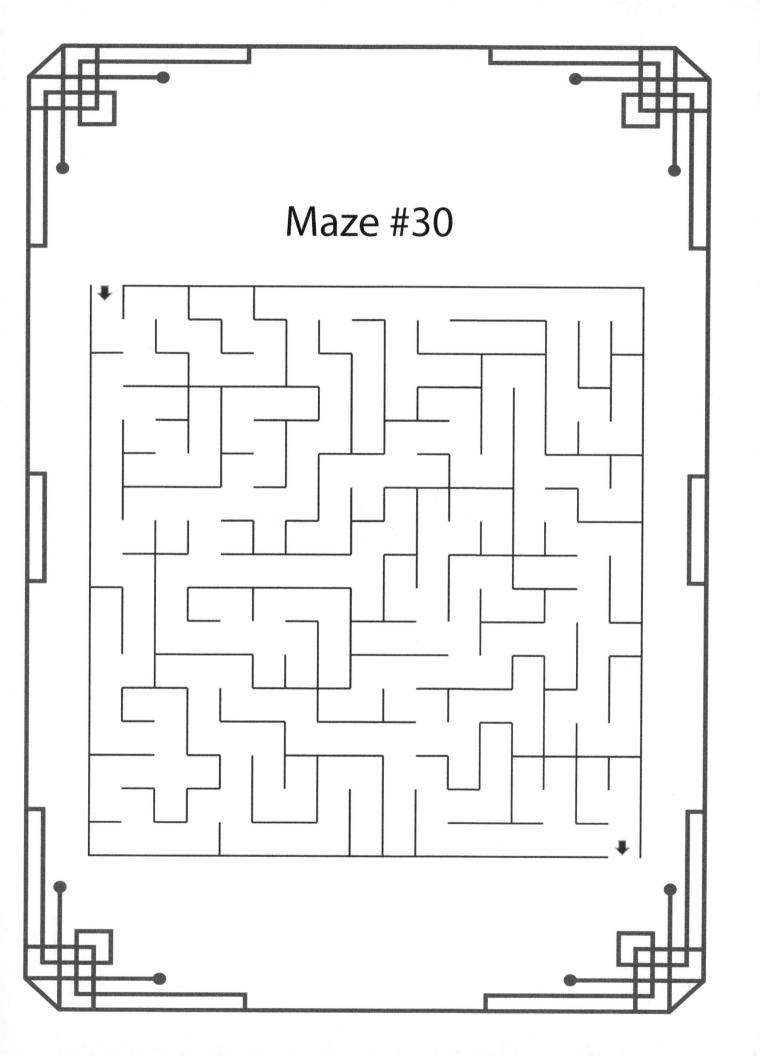

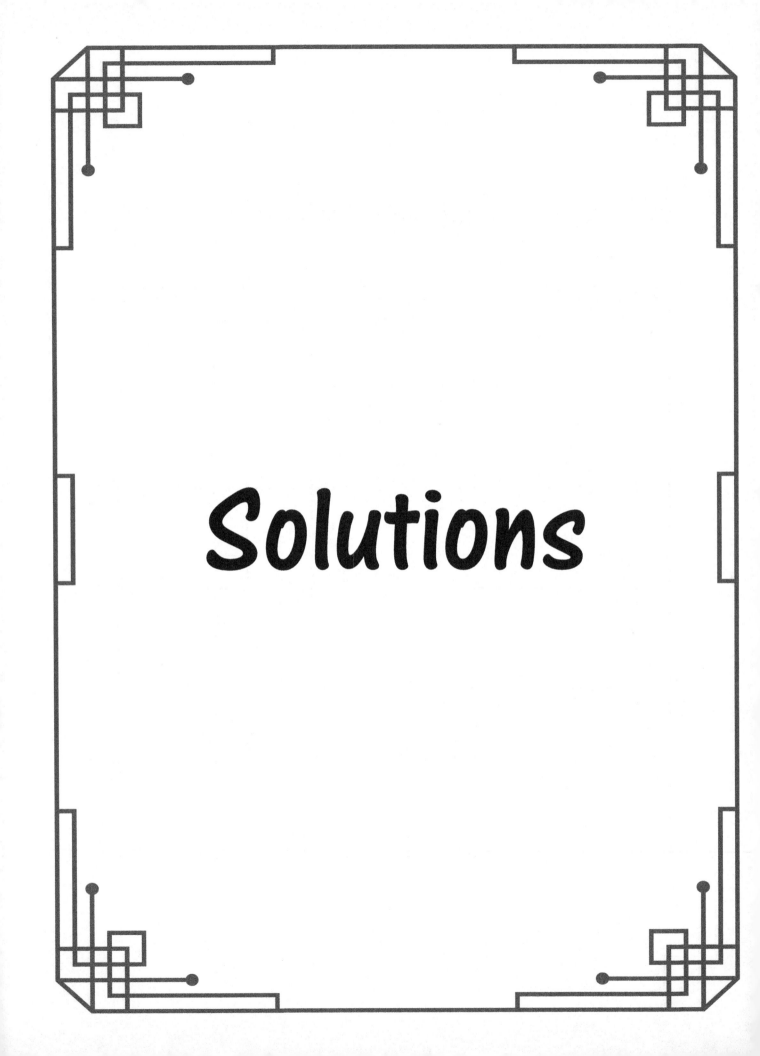

Solutions

Solution #1

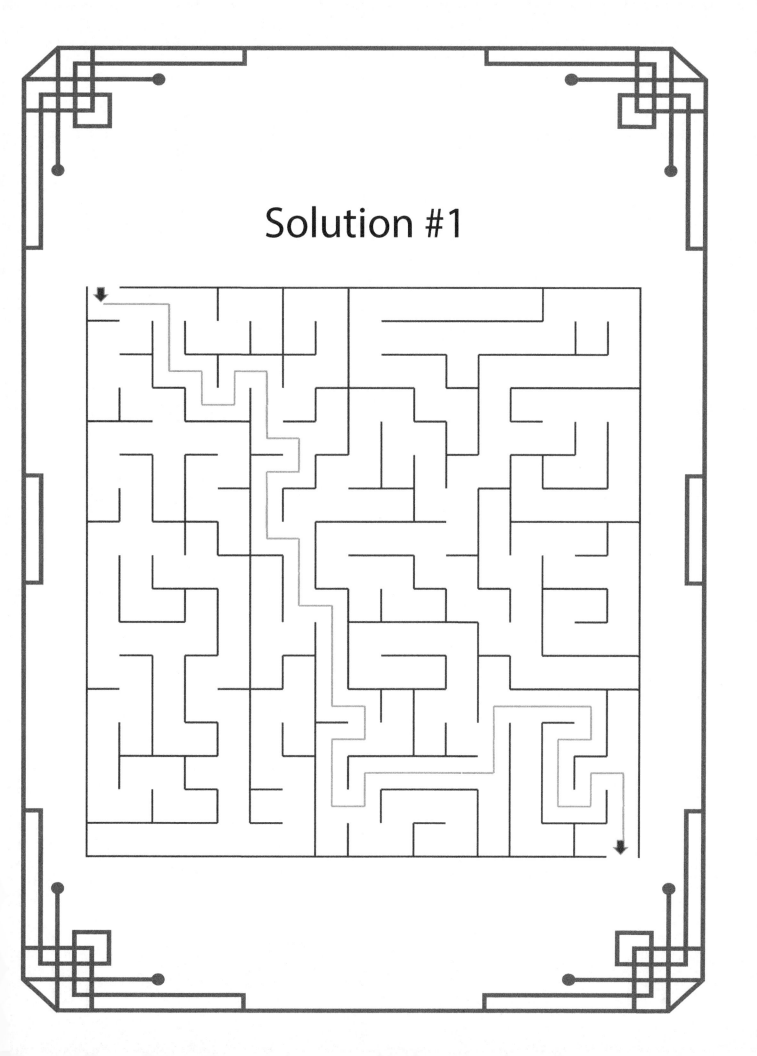

Solution #2

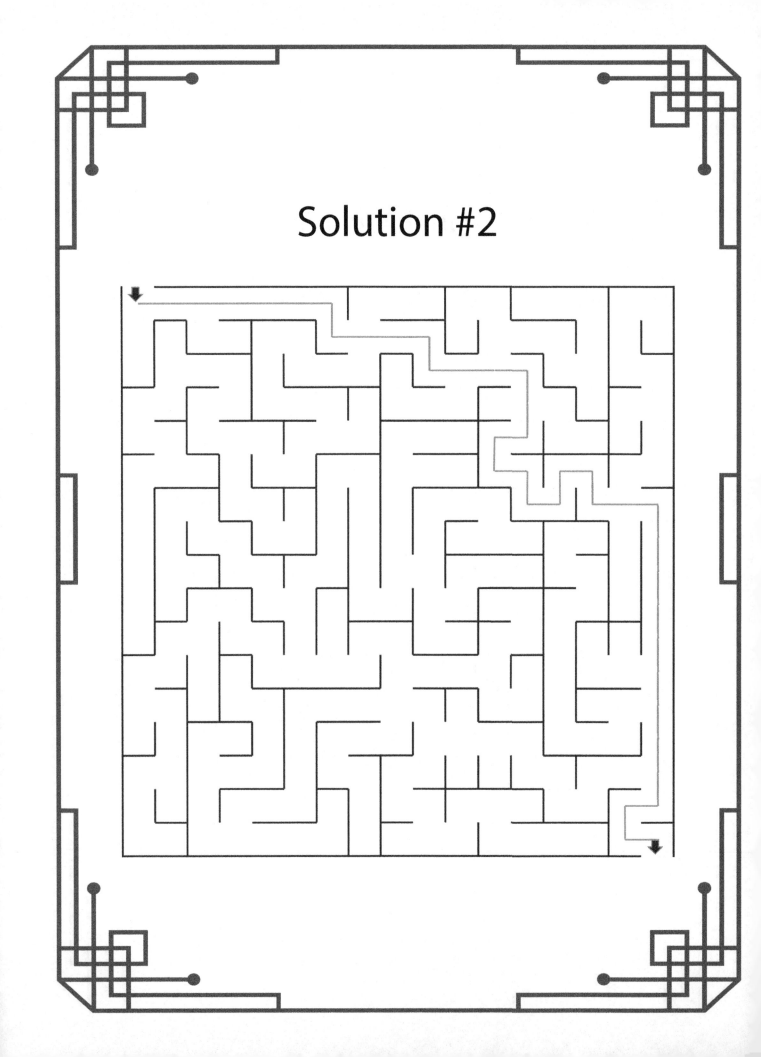

Solution #3

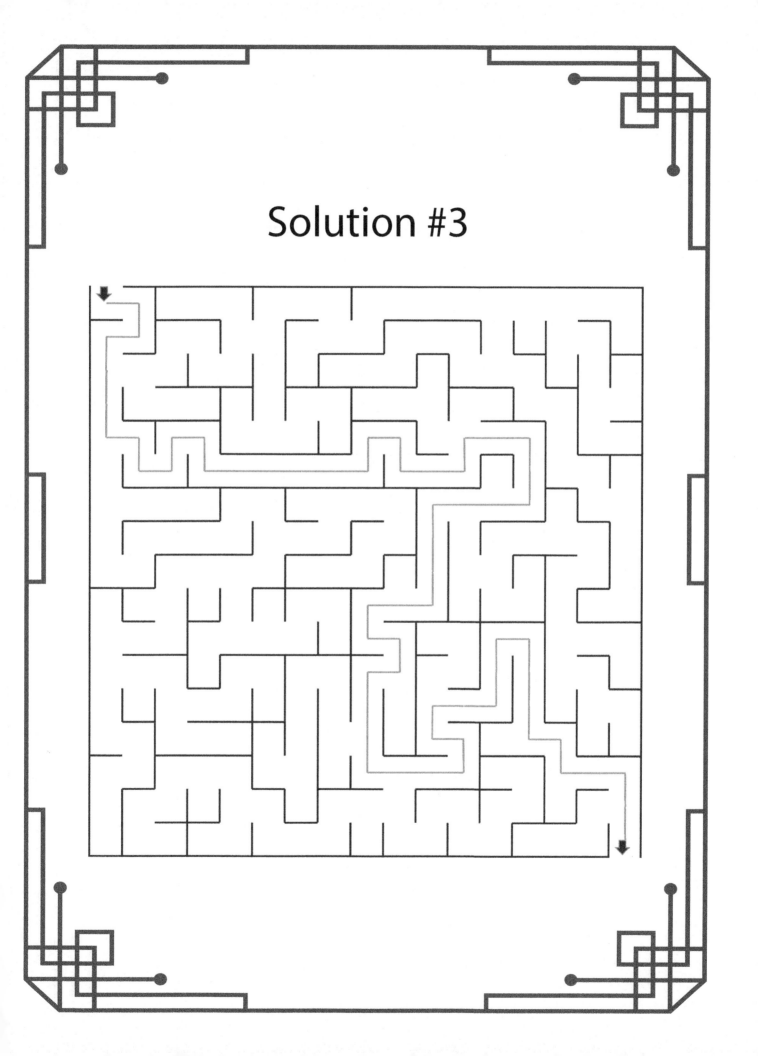

Solution #4

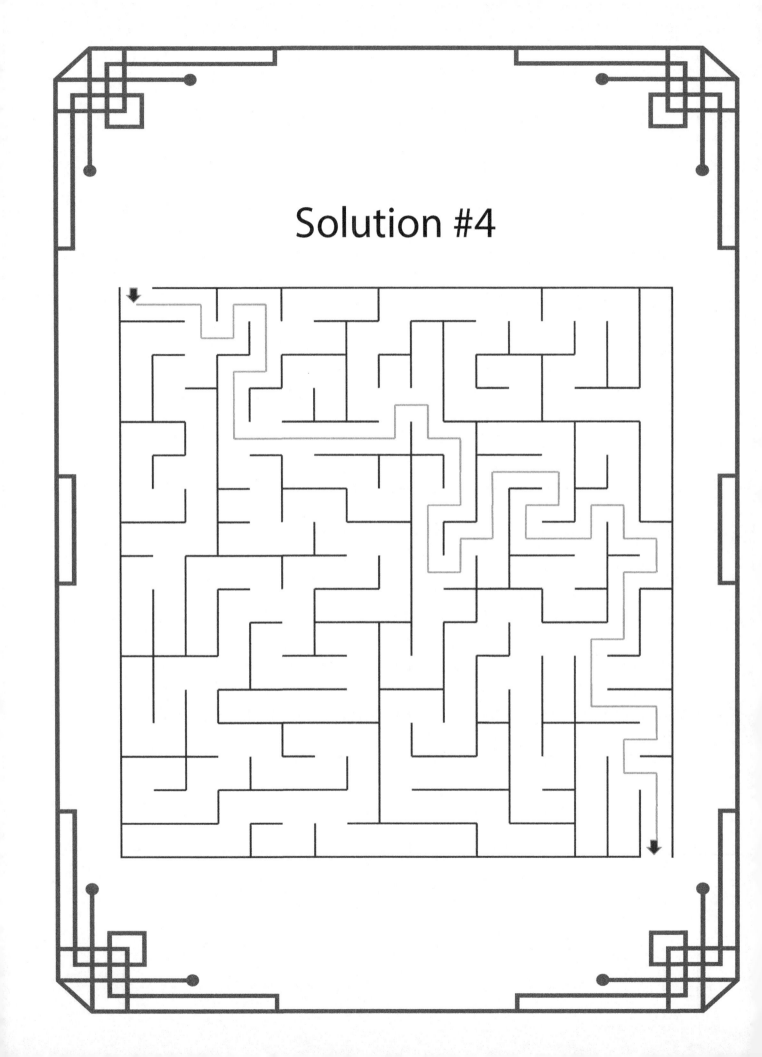

Solution #5

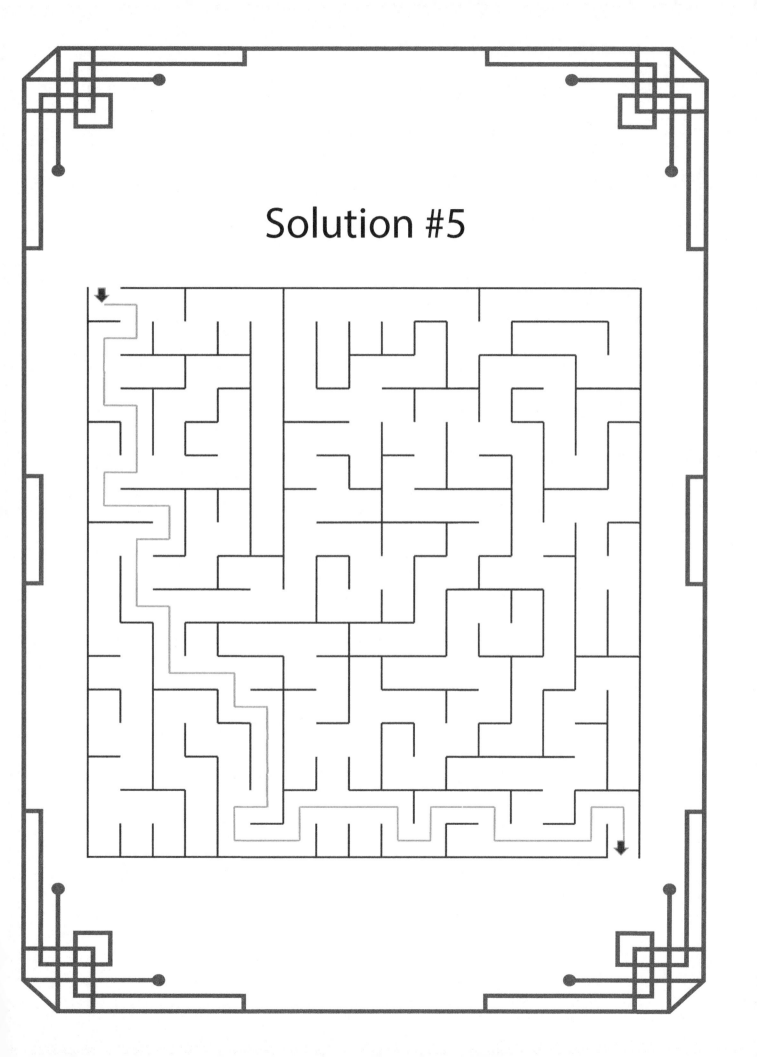

Solution #6

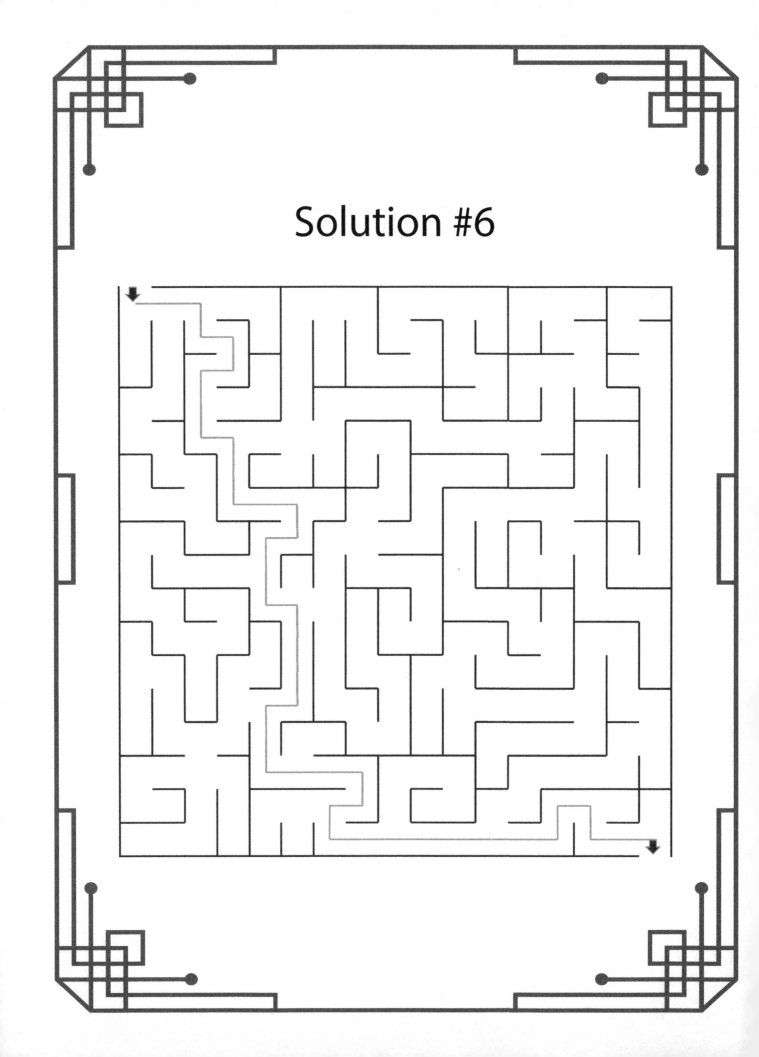

Solution #7

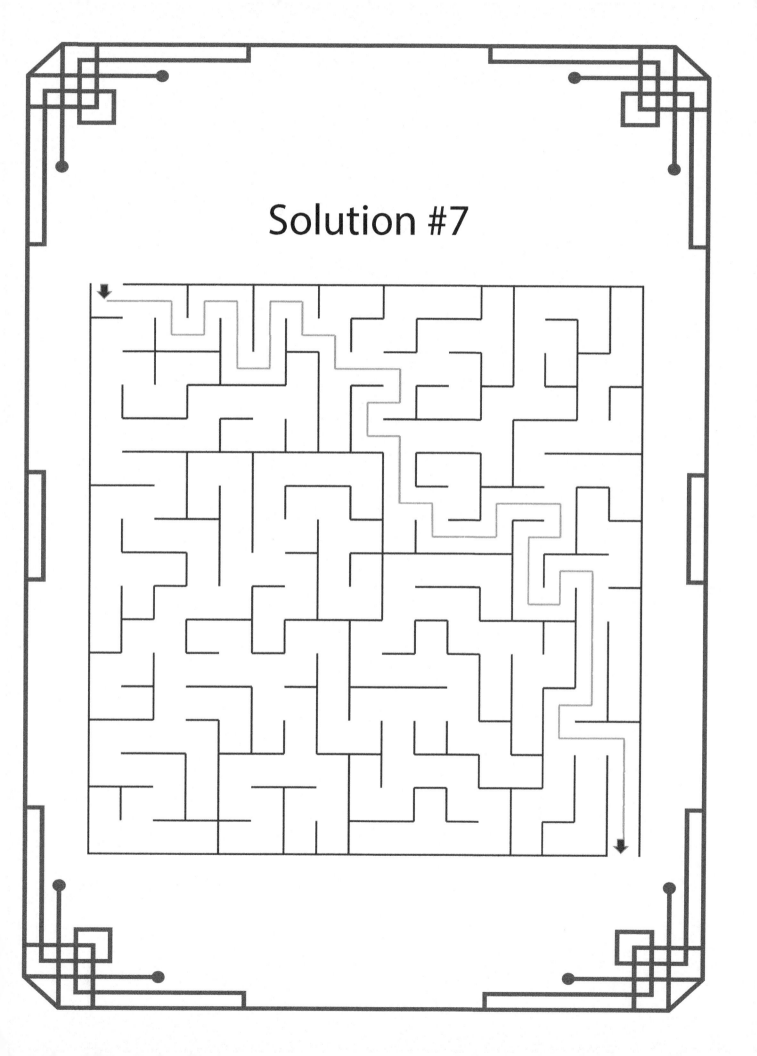

Solution #8

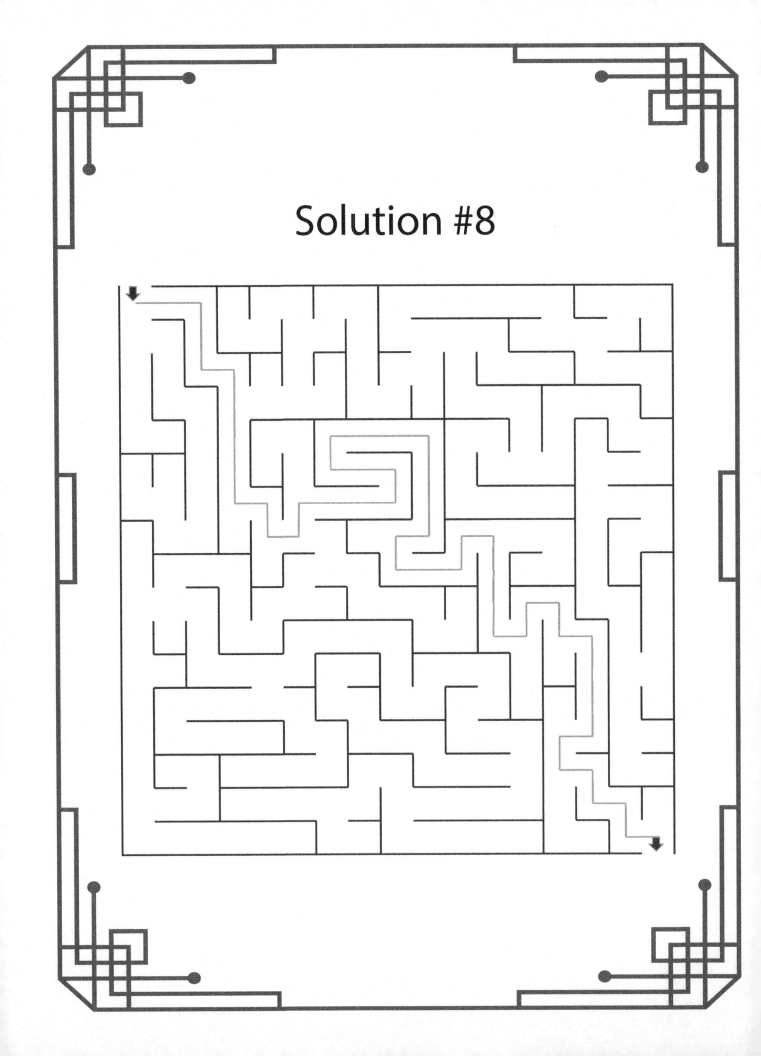

Solution #9

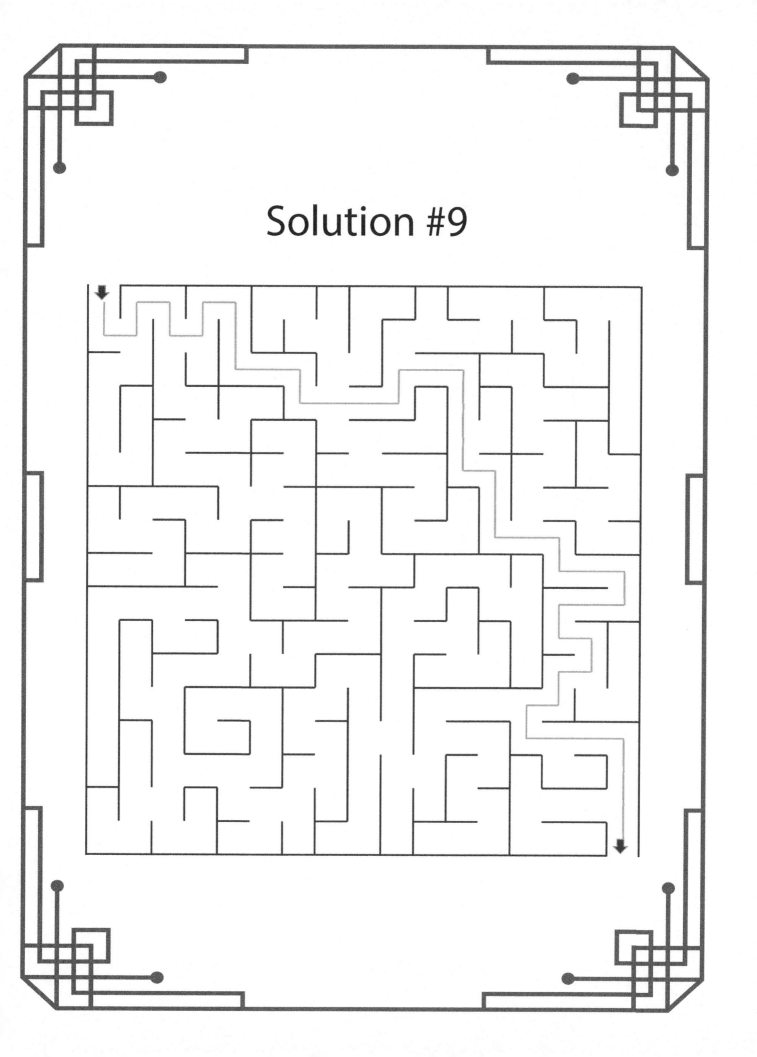

Solution #10

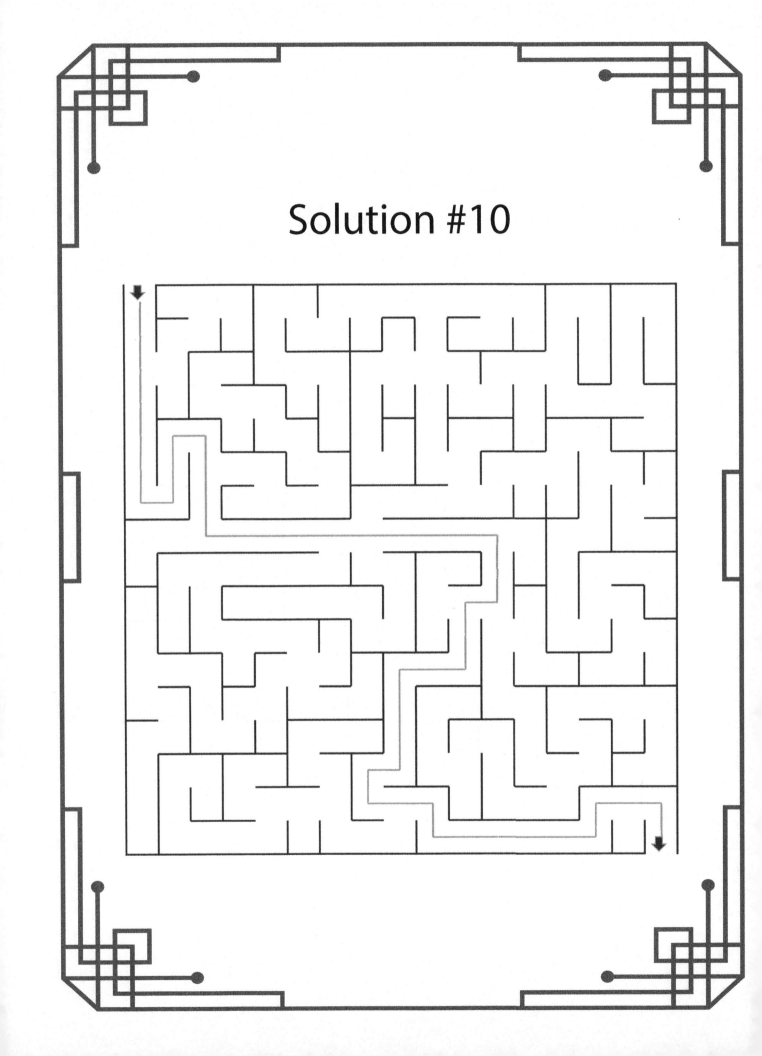

Solution #11

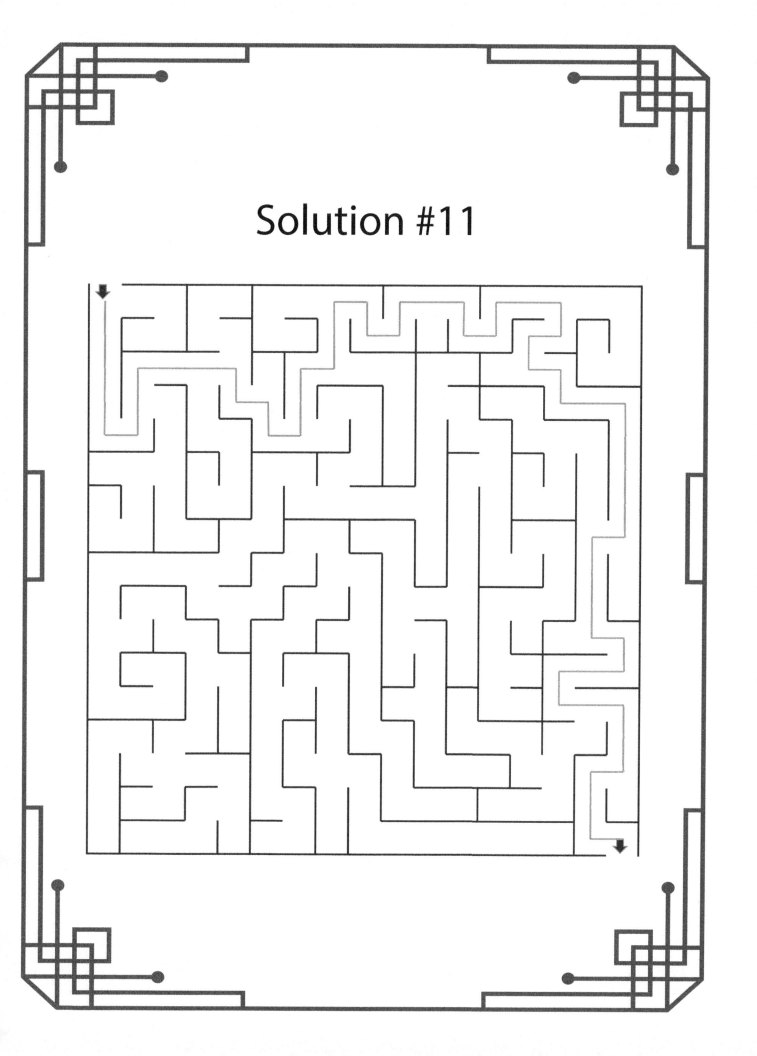

Solution #12

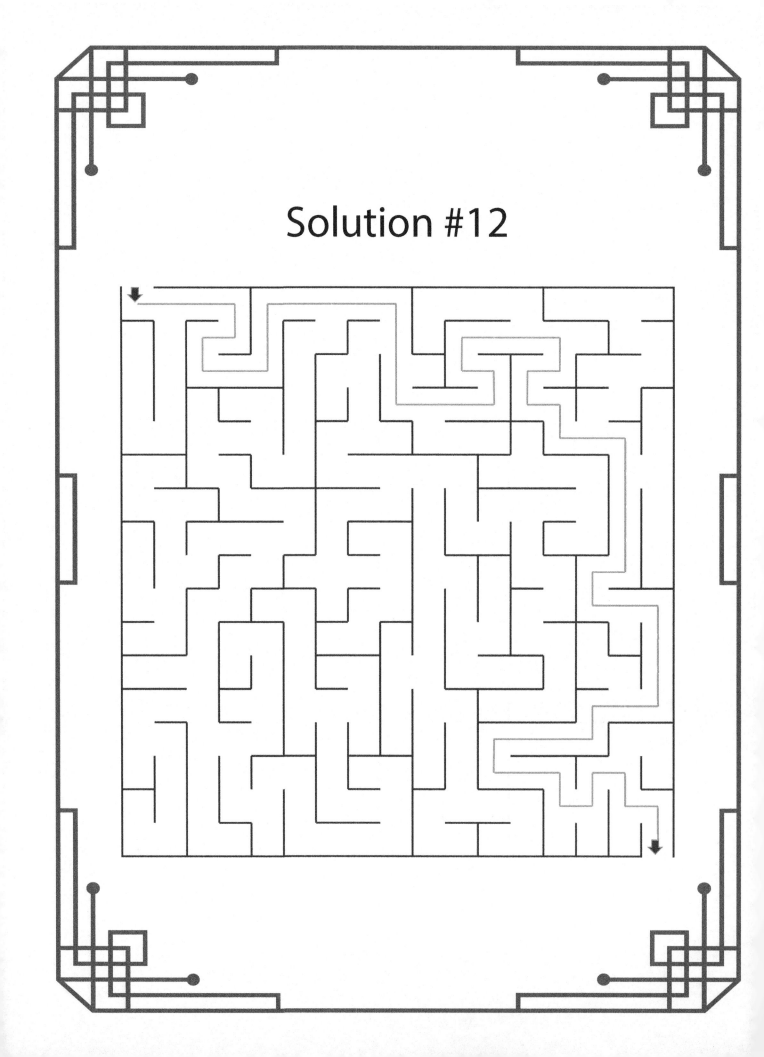

Solution #13

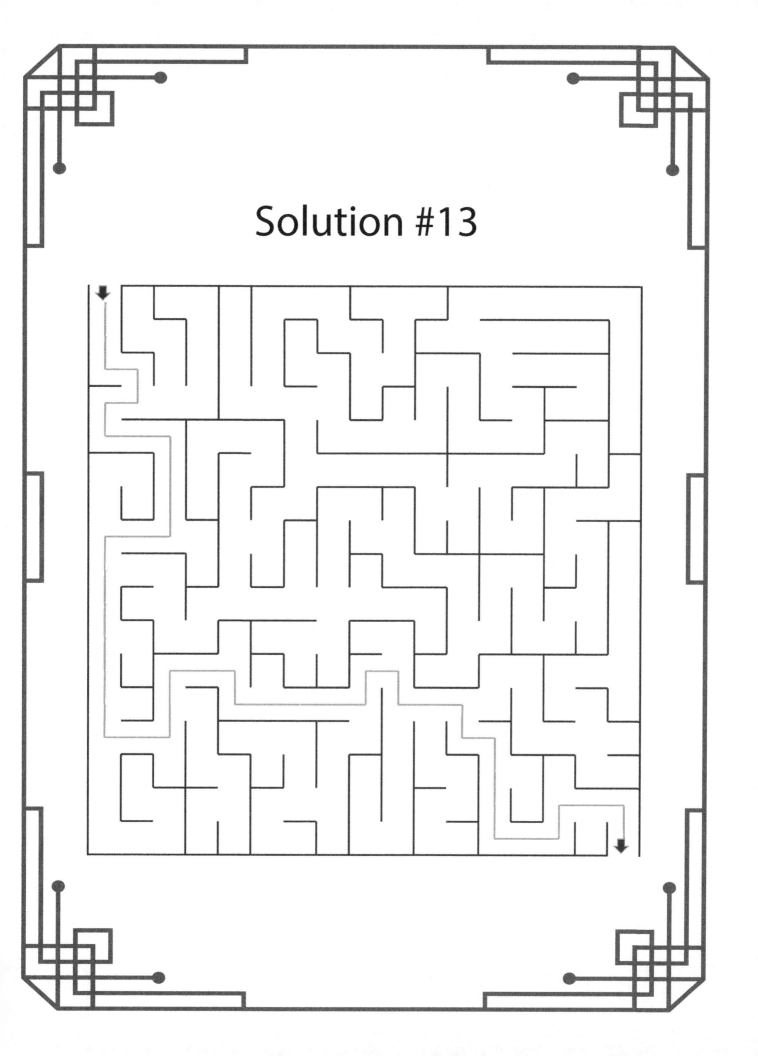

Solution #14

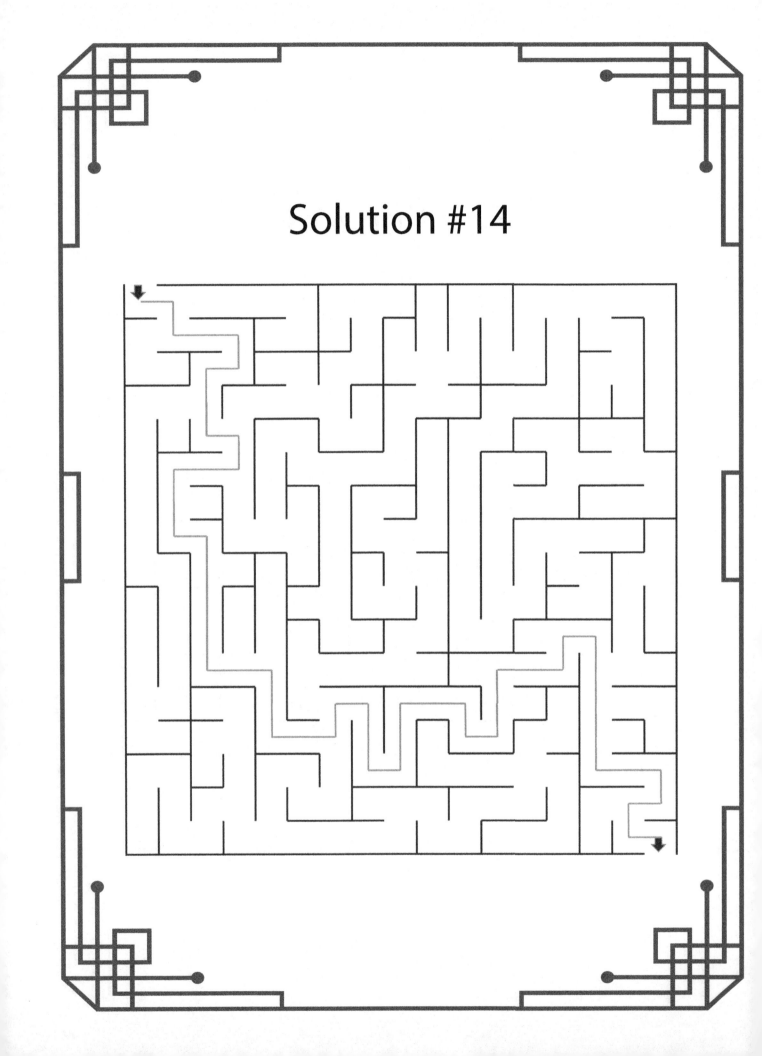

Solution #15

Solution #16

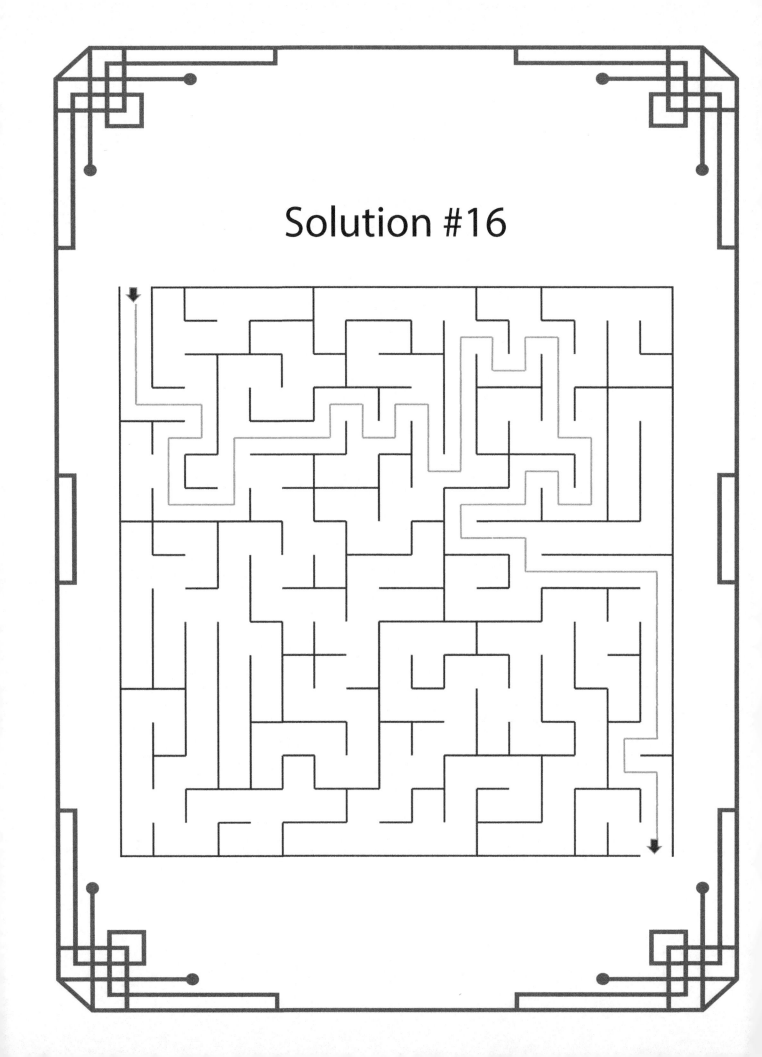

Solution #17

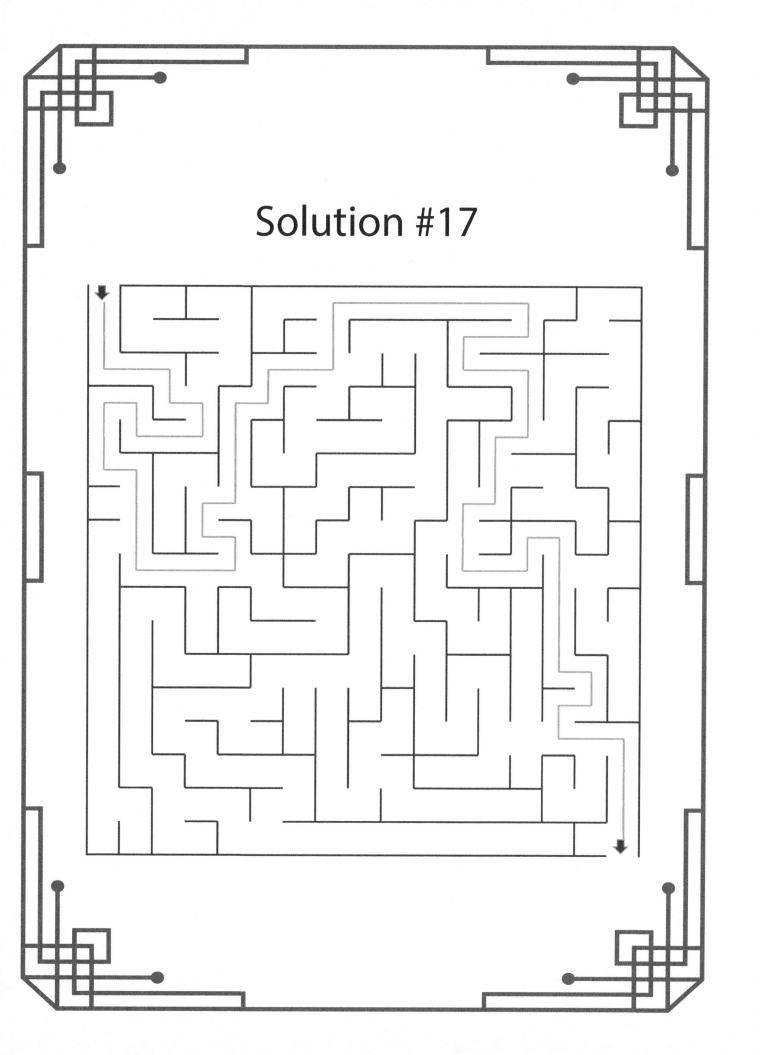

Solution #18

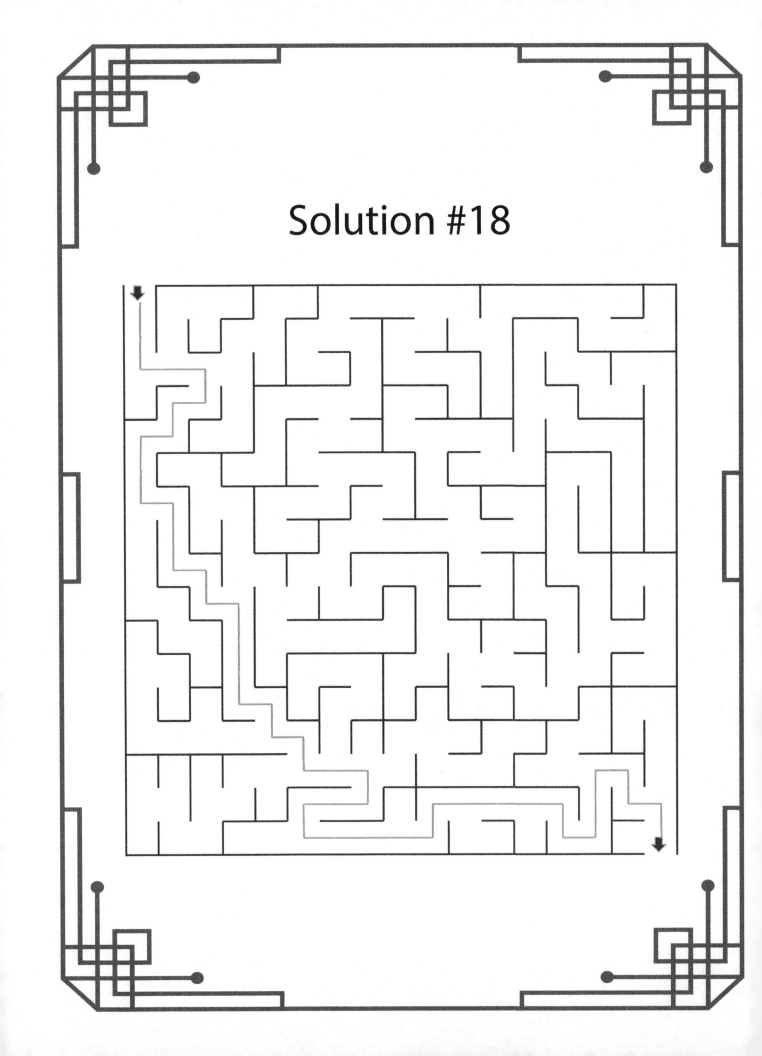

Solution #19

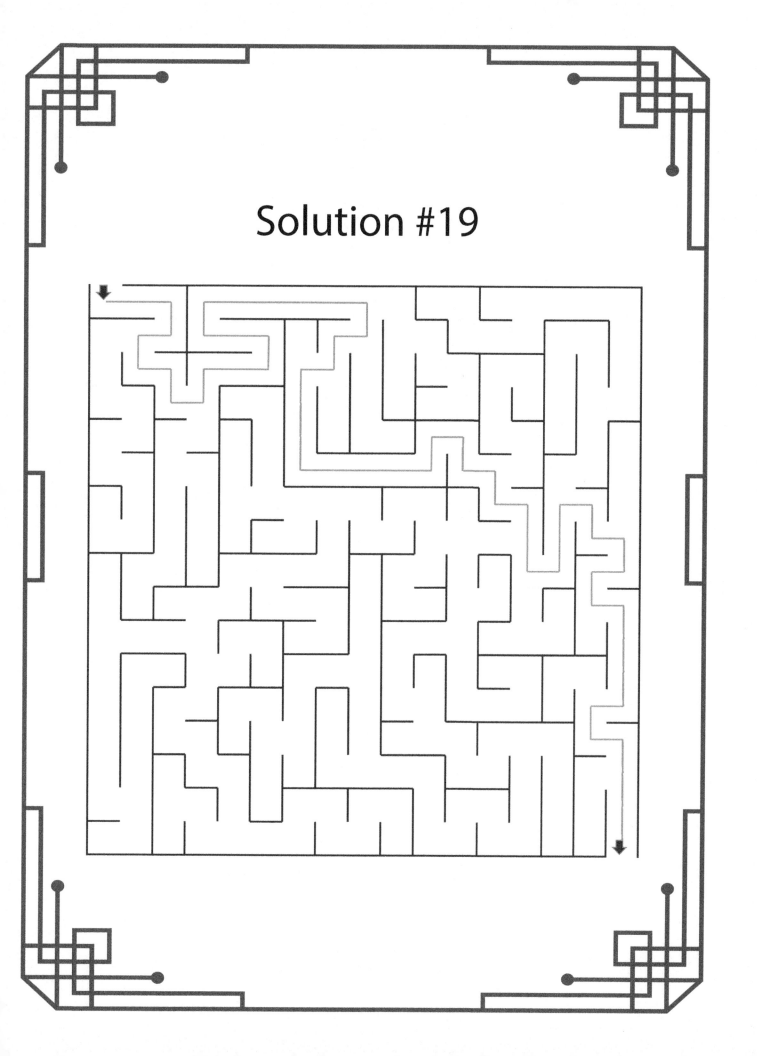

Solution #20

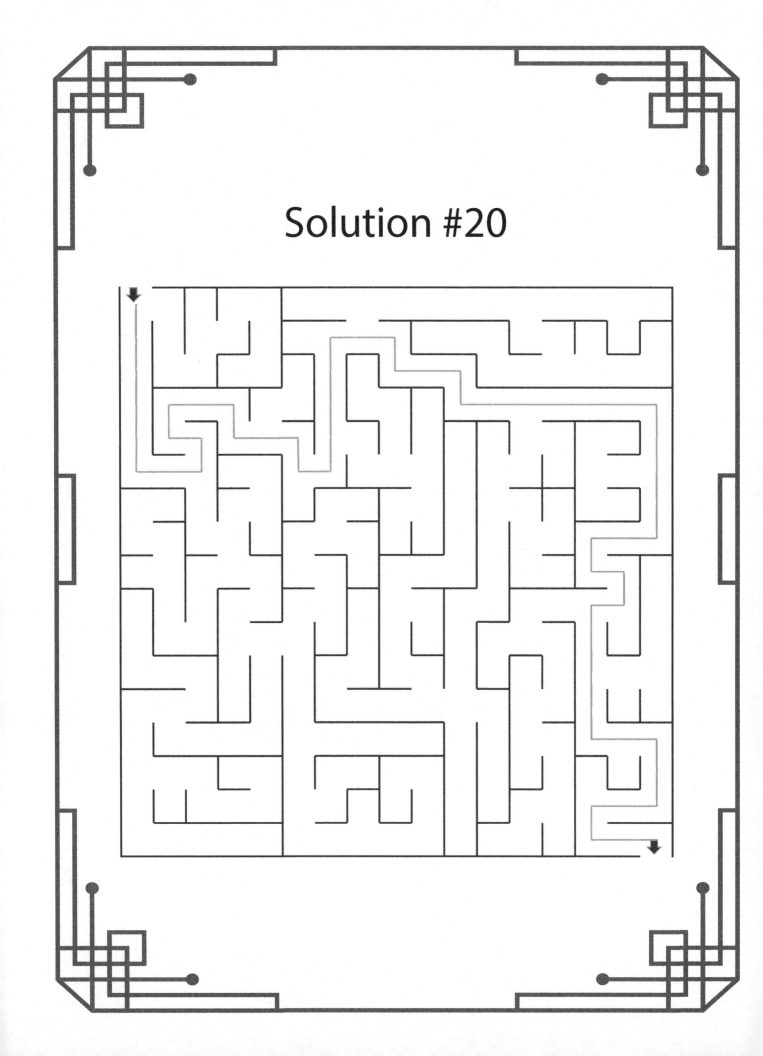

Solution #21

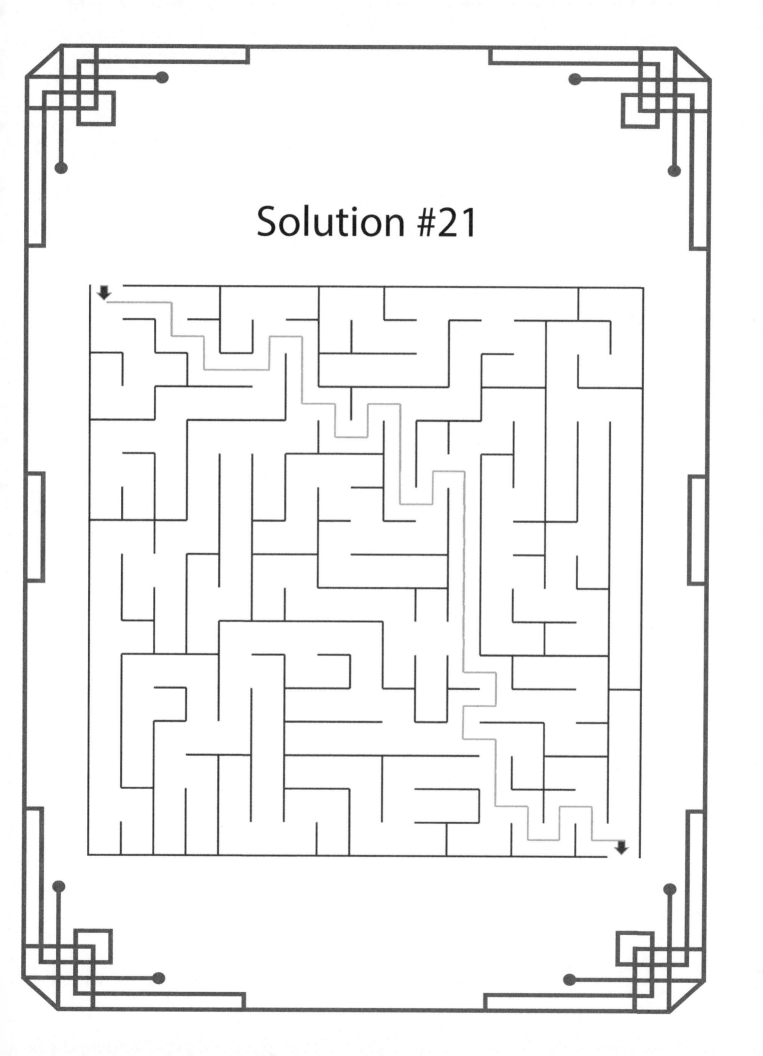

Solution #22

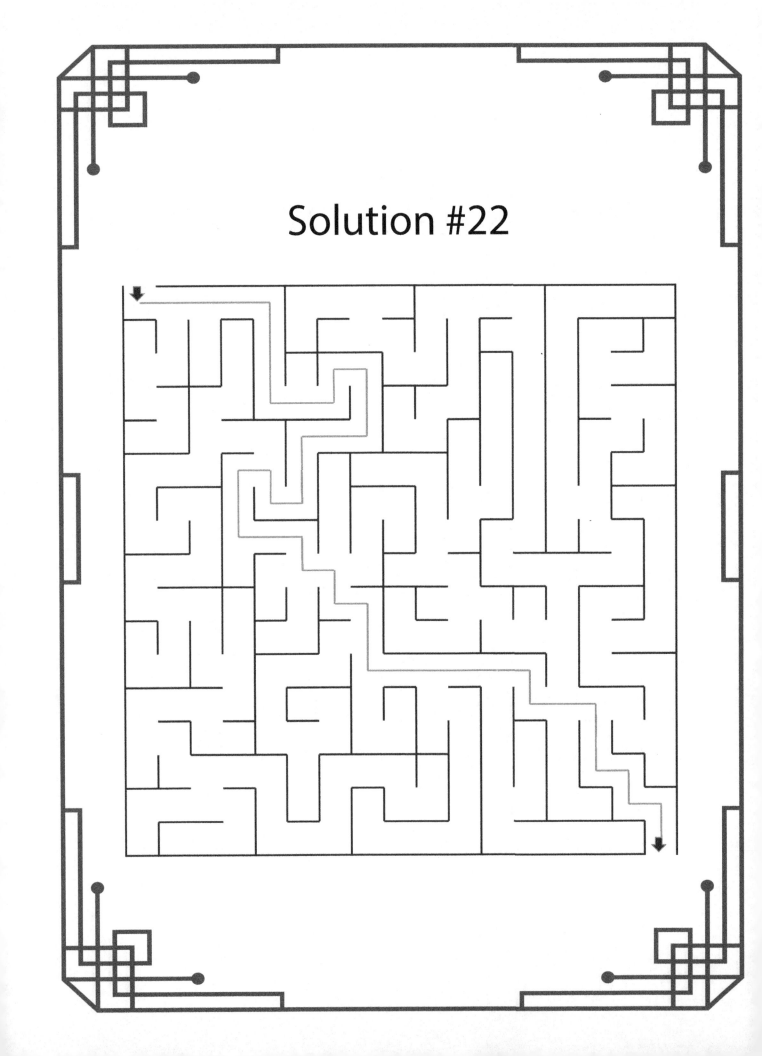

Solution #23

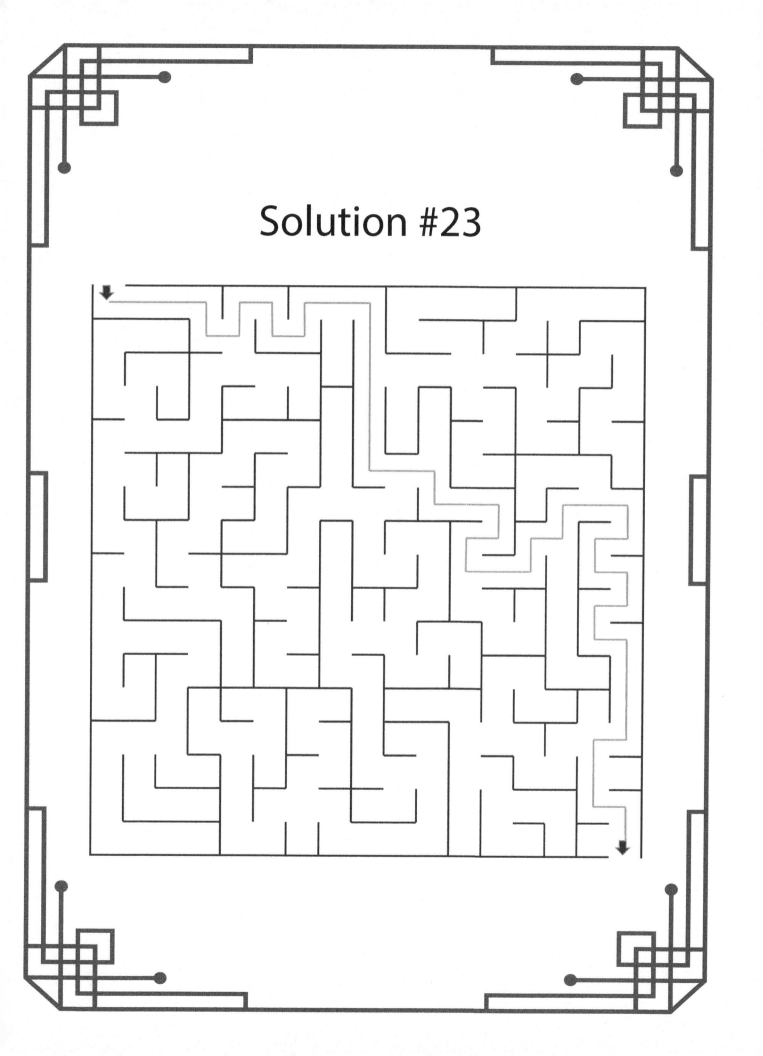

Solution #24

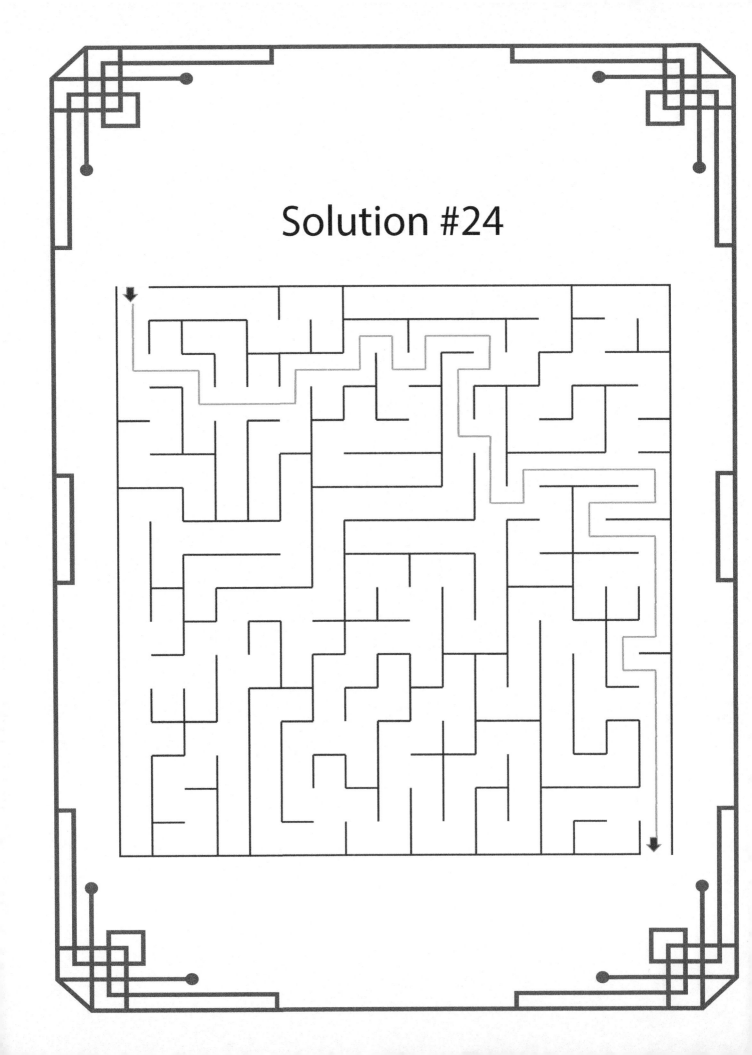

Solution #25

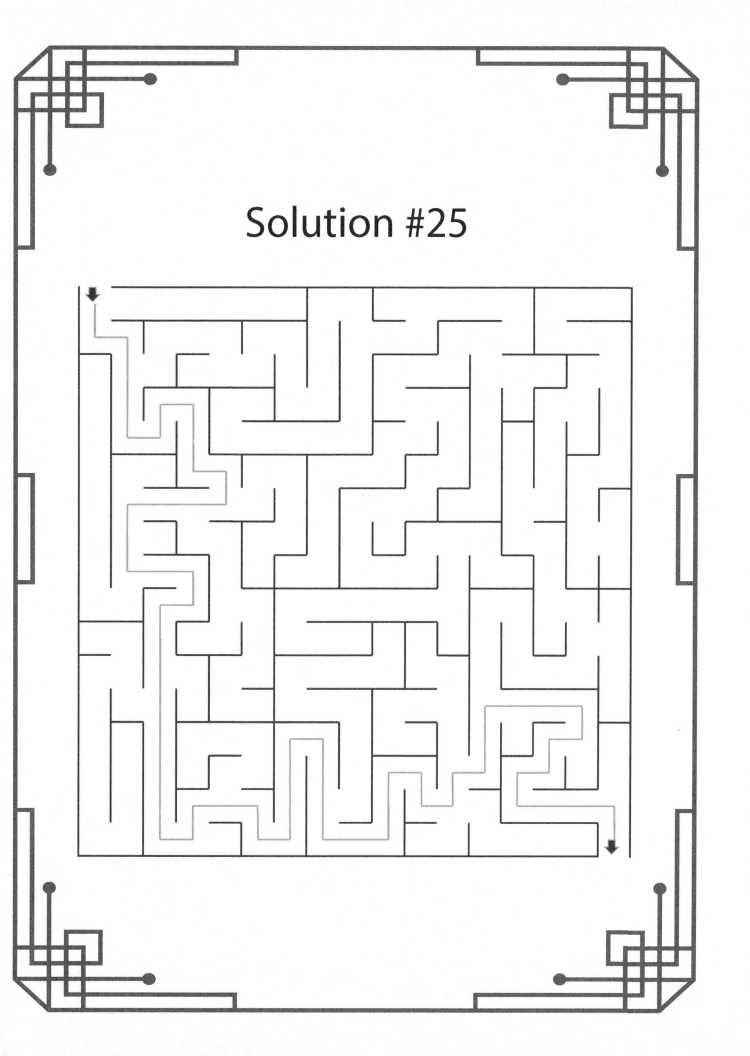

Solution #26

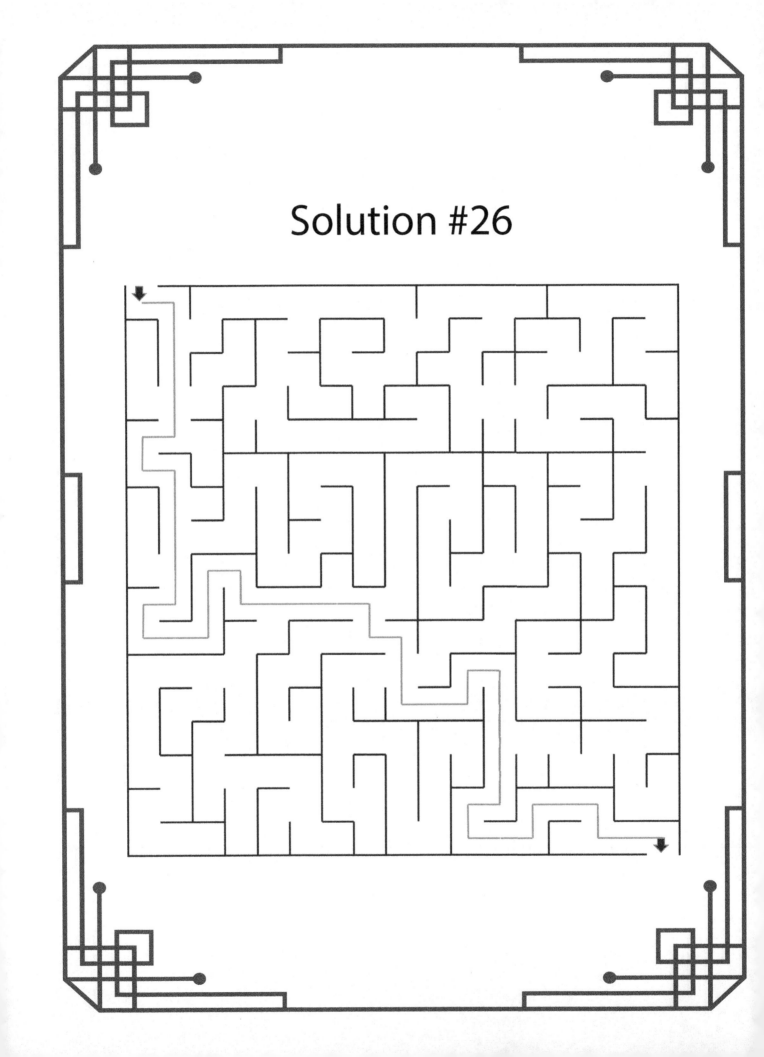

Solution #27

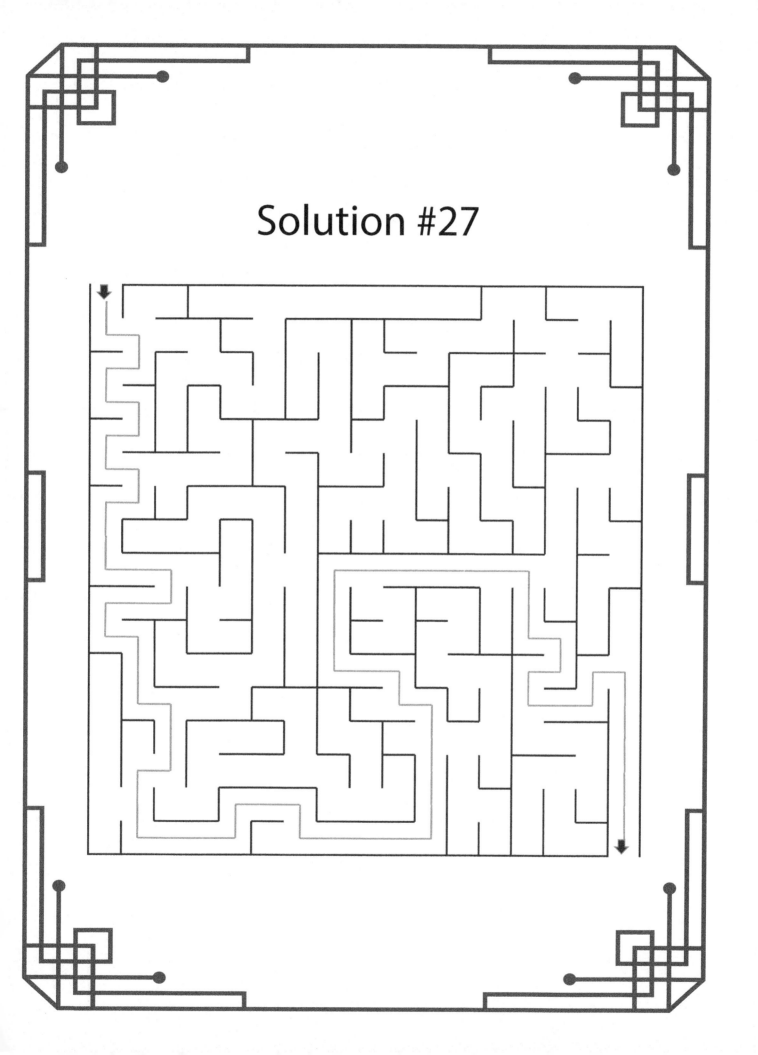

Solution #28

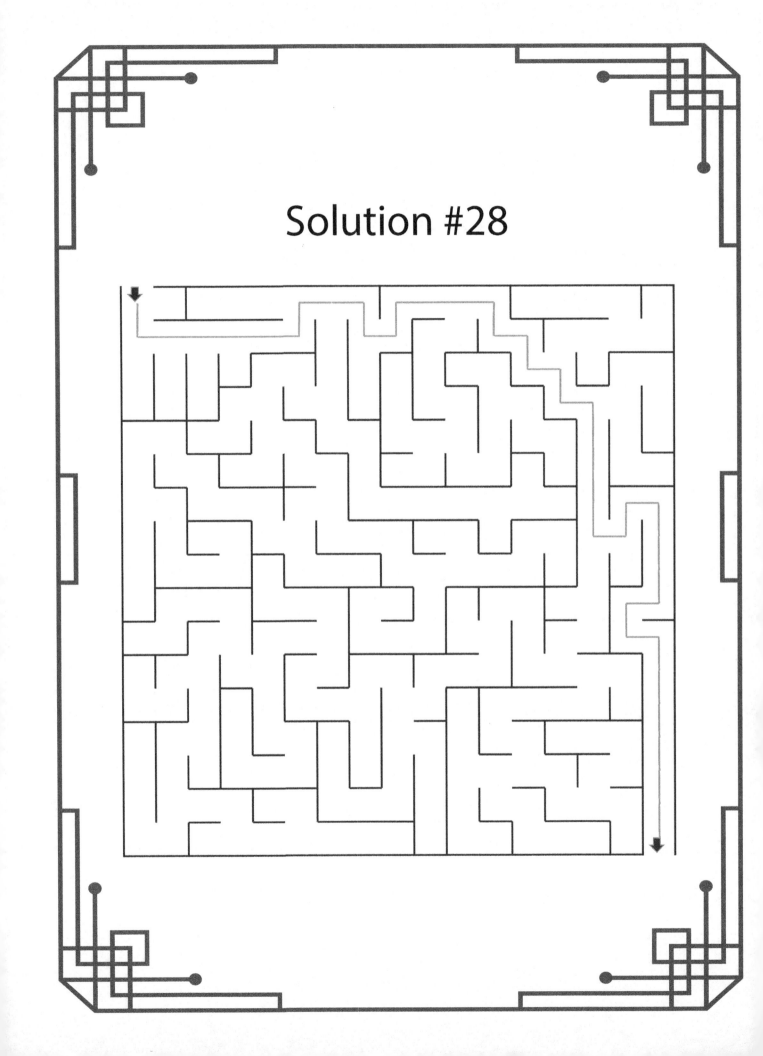

Solution #29

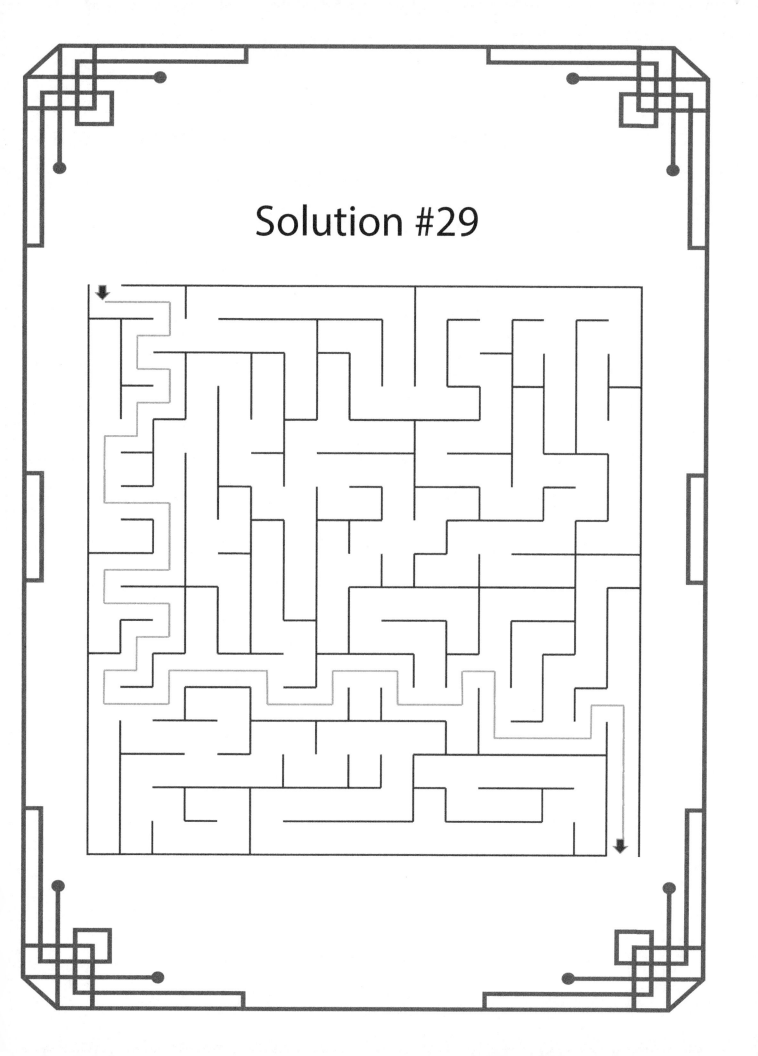

Solution #30

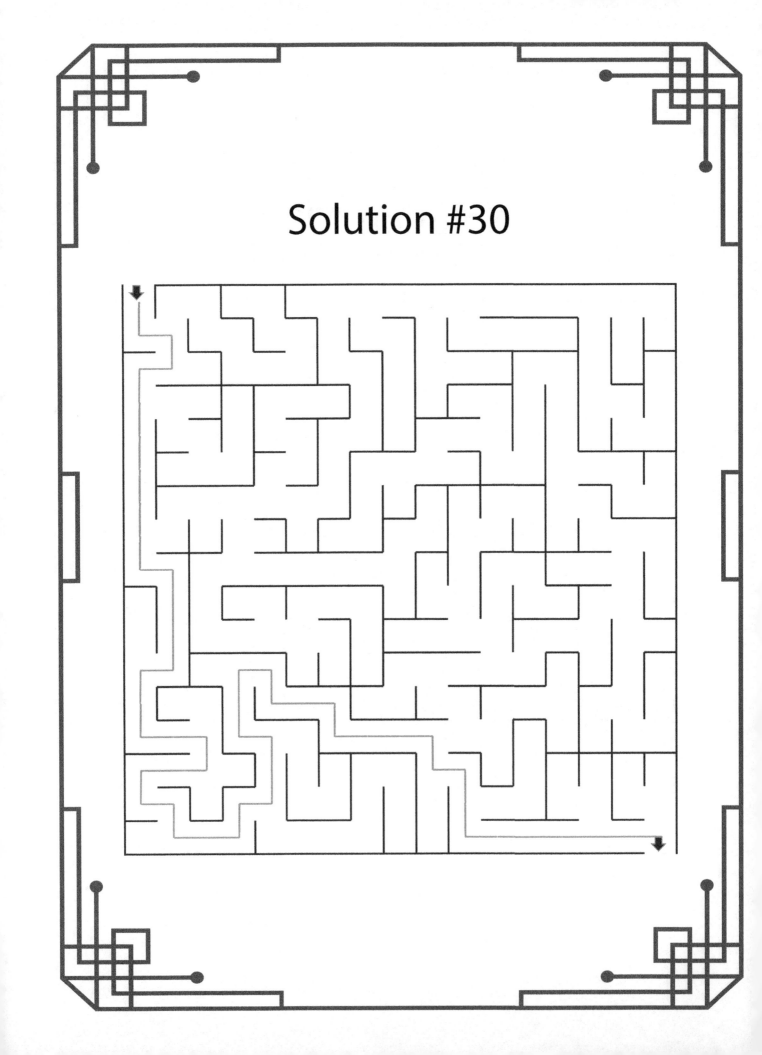

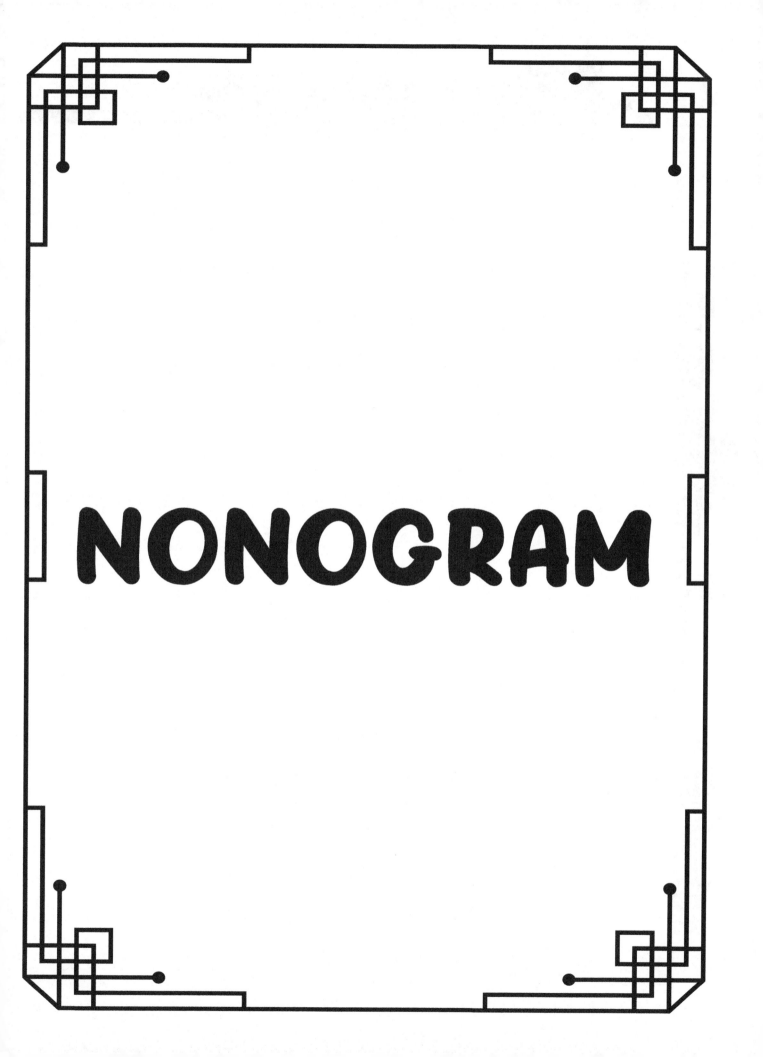

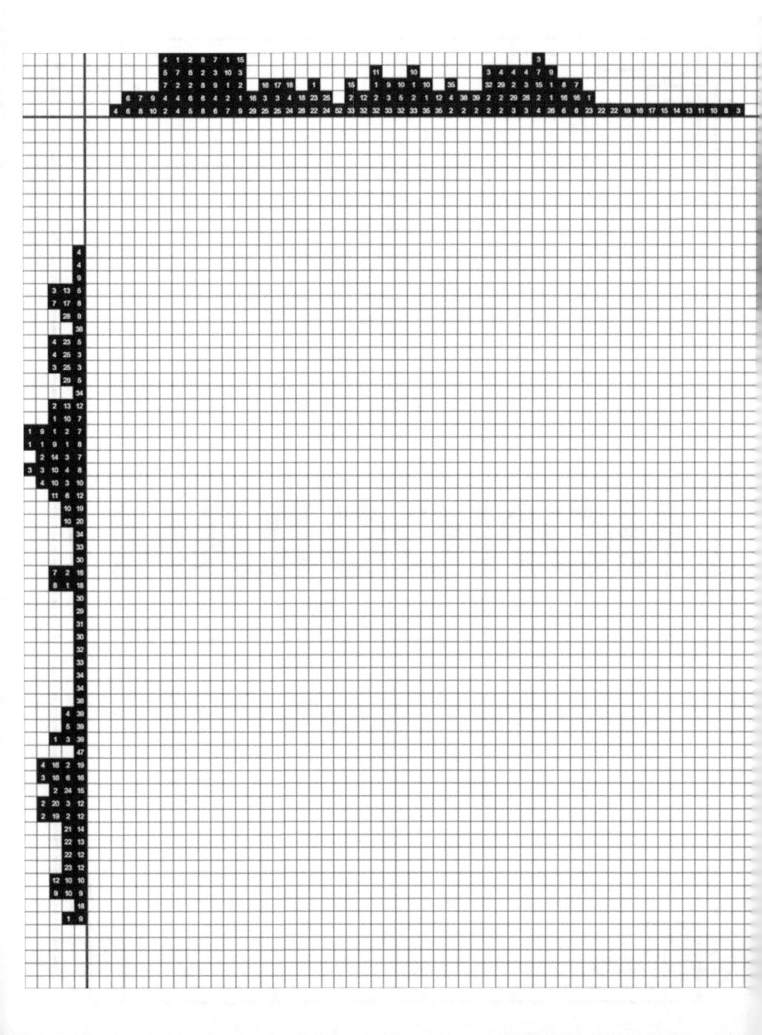

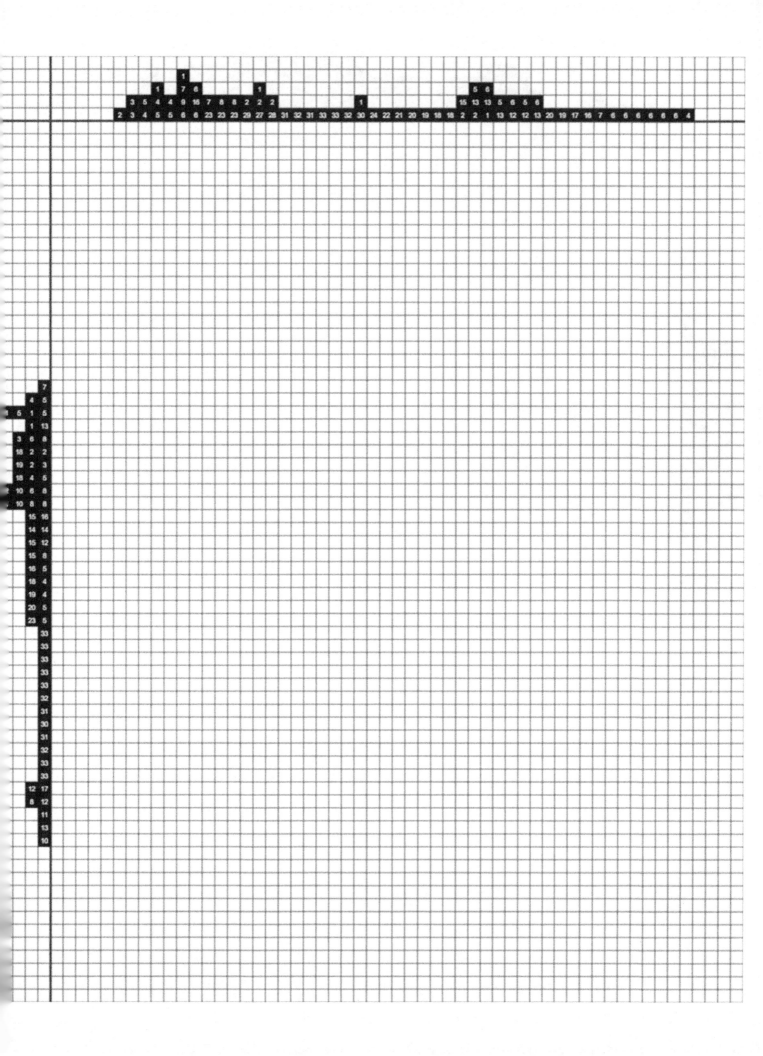

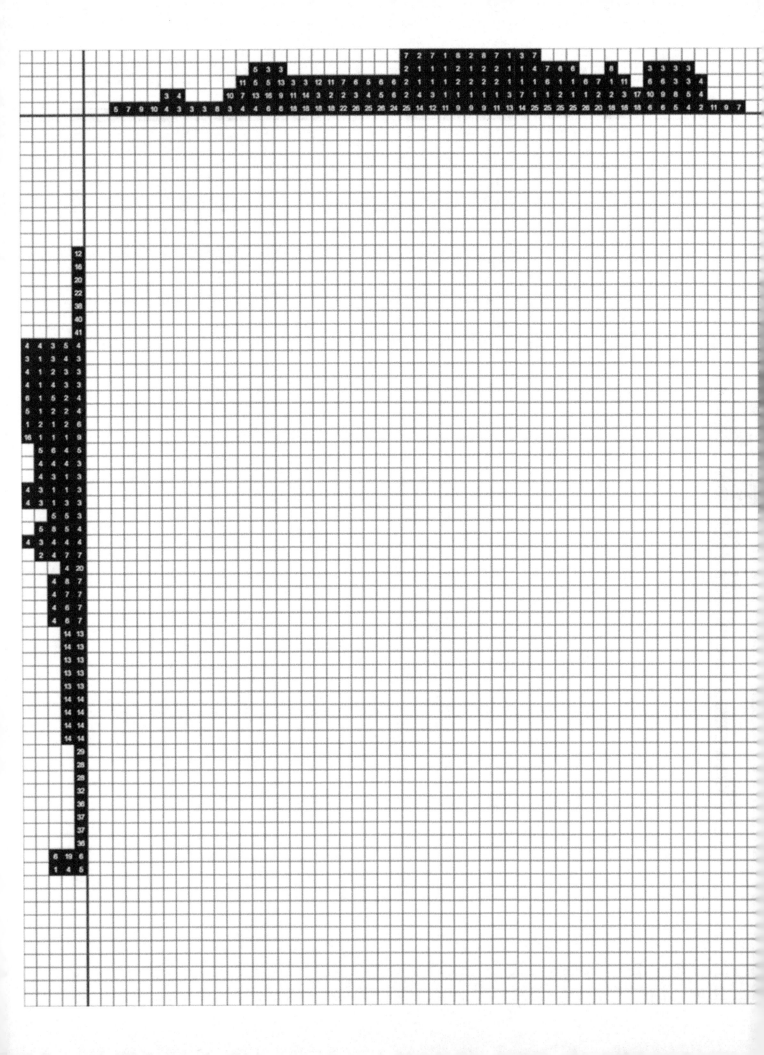

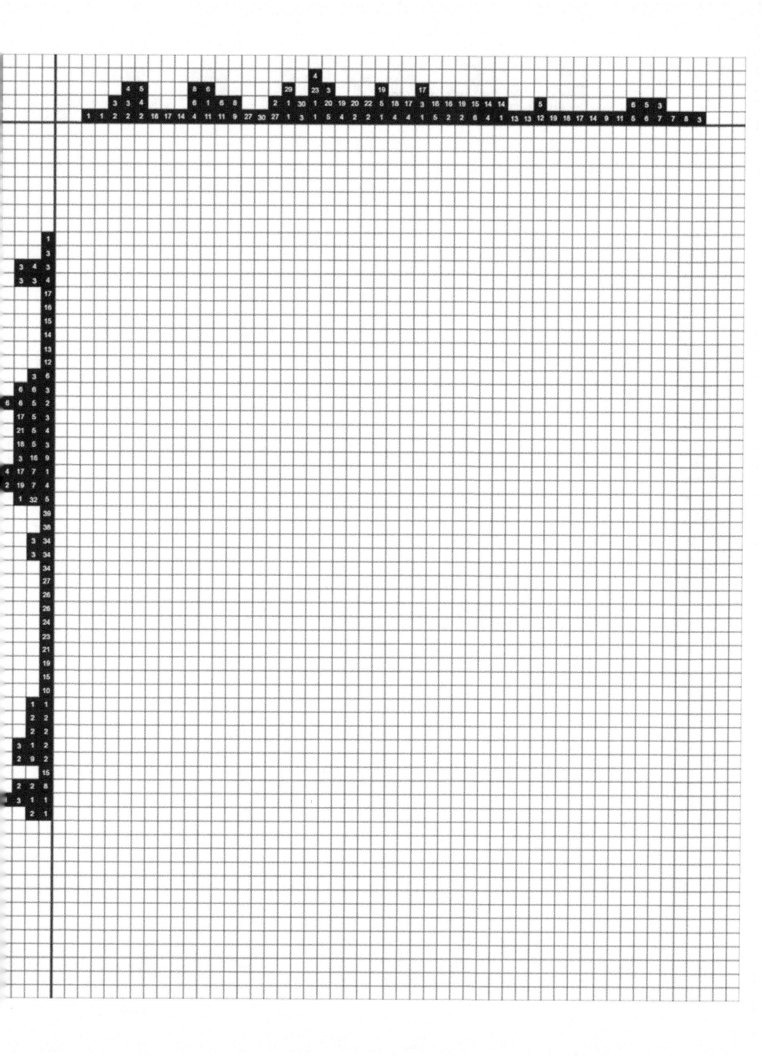

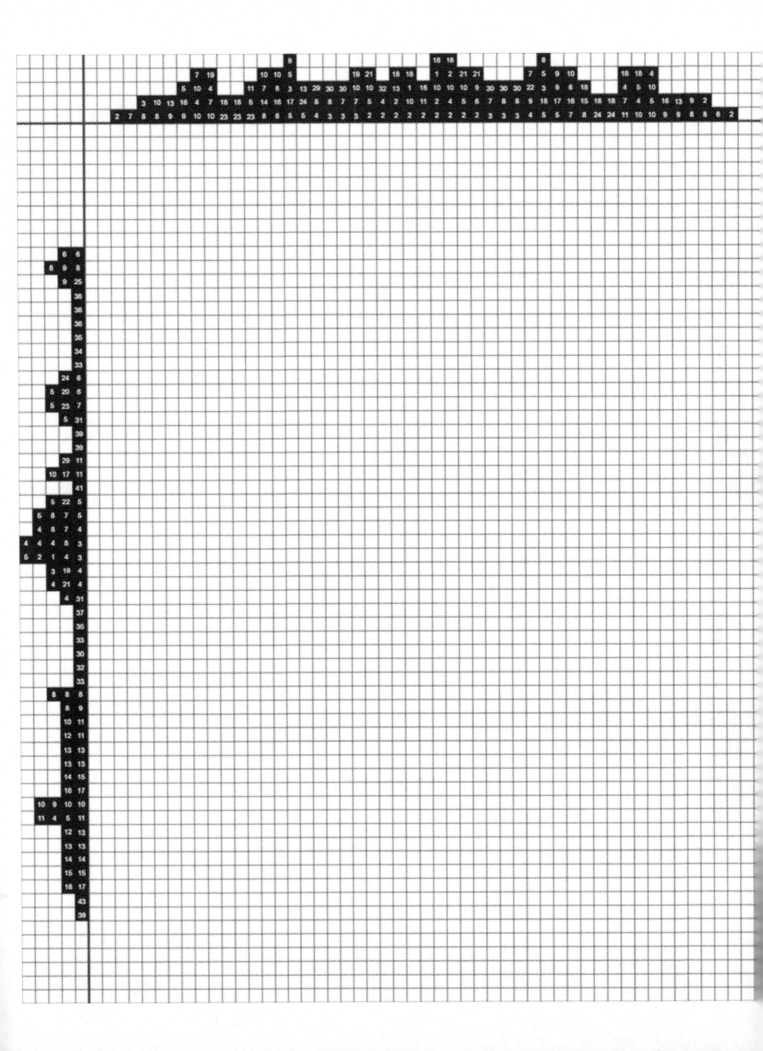

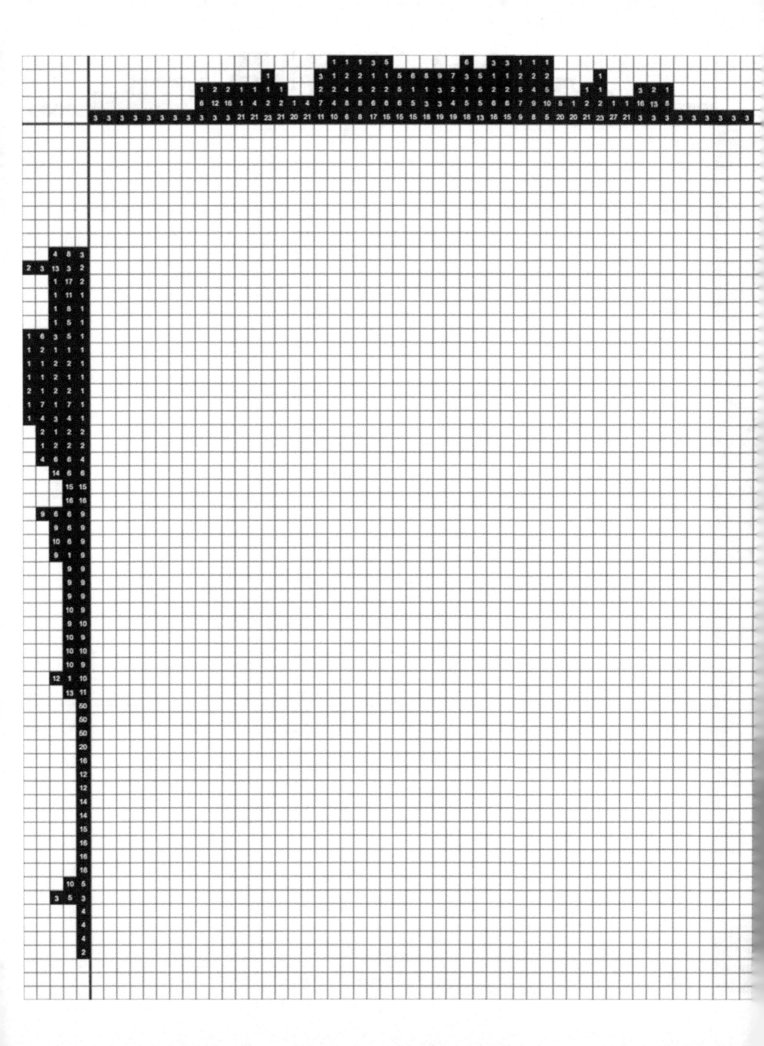

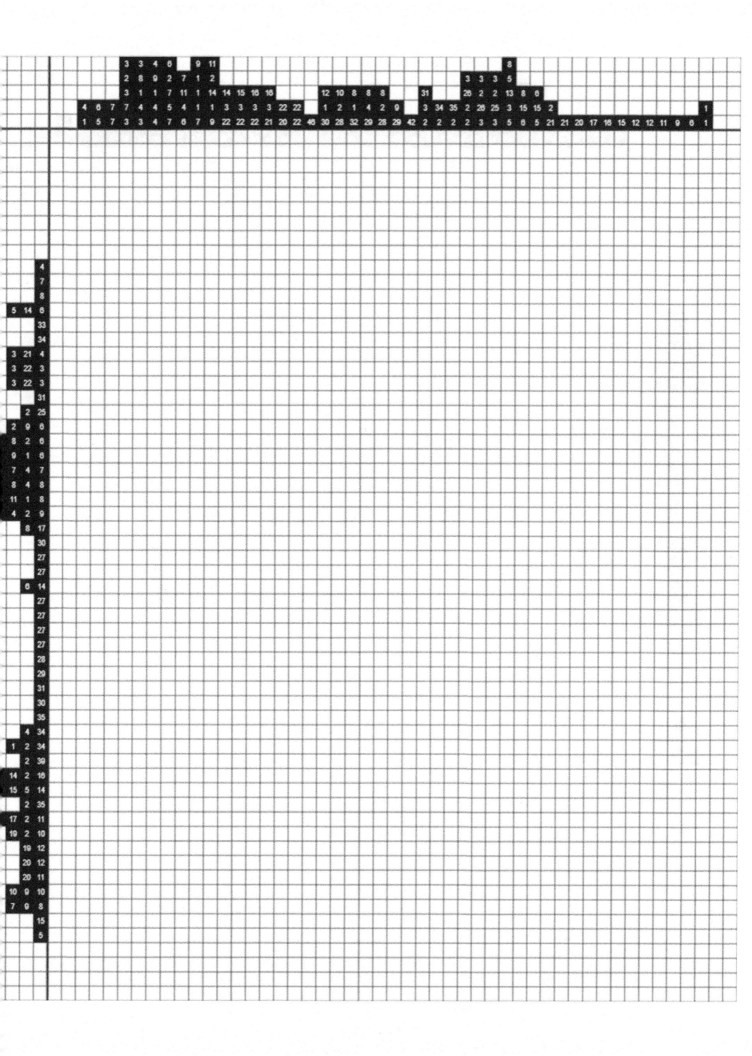

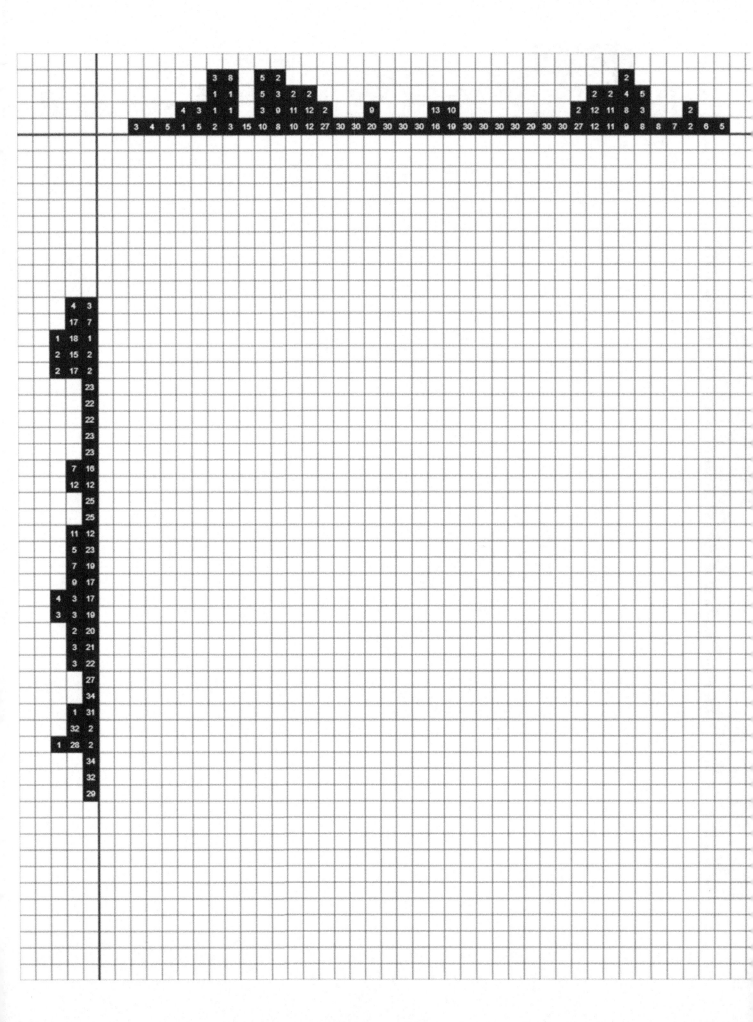

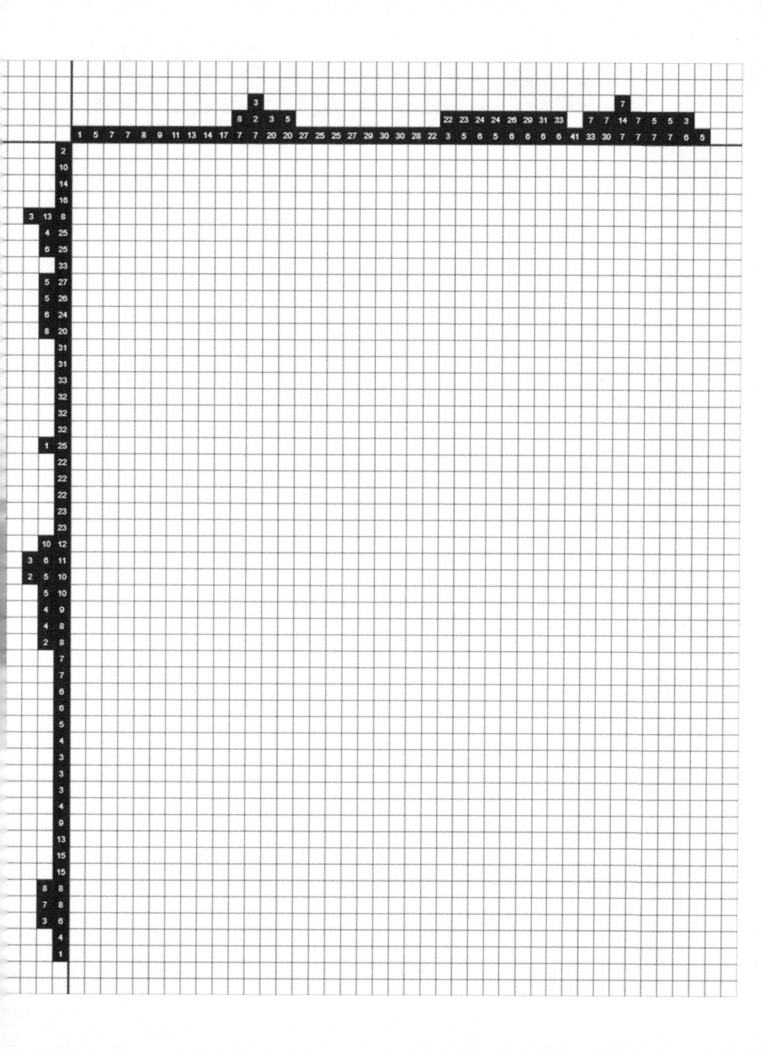

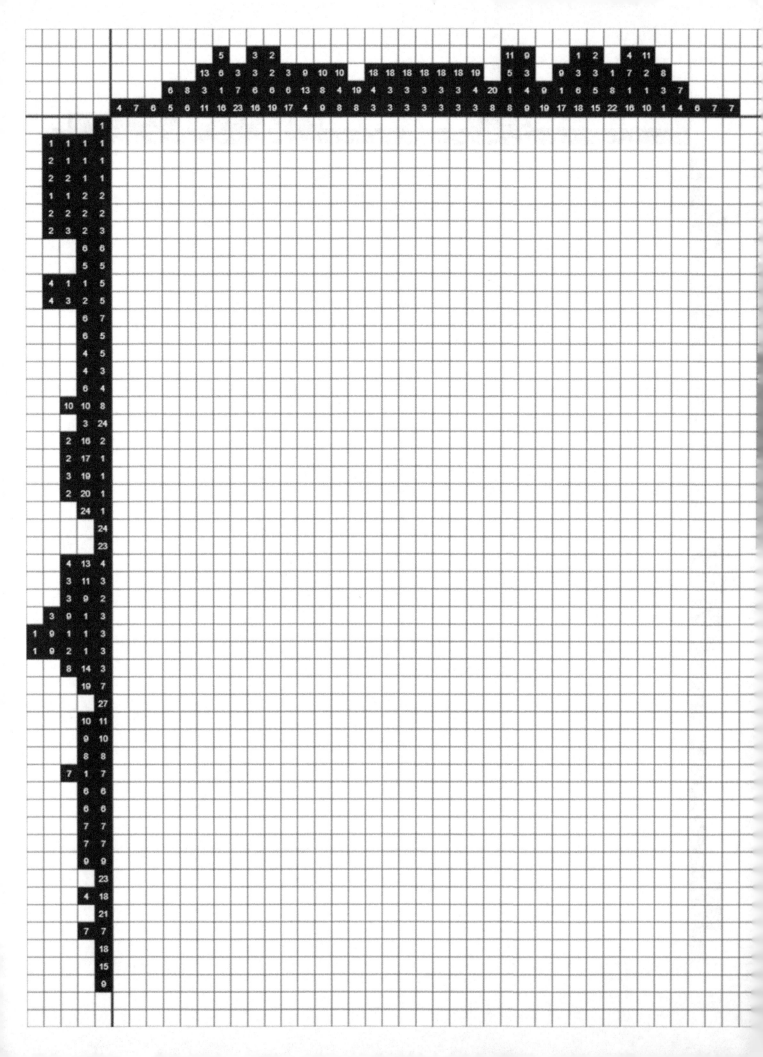

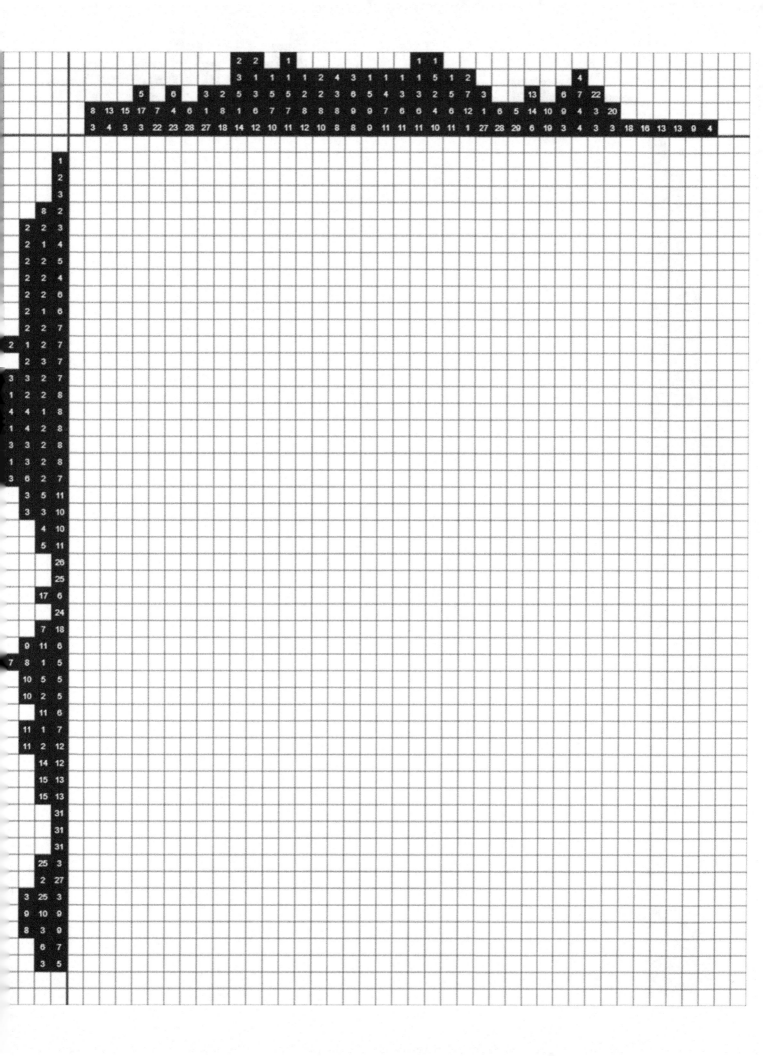

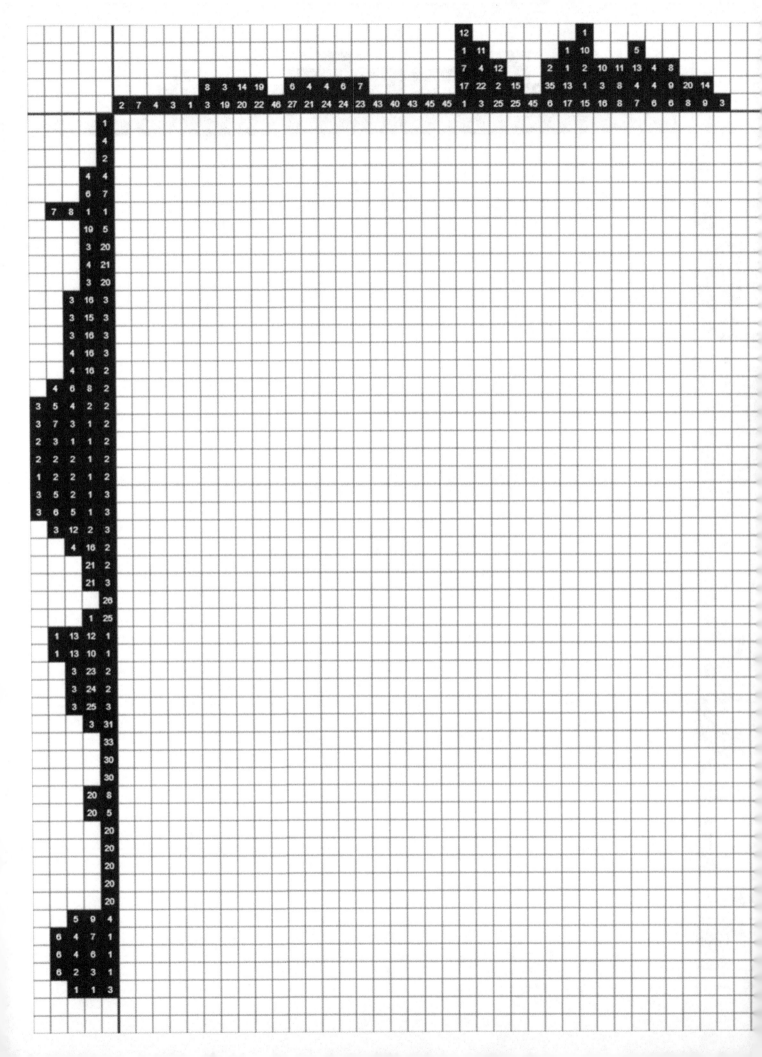

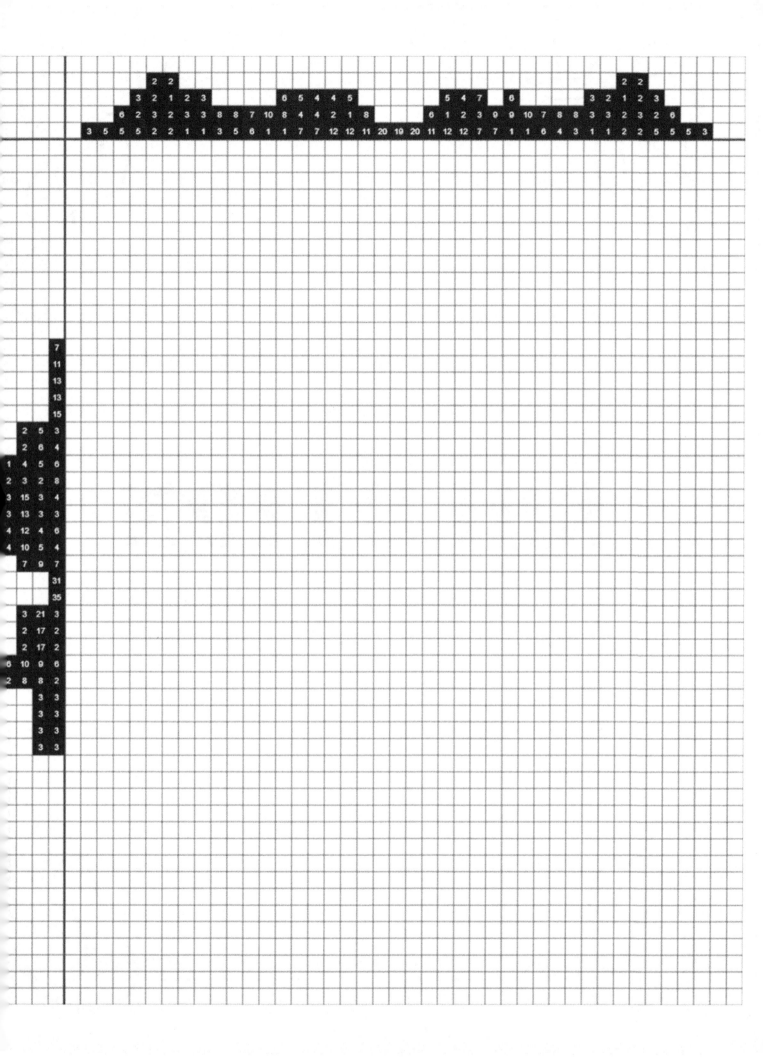

SOLUTION

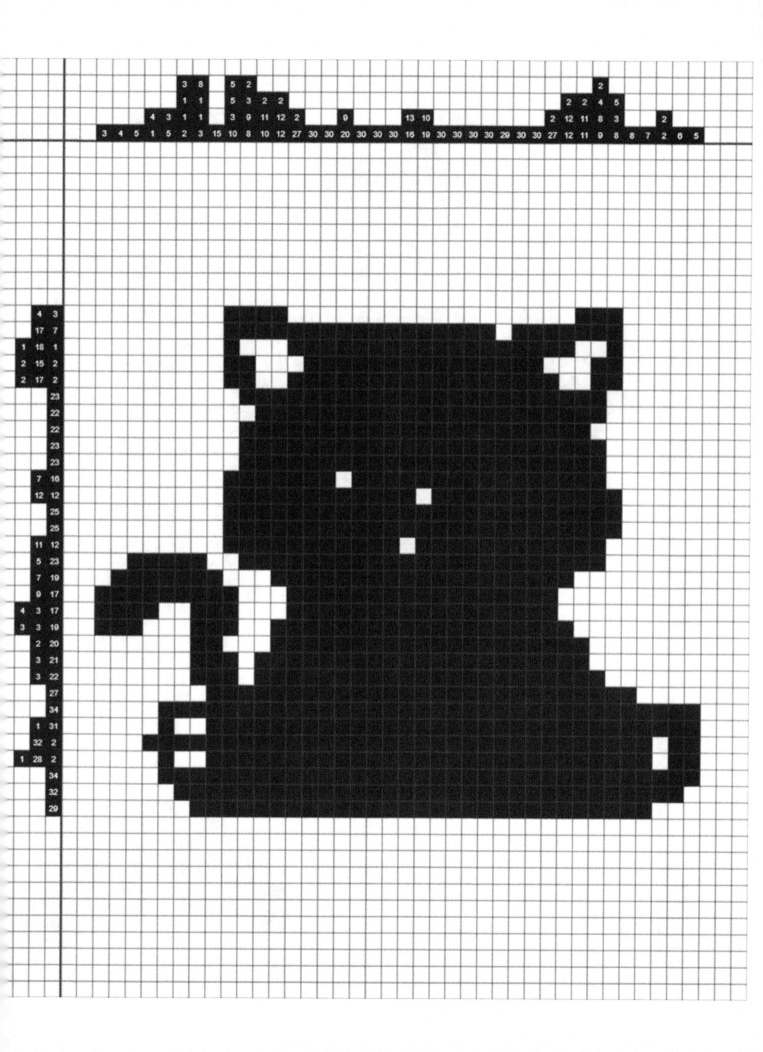

SUDOKU

SUDOKU-1

	6		8					9
		3	9			2		7
	1			6	2	8		
		8	5					
				7				
9				4			8	2
		2		1				
	3							
			3		4		5	1

SUDOKU-2

8			6	3		2		
		3			1			
			5			6		
	8			4	9		5	
		1						
9	2				8			
		8		5				2
						4	7	
1					7			3

SUDOKU-3

7		2	8					1
			4				9	2
					7			
	8	6			1			9
			8		2			
	9				3		2	7
	2	1		7				6
				5				
			9					8

SUDOKU-4

4		6	9					8
			2	5		9		
3		1		4		2		9
		7						
8		2	5		3			4
						7		1
					6			
9	6					5	4	

SUDOKU-5

		3				7		4
	9					5		
1		6						
			5				3	9
4	1		3				5	6
		9	7					
8			2	9		1		
				3		2		

SUDOKU-6

3			2					
		9						
7		2	6				8	
9						3		4
	8		5		3			7
						9		6
	3	8				6	4	5
					4			2
	1						7	

SUDOKU-7

		4	9	6				
6	8			2	1		4	
								2
	3				5	1		
		8						
	2						5	7
				3	9			
1		6						
			9				7	6

SUDOKU-8

					9			7
		1		4	9			8
		3						
		4						
			1				2	4
9	1		5			8		
	2	8			7			1
1	3				7			
	4					3		

SUDOKU-9

	2						7	
9	3			2		5		6
						1		3
	8		7		1		4	
		4			3			
5			9	4				7
4		8		3			5	
		2				3		

SUDOKU-10

	2			6			1	
	6				1	3		
	5	9			2			
		4	3	5		8		
7							5	
		2			4			
								8
9				7				
		3			9			7

SUDOKU-11

7			4	2	9	3		
		1						
							6	7
		7		5				
	5	3			8	2	4	6
8							9	
							3	
	8		7	4				
		4		6	1			

SUDOKU-12

8			5					
9		5		2	6		8	
		1	4		8	2		
							9	1
			3					
3			7		4			
			7				4	
			6		2			
		8					7	2

SUDOKU-13

	5		6				9	1
	4			9				
						3		2
		7				8	1	9
5			7					
		6		2			7	
	7		9					4
1	8		4			7	2	

SUDOKU-14

			7	1	8			
9								1
				2		5	7	
		6					9	
	1			6	5			
	2			7			1	
			1					8
8		5	4					2
1			2			4		7

SUDOKU-15

3	6					2		
	8				4			7
		5	8					
		7		9				5
				1		8		
9	1	2					7	4
	5			7				
			2					
	7		5			4		

SUDOKU-16

	7							2
				8	5			
		8	9	1	6			
5			3				4	9
			4	9				
			5					6
			8					
		9	7	5	1			
		1		9			7	

SUDOKU-17

	2				3	9		
4			8					
6				1	7	5		
		1					7	
9	5					8	4	
2								
							2	
		5		7				3
1	6			8				5

SUDOKU-18

	5			6			3	
		8				6	7	1
			3					
9	6		1					8
		2					4	6
			8	1		3		
3	2				5	1		
	1	4		9				5

SUDOKU-19

3		8			6		9	
5				9	8			
9				6				
				4	7			
	1		9					
		3		5		9		
	7						3	5
			4		8			
				1	5			

SUDOKU-20

1	4	6	2					
9				8				
				1		4		
		6	2		3			
3		9				1		
		4	9		6			7
5			3		2	4		
8			1			6		3

SUDOKU-21

4							9	
						4		
2				3				5
		5		2		8		
	9				5			
	1							3
	8	1						6
		4						7
7	6		9					2

SUDOKU-22

5		7						2
			1	2		9		
	6			5		8		
7				8				
	8	9			6			5
		2			4			
	6							7
						1	4	
		3				9		

SUDOKU-23

	5			9	1			
3								
8		1						
		4					3	
			6	3			1	
				2			7	6
2		7		5			4	9
4				3	8			1
		5	4			7		

SUDOKU-24

	2			7	8	3		
				4	3	6		
		6						
	7	4		5				
		2		9			1	4
								5
		3	9				8	
							9	
9	5			1	6			2

SUDOKU-25

7		3						
6	8							
		1				4		3
	1				8	5		
							8	1
					4		2	6
		4	9	5				2
			3	1				
5	7				6			

SUDOKU-26

3		8						
			2					
5			1	9		7		
1	6		5				4	2
	2			4	8			
	4	1	7					6
8				5				1
			6					8

SUDOKU-27

2				6				
	6					1		
	9	5	1					
1	4			5				3
5		8			9			7
						4		
3		4			8		2	
			6					
7	1		3					5

SUDOKU-28

5	8							
			8		9		4	
		3						1
	1		4					
	4						3	6
6		2						
7			3			1		
8		6		7				3
						4		5

SUDOKU-29

		2				8		
				2				5
	3	9			4			
			6	8	7	5		
				1	6			
		2		5				3
	1					3		
		8				9	6	
	6		7			5	1	

SUDOKU-30

8		5					9	
3	6				7			
		1		5		7		8
			3				1	
			5					
7						2		
	8							
			6	2	4		5	
9		4			8	3		

SUDOKU-31

1	7							
				6		4		
	6		5			9		
	2					3		
5								
			9	2	1			
								9
		1	6		7			8
	1	2	7		4			5

SUDOKU-32

3			5		4			1
		3		9				
6								
2	5		7		3		6	
	1							
	7			1	5			
1	4			9	6	2		3
			1	8				6

SUDOKU-33

	2	7			1		3	
						7		
1		5		8				
	6			3		4		
3			1				5	
				7	4			
	3		9			8		
4			6					
							4	7

SUDOKU-34

4	5			6		8		
	8	9					3	
					1	2		
			8	4		5		
		4	7					2
		5						
8				3				4
7			9			6		1

SUDOKU-35

	6	5		2	7		4	
8		2						
						3		6
						9		8
			1	6				
			5				6	
		7			4			
		8	7		9	5		
	4						3	

SUDOKU-36

2					5		8	
			6					1
7		1				5		
			2		3			
	1		9					2
8		7				4		
		6		2				
							1	6
			9			8		3

SUDOKU-37

4				5			9	
			1			3	5	
		9	7					4
		8				2	3	
	9	2						7
	6		5	9				
								1
				6	8			5
6			9		7			

SUDOKU-38

8					3			
7		2	4			8	9	
	5							1
	2		3		1	4	7	
	6					2		
	4	9	8					
		7				5		
6				5				9

SUDOKU-39

1			4				3	
	9			1		4		
		2						
2		3						8
		5				7		9
	8		6					
				5	6			
3	1			9	8			
			7			1		

SUDOKU-40

9			6				1	
			8					
					7	3	5	
7	8						4	
		4				2		
	5		4	3				
				5				
3		1	9					
			6			8	3	2

SUDOKU-41

3		2					6	
	8			3		4	2	
		1				5		
5			3				8	9
					7			
	3			4				
	6		2		5		9	
9				7				
		5	8				4	

SUDOKU-42

8		6	7			9		
							4	5
3				4				
		1	3					2
	6				4			
	3	4		2	6			
	1			3				
			6		7			1
		7					2	6

SUDOKU-43

7								
	1		9			3		
				5	1	7	6	
		4						9
			3			5	4	
		2	6					1
	9		8					
2		1			3			
						2	7	8

SUDOKU-44

		3	6			4	9	
			4	1				
	9					7		
7				2		9		6
		9			8		4	5
	5							
		2	1	3				
		8	7			6	3	

SUDOKU-45

5			8		4		1	
6				2		8		
				7				
	6		4	3		9	8	1
	3							
			6			4		
			9					7
9		8				2		
		2	1					

SUDOKU-46

4			3					1
5		9					6	2
3	6		8					
					6		3	4
				4		6		9
			7					
		5	9					3
			5		7	4		
2						9		

SUDOKU-47

		4						
			2					9
			8	6				
	9		5	3				
	8				7	5		2
1							6	
	4	7		9	8	2		
2		3						4
							1	5

SUDOKU-48

5	7	2						
				5		6		8
			2					7
	8					7	5	1
	1		5	4				
	2			8				4
	6					2		
7			8		3			
		3				4		

SUDOKU-49

2				1				6
	3				9			
1			8	7	5	2		
	6							
		5			7			
		8	3	2		6		5
3								4
5							2	
		1		3				

SUDOKU-50

	7		5		4		3	
		9		7				
	4		8			5		
			6					9
	3							
1				8				6
	2	5				9		
		3	6					5
			2			8		7

SOLUTION-1

2	6	5	7	8	3	4	1	9
4	8	3	9	5	1	2	6	7
7	1	9	4	6	2	8	3	5
6	2	8	5	3	9	1	7	4
3	4	1	2	7	8	5	9	6
9	5	7	1	4	6	3	8	2
5	9	2	8	1	7	6	4	3
1	3	4	6	9	5	7	2	8
8	7	6	3	2	4	9	5	1

SOLUTION-2

8	5	9	6	3	4	2	1	7
2	6	3	8	7	1	9	4	5
7	1	4	5	9	2	6	3	8
6	8	7	2	4	9	3	5	1
4	3	1	7	6	5	8	2	9
9	2	5	3	1	8	7	6	4
3	7	8	4	5	6	1	9	2
5	9	2	1	8	3	4	7	6
1	4	6	9	2	7	5	8	3

SOLUTION-3

7	4	2	5	8	9	6	3	1
3	6	8	1	4	7	5	9	2
5	1	9	2	3	6	7	8	4
2	8	6	7	5	1	3	4	9
4	3	7	8	9	2	1	6	5
1	9	5	4	6	3	8	2	7
9	2	1	3	7	8	4	5	6
8	7	4	6	2	5	9	1	3
6	5	3	9	1	4	2	7	8

SOLUTION-4

4	2	6	9	3	7	1	5	8
7	8	3	2	5	1	9	4	6
5	1	9	8	6	4	3	2	7
3	5	1	6	4	8	2	7	9
6	4	7	1	9	2	5	8	3
8	9	2	5	7	3	6	1	4
2	3	5	4	8	9	7	6	1
1	7	4	3	2	6	8	9	5
9	6	8	7	1	5	4	3	2

SOLUTION-5

5	8	3	9	2	1	7	6	4
7	9	2	6	3	4	5	8	1
1	4	6	7	5	8	3	9	2
2	6	8	5	1	7	4	3	9
4	1	7	3	8	9	2	5	6
9	3	5	4	6	2	8	1	7
3	2	9	1	7	5	6	4	8
8	5	4	2	9	6	1	7	3
6	7	1	8	4	3	9	2	5

SOLUTION-6

3	5	1	4	2	8	7	6	9
8	6	9	3	7	5	2	4	1
7	4	2	6	9	1	5	8	3
9	2	6	1	8	7	3	5	4
1	8	4	5	6	3	9	2	7
5	7	3	2	4	9	8	1	6
2	3	8	7	1	6	4	9	5
6	9	7	8	5	4	1	3	2
4	1	5	9	3	2	6	7	8

SOLUTION-7

2	5	4	9	6	7	3	1	8
6	8	9	3	2	1	7	4	5
7	1	3	8	5	4	6	9	2
4	3	7	2	8	5	1	6	9
5	6	8	7	1	9	2	3	4
9	2	1	4	3	6	8	5	7
8	7	5	6	4	3	9	2	1
1	9	6	5	7	2	4	8	3
3	4	2	1	9	8	5	7	6

SOLUTION-8

4	5	2	8	6	9	3	1	7
3	7	1	5	2	4	9	6	8
8	9	6	3	7	1	2	4	5
2	6	5	4	8	3	1	7	9
7	8	3	9	1	6	5	2	4
9	1	4	7	5	2	6	8	3
5	2	8	6	3	7	4	9	1
1	3	9	2	4	8	7	5	6
6	4	7	1	9	5	8	3	2

SOLUTION-9

7	4	5	6	1	8	9	3	2
8	2	6	3	5	9	4	7	1
9	3	1	4	2	7	5	8	6
2	6	7	5	8	4	1	9	3
3	8	9	7	6	1	2	4	5
1	5	4	2	9	3	7	6	8
5	1	3	9	4	6	8	2	7
4	7	8	1	3	2	6	5	9
6	9	2	8	7	5	3	1	4

SOLUTION-10

3	2	7	4	6	8	9	1	5
4	6	8	5	9	1	3	7	2
1	5	9	7	3	2	6	8	4
6	9	4	3	5	7	8	2	1
7	3	1	2	8	6	4	5	9
5	8	2	9	1	4	7	3	6
2	7	5	6	4	3	1	9	8
9	1	6	8	7	5	2	4	3
8	4	3	1	2	9	5	6	7

SOLUTION-11

7	6	8	4	2	9	3	5	1
5	3	1	6	8	7	4	2	9
4	9	2	3	1	5	8	6	7
2	4	7	9	5	6	1	8	3
9	5	3	1	7	8	2	4	6
8	1	6	2	3	4	7	9	5
1	7	5	8	9	2	6	3	4
6	8	9	7	4	3	5	1	2
3	2	4	5	6	1	9	7	8

SOLUTION-12

8	2	6	5	1	7	4	3	9
9	4	5	3	2	6	1	8	7
7	3	1	4	9	8	2	5	6
6	7	4	2	8	5	3	9	1
5	8	2	1	3	9	7	6	4
3	1	9	7	6	4	5	2	8
2	6	3	8	7	1	9	4	5
4	9	7	6	5	2	8	1	3
1	5	8	9	4	3	6	7	2

SOLUTION-13

7	5	2	6	3	8	4	9	1
8	4	3	2	9	1	6	5	7
6	9	1	5	4	7	3	8	2
4	2	7	3	5	6	8	1	9
5	3	8	7	1	9	2	4	6
9	1	6	8	2	4	5	7	3
3	7	5	9	8	2	1	6	4
2	6	4	1	7	5	9	3	8
1	8	9	4	6	3	7	2	5

SOLUTION-14

6	5	4	7	1	8	3	2	9
9	7	2	5	4	3	6	8	1
3	8	1	6	9	2	5	7	4
4	3	6	8	2	1	7	9	5
7	1	8	9	6	5	2	4	3
5	2	9	3	7	4	8	1	6
2	4	7	1	5	6	9	3	8
8	9	5	4	3	7	1	6	2
1	6	3	2	8	9	4	5	7

SOLUTION-15

3	6	4	1	5	7	2	9	8
1	8	9	3	2	4	5	6	7
7	2	5	8	6	9	1	4	3
8	3	7	4	9	2	6	1	5
5	4	6	7	3	1	9	8	2
9	1	2	6	8	5	3	7	4
4	5	1	9	7	3	8	2	6
6	9	3	2	4	8	7	5	1
2	7	8	5	1	6	4	3	9

SOLUTION-16

1	7	6	4	3	5	8	9	2
4	9	3	2	7	8	5	6	1
5	2	8	9	1	6	4	3	7
8	5	7	3	6	2	1	4	9
6	3	2	1	4	9	7	5	8
9	1	4	5	8	7	3	2	6
7	6	5	8	2	3	9	1	4
2	4	9	7	5	1	6	8	3
3	8	1	6	9	4	2	7	5

SOLUTION-17

5	2	8	6	4	3	9	1	7
4	1	7	8	5	9	2	3	6
6	3	9	2	1	7	5	8	4
3	8	1	4	2	5	6	7	9
9	5	6	7	3	1	8	4	2
2	7	4	9	6	8	3	5	1
7	4	3	5	9	6	1	2	8
8	9	5	1	7	2	4	6	3
1	6	2	3	8	4	7	9	5

SOLUTION-18

2	5	7	4	6	1	8	3	9
4	3	8	5	2	9	6	7	1
6	9	1	3	7	8	4	5	2
7	4	5	2	8	6	9	1	3
9	6	3	1	5	4	7	2	8
1	8	2	9	3	7	5	4	6
5	7	6	8	1	2	3	9	4
3	2	9	6	4	5	1	8	7
8	1	4	7	9	3	2	6	5

SOLUTION-19

3	4	8	7	2	6	5	9	1
5	6	7	1	4	9	8	2	3
9	2	1	5	8	3	6	7	4
6	5	9	8	3	4	7	1	2
4	1	2	9	6	7	3	5	8
7	8	3	2	5	1	9	4	6
8	7	4	6	9	2	1	3	5
1	3	5	4	7	8	2	6	9
2	9	6	3	1	5	4	8	7

SOLUTION-20

1	4	6	2	9	5	7	3	8
9	5	3	7	1	8	2	6	4
7	8	2	4	6	3	5	9	1
6	7	5	8	3	1	9	4	2
4	1	8	6	2	9	3	7	5
3	2	9	5	4	7	8	1	6
2	3	4	9	8	6	1	5	7
5	6	1	3	7	2	4	8	9
8	9	7	1	5	4	6	2	3

SOLUTION-21

4	8	3	6	7	5	2	9	1
5	7	6	2	9	1	4	3	8
2	9	1	8	3	4	7	6	5
3	4	7	5	6	2	1	8	9
6	2	9	3	1	8	5	7	4
8	1	5	7	4	9	6	2	3
9	5	8	1	2	7	3	4	6
1	3	2	4	8	6	9	5	7
7	6	4	9	5	3	8	1	2

SOLUTION-22

5	9	7	4	6	8	3	1	2
8	4	3	7	1	2	5	9	6
2	6	1	9	5	3	8	7	4
7	5	4	2	8	9	6	3	1
3	8	9	1	7	6	4	2	5
6	1	2	5	3	4	7	8	9
4	3	6	8	9	1	2	5	7
9	7	8	6	2	5	1	4	3
1	2	5	3	4	7	9	6	8

SOLUTION-23

7	5	6	2	9	1	4	8	3
3	9	2	8	6	4	1	5	7
8	4	1	5	7	3	6	9	2
6	2	4	7	1	8	9	3	5
9	7	8	6	3	5	2	1	4
5	1	3	9	4	2	8	7	6
2	8	7	1	5	6	3	4	9
4	6	9	3	8	7	5	2	1
1	3	5	4	2	9	7	6	8

SOLUTION-24

1	2	5	6	7	8	3	4	9
7	8	9	2	4	3	6	5	1
3	4	6	5	1	9	2	7	8
6	7	4	8	5	1	9	2	3
5	3	2	7	9	6	8	1	4
8	9	1	4	3	2	7	6	5
4	6	3	9	2	5	1	8	7
2	1	7	3	8	4	5	9	6
9	5	8	1	6	7	4	3	2

SOLUTION-25

7	4	3	5	2	1	6	9	8
6	8	9	7	4	3	2	1	5
2	5	1	8	6	9	4	7	3
3	1	6	2	9	8	5	4	7
4	2	7	6	3	5	9	8	1
8	9	5	1	7	4	3	2	6
1	3	4	9	5	7	8	6	2
9	6	8	3	1	2	7	5	4
5	7	2	4	8	6	1	3	9

SOLUTION-26

3	7	8	5	4	6	2	1	9
6	1	9	3	2	7	5	8	4
5	2	4	8	1	9	6	7	3
1	6	7	9	5	8	3	4	2
4	8	3	6	7	2	1	9	5
9	5	2	1	3	4	8	6	7
2	4	1	7	8	3	9	5	6
8	3	6	4	9	5	7	2	1
7	9	5	2	6	1	4	3	8

SOLUTION-27

2	7	1	9	6	3	5	8	4
8	6	3	5	2	4	1	7	9
4	9	5	1	8	7	3	6	2
1	4	7	8	5	6	2	9	3
5	2	8	4	3	9	6	1	7
6	3	9	2	7	1	4	5	8
3	5	4	7	1	8	9	2	6
9	8	2	6	4	5	7	3	1
7	1	6	3	9	2	8	4	5

SOLUTION-28

5	8	7	6	1	4	3	9	2
2	6	1	8	3	9	5	4	7
4	9	3	5	7	2	6	8	1
3	1	8	4	2	6	7	5	9
9	4	5	7	8	1	2	3	6
6	7	2	9	5	3	8	1	4
7	2	4	3	9	5	1	6	8
8	5	6	1	4	7	9	2	3
1	3	9	2	6	8	4	7	5

SOLUTION-29

4	5	2	3	1	7	8	6	9
8	7	1	6	2	9	3	4	5
6	3	9	5	8	4	1	7	2
2	9	3	4	6	8	7	5	1
5	8	7	9	3	1	6	2	4
1	4	6	2	7	5	9	8	3
9	1	5	8	4	6	2	3	7
7	2	8	1	5	3	4	9	6
3	6	4	7	9	2	5	1	8

SOLUTION-30

8	7	5	1	4	3	6	9	2
3	6	2	8	9	7	5	4	1
4	9	1	2	5	6	7	3	8
5	4	8	3	6	2	9	1	7
6	2	9	5	7	1	4	8	3
7	1	3	4	8	9	2	6	5
2	8	6	9	3	5	1	7	4
1	3	7	6	2	4	8	5	9
9	5	4	7	1	8	3	2	6

SOLUTION-31

1	7	4	9	2	8	6	5	3
2	9	5	3	1	6	8	4	7
3	6	8	4	5	7	2	9	1
7	2	9	8	4	1	5	3	6
5	4	1	6	7	3	9	8	2
8	3	6	5	9	2	1	7	4
6	8	7	2	3	5	4	1	9
4	5	3	1	6	9	7	2	8
9	1	2	7	8	4	3	6	5

SOLUTION-32

3	7	2	6	5	8	4	9	1
5	8	4	3	1	9	6	2	7
6	9	1	4	7	2	3	8	5
2	5	9	7	4	3	1	6	8
4	1	6	8	2	5	7	3	9
8	3	7	9	6	1	5	4	2
9	6	5	2	3	7	8	1	4
1	4	8	5	9	6	2	7	3
7	2	3	1	8	4	9	5	6

SOLUTION-33

8	2	7	4	6	1	9	3	5
6	4	3	2	5	9	7	8	1
1	9	5	7	8	3	6	2	4
5	6	1	8	3	2	4	7	9
3	7	4	1	9	6	2	5	8
2	8	9	5	7	4	1	6	3
7	3	2	9	4	5	8	1	6
4	5	8	6	1	7	3	9	2
9	1	6	3	2	8	5	4	7

SOLUTION-34

4	5	2	3	6	7	8	1	9
1	8	9	4	5	2	7	3	6
6	7	3	8	9	1	2	4	5
9	2	7	6	8	4	1	5	3
5	6	4	7	1	3	9	8	2
3	1	8	5	2	9	4	6	7
8	9	1	2	3	6	5	7	4
2	4	6	1	7	5	3	9	8
7	3	5	9	4	8	6	2	1

SOLUTION-35

9	6	5	3	2	7	8	4	1
8	3	2	6	4	1	7	9	5
4	7	1	9	8	5	3	2	6
2	1	6	4	7	3	9	5	8
5	9	3	1	6	8	4	7	2
7	8	4	5	9	2	1	6	3
3	5	7	2	1	4	6	8	9
6	2	8	7	3	9	5	1	4
1	4	9	8	5	6	2	3	7

SOLUTION-36

2	6	3	4	1	5	9	8	7
4	8	5	6	7	9	3	2	1
7	9	1	8	3	2	5	6	4
6	5	9	2	4	3	1	7	8
3	1	4	9	8	7	6	5	2
8	2	7	5	6	1	4	3	9
1	4	6	3	2	8	7	9	5
9	3	8	7	5	4	2	1	6
5	7	2	1	9	6	8	4	3

SOLUTION-37

4	1	6	8	5	3	7	9	2
8	2	7	1	4	9	3	5	6
3	5	9	7	2	6	8	1	4
5	4	8	6	7	1	2	3	9
1	9	2	3	8	4	5	6	7
7	6	3	5	9	2	1	4	8
9	7	4	2	3	5	6	8	1
2	3	1	4	6	8	9	7	5
6	8	5	9	1	7	4	2	3

SOLUTION-38

8	9	1	6	2	3	7	5	4
7	3	2	4	1	5	8	9	6
4	5	6	9	8	7	1	3	2
3	7	5	2	4	8	9	6	1
9	2	8	3	6	1	4	7	5
1	6	4	5	7	9	2	8	3
5	4	9	8	3	2	6	1	7
2	1	3	7	9	6	5	4	8
6	8	7	1	5	4	3	2	9

SOLUTION-39

1	5	7	4	8	2	9	3	6
8	9	6	5	1	3	4	7	2
4	3	2	7	9	6	5	8	1
2	7	3	9	5	4	1	6	8
6	4	5	8	3	1	7	2	9
9	8	1	6	2	7	3	4	5
7	2	8	1	4	5	6	9	3
3	1	4	2	6	9	8	5	7
5	6	9	3	7	8	2	1	4

SOLUTION-40

9	4	2	6	5	3	7	1	8
5	7	3	1	8	4	6	2	9
6	1	8	2	9	7	3	5	4
7	8	6	5	1	2	9	4	3
1	3	4	8	7	9	2	6	5
2	5	9	4	3	6	1	8	7
8	6	7	3	2	5	4	9	1
3	2	1	9	4	8	5	7	6
4	9	5	7	6	1	8	3	2

SOLUTION-41

3	5	2	1	8	4	9	6	7
7	8	6	5	3	9	4	2	1
4	9	1	7	6	2	5	3	8
5	4	7	3	2	1	6	8	9
6	2	8	9	5	7	3	1	4
1	3	9	6	4	8	2	7	5
8	6	4	2	1	5	7	9	3
9	1	3	4	7	6	8	5	2
2	7	5	8	9	3	1	4	6

SOLUTION-42

8	4	6	7	5	2	9	1	3
1	7	9	8	6	3	2	4	5
3	5	2	9	4	1	6	7	8
5	9	1	3	7	8	4	6	2
2	6	8	5	9	4	1	3	7
7	3	4	1	2	6	8	5	9
6	1	5	2	3	9	7	8	4
4	2	3	6	8	7	5	9	1
9	8	7	4	1	5	3	2	6

SOLUTION-43

7	2	6	4	3	8	1	9	5
4	1	5	9	6	7	3	8	2
8	3	9	2	5	1	7	6	4
3	7	4	1	8	5	6	2	9
1	6	8	3	9	2	5	4	7
9	5	2	6	7	4	8	3	1
5	9	7	8	2	6	4	1	3
2	8	1	7	4	3	9	5	6
6	4	3	5	1	9	2	7	8

SOLUTION-44

5	2	3	6	8	7	4	9	1
8	6	7	4	1	9	5	2	3
4	9	1	2	5	3	7	6	8
2	8	5	9	6	4	3	1	7
7	3	4	5	2	1	9	8	6
6	1	9	3	7	8	2	4	5
3	5	6	8	4	2	1	7	9
9	7	2	1	3	6	8	5	4
1	4	8	7	9	5	6	3	2

SOLUTION-45

5	2	3	8	9	4	7	1	6
6	7	9	3	2	1	8	4	5
4	8	1	6	5	7	3	2	9
2	6	7	4	3	5	9	8	1
8	3	4	7	1	9	5	6	2
1	9	5	2	6	8	4	7	3
3	4	6	9	8	2	1	5	7
9	1	8	5	7	6	2	3	4
7	5	2	1	4	3	6	9	8

SOLUTION-46

4	2	7	3	6	5	8	9	1
5	8	9	4	7	1	3	6	2
3	6	1	8	9	2	5	4	7
8	9	2	1	5	6	7	3	4
7	5	3	2	4	8	6	1	9
1	4	6	7	3	9	2	5	8
6	7	5	9	2	4	1	8	3
9	3	8	5	1	7	4	2	6
2	1	4	6	8	3	9	7	5

SOLUTION-47

6	2	4	7	5	9	3	8	1
7	3	8	2	4	1	6	5	9
9	5	1	8	6	3	4	2	7
4	9	2	5	3	6	1	7	8
3	8	6	9	1	7	5	4	2
1	7	5	4	8	2	9	6	3
5	4	7	1	9	8	2	3	6
2	1	3	6	7	5	8	9	4
8	6	9	3	2	4	7	1	5

SOLUTION-48

5	7	2	3	6	8	1	4	9
1	3	9	7	5	4	6	2	8
6	4	8	2	1	9	5	3	7
4	8	6	9	3	2	7	5	1
3	1	7	5	4	6	8	9	2
9	2	5	1	8	7	3	6	4
8	6	1	4	9	5	2	7	3
7	5	4	8	2	3	9	1	6
2	9	3	6	7	1	4	8	5

SOLUTION-49

2	5	7	4	1	3	8	9	6
8	3	4	2	6	9	5	1	7
1	9	6	8	7	5	2	4	3
7	6	3	5	9	1	4	8	2
4	2	5	6	8	7	1	3	9
9	1	8	3	2	4	6	7	5
3	7	2	1	5	8	9	6	4
5	8	9	7	4	6	3	2	1
6	4	1	9	3	2	7	5	8

SOLUTION-50

6	7	8	5	2	4	9	3	1
2	5	9	1	3	7	4	6	8
3	4	1	8	9	6	5	7	2
4	8	7	6	1	5	3	2	9
5	3	6	9	7	2	1	8	4
1	9	2	3	4	8	7	5	6
7	2	5	4	8	1	6	9	3
8	1	3	7	6	9	2	4	5
9	6	4	2	5	3	8	1	7

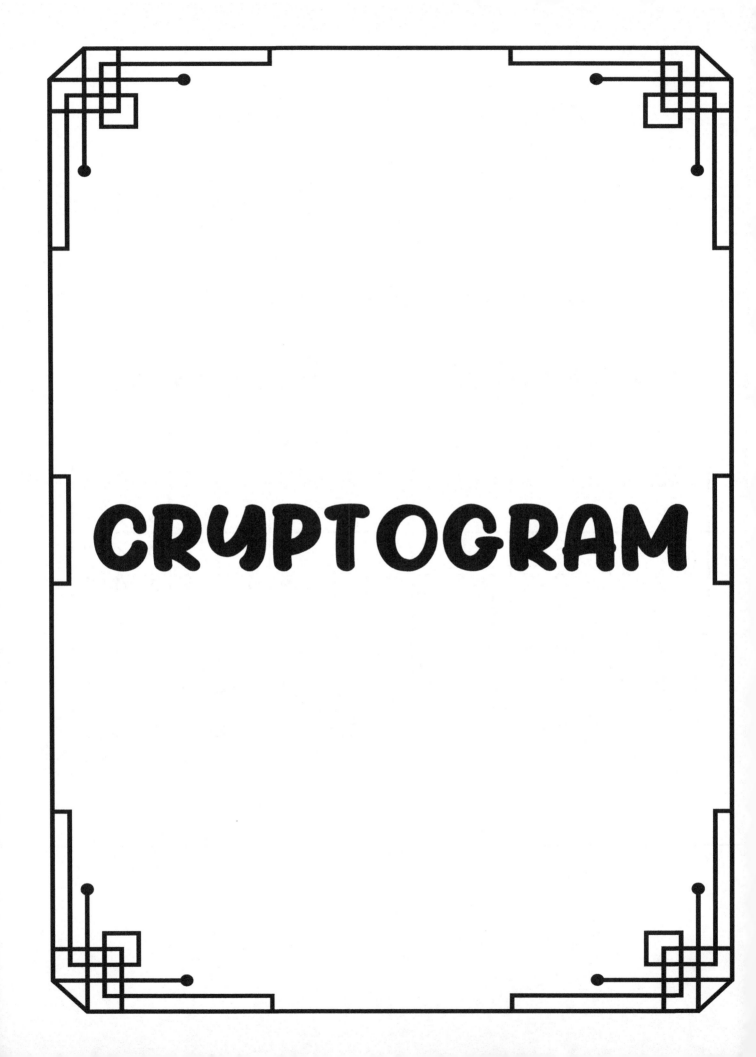

CRYPTOGRAM

CRYPTOGRAM

1.

G	N	U	S	R		G	R	J	J	V	P		U	N	S	S	P

I	N	W	R		U	R	R	J		F	J	M	E	J		G	M

G	D	N	W	R	S		M	H	H		G	I	R		Q	N	B	B	S	R

N	G		P	Q	R	R	B	P		Z	Q		G	M		1	6	0

F	O	/	I	D	.

2.

H	T	M	I	H		L	R	Q	O		N	D	M	F

G	D	H	O	H	.

CRYPTOGRAM

3.

B	J	B	L	Q		W	B	L	H	P	G	,

V	G	A	O	K	Y	V	G	M		V	Y	B	G	F	V	A	U	O

F	I	V	G	H	,		Z	U	H		U		K	G	V	D	K	B

B	Q	B		&		F	P	G	M	K	B		W	L	V	G	F

U	O	P	G	M		I	V	F	Z		F	Z	B	V	L

T	V	G	M	B	L	W	L	V	G	F	.

--

CRYPTOGRAM

4.

K	V	I		G	I	J	M	R	E	R	K	P	D	L		D	H

P	L	G	I	F	I	L	G	I	L	J	I		N	R	Z

N	E	P	K	K	I	L		D	L		V	I	Q	F

(	Q	R	E	P	U	C	R	L	R	)		F	R	F	I	E	.

5.

V	W	M		S	Q	K	T	Z	A	J		U	R	G		V	W	M

G	A	G	V	M	F		G	W	A	Z		S	O		V	W	M

V	A	V	R	L	A	J	,		R	L	H		G	W	M

Z	F	S	C	A	H	M	H		V	U	M	L	V	K	-	O	A	C	M

K	M	R	F	G		S	O		G	M	F	C	A	J	M	.

CRYPTOGRAM

6.

| | C | | A | P | Y | A | T | | R | C | B | , | | I | C | B |

| | T | S | B | P | C | | P | C | R | E | C | , | | T | S | Q | W | O |

| | L | T | Y | | D | Y | A | S | D | W | | H | S | D |

| | W | D | K | B | F | K | B | X | | S | B | Y | | Q | K | L | Y | D | | S | H |

| | G | Y | Y | D | | K | B | | 4 | . | 1 | 1 | | O | Y | A | S | B | W | O | . |

CRYPTOGRAM

7.

F	J	R	S		A	B	J	X	K	Y	G		U	S	J	I	R	Y	M	A

K		L	M	D		V	K	F	M	S		J	Q		X	R	Y	R	A

M	O	M	S	F		B	D	J		D	M	M	H	A		A	J

B	G	K	B		Z	B		I	J	M	A	L	'	B

I	Z	P	M	A	B		Z	B	A	M	V	Q	.

--

8.

I	C	W	A	Q	D	J	F	P	Y		E	P	Z	P	W	K		Q	D

K	D	J	Z	P	D	L		F	P	B		S	R	K	U		B	Q	V

F	C	D	L	U	K	L		U	S	S	Y	B	.

--

CRYPTOGRAM

9.

| S | B | P | | O | P | D | N | G | | N | A | | S | B | P |

| M | Z | L | S | C | M | J | F | M | D | | X | C | N | K | D |

| L | D | M | V | P | | F | L | | L | N | | H | N | K | P | C | A | Z | J |

| N | D | J | I | | 1 | / | 1 | 4 | , | 0 | 0 | 0 | S | B | | N | A | | M | D |

| N | Z | D | Q | P | | F | L | | P | D | N | Z | Y | B | | S | N |

| V | F | J | J | | M | | B | Z | G | M | D | . |

--

10.

| Z | A | C | | A | N | W | O | E | | I | H | O | U | E | | U | V |

| O | I | G | N | Z | | 7 | 5 | % | | D | O | Z | C | H | . |

--

CRYPTOGRAM

11.

| N | F | U | | R | Q | K | U | H | | J | R | H | H | T | | W | Q |

| Y | U | Q | U | I | E | U | H | R | | R | V | U | | Q | U | R | V | H | A |

| 2 | 0 | | N | W | B | U | T | | N | R | H | H | U | V | | N | F | R | Q |

| Q | W | R | K | R | V | R | | J | R | H | H | T | . |

--

12.

| R | | P | Q | W | H | K | O | Y | N | | J | U | Y | Y |

| E | K | I | W | E | I | U | X | R | X | K | | U | X | H | | O | Q | Q | C |

| R | F | C | | K | R | X | | U | X | | R | I | R | U | F | . |

--

CRYPTOGRAM

13.

B	F	Y		L	F	Z	S	B	Y	L	B		O	S	W	B	W	L	F

U	Z	D	V	S	G	F		N	V	L		G	F	V	S	E	Y	L

W	,		N	F	Z		N	V	L		4		X	Y	Y	B		9

W	D	G	F	Y	L	.

--

CRYPTOGRAM

14.

| T | | R | I | D | Z | O | E | ' | R | | H | O | G | | D | R | | Q | F | J |

| T | | W | F | Y | O | , | | G | P | J | | E | T | J | W | O | E | | T |

| J | E | T | I | | X | F | E | | D | J | R | | X | F | F | Z | . |

| J | W | O | N | | T | E | O | | T | R |

| D | Q | Z | D | M | D | Z | P | T | K | | T | R |

| R | Q | F | H | X | K | T | C | O | R | , | | H | D | J | W | | Q | F |

| J | H | F | | O | M | O | E | | G | O | D | Q | B | | J | W | O |

| R | T | Y | O | . | | R | F | Y | O | | J | E | F | I | D | A | T | K |

| R | I | D | Z | O | E | R | | W | T | M | O | | G | P | D | K | J |

| H | O | G | R | | F | M | O | E | | O | D | B | W | J | O | O | Q |

| X | O | O | J | | T | A | E | F | R | R | . |

CRYPTOGRAM

15.

| Q | F | O | X | Q | U | O | | N | D | C | O | | Y | V | Q | L | | H | C |

| Q | | T | Q | P | H | X | | N | O | Q | U | R | O |

| I | Q | Y | O | I | Q | N | N | : | | 7 | | V | D | W | G | B | O | Y | . |

--

16.

| L | M | Y | X | P | K | | V | D | | K | U | Y | | Q | O | Z | G |

| Y | O | B | Z | V | D | U | | A | Q | M | L | | K | U | X | K |

| Y | O | L | D | | V | O | | K | U | Y | | Z | Y | K | K | Y | M | D |

| " | P | K | . | " |

--

CRYPTOGRAM

17.

| M | Q | K | | L | I | M | | I | O | K | F | | M | Q | K |

| S | K | M | M | K | F | | " | G | " | | G | W | | P | D | S | S | K | L |

| D | | M | G | M | M | S | K | . |

--

18.

| L | O | | P | R | D | Y | , | | L | R | | L | G |

| L | M | M | N | E | D | M | | R | U | | G | Q | N | D | J | | L | O |

| B | J | U | O | R | | U | B | | D | | A | N | D | A |

| Z | N | J | G | U | O | . |

--

CRYPTOGRAM

19.

W	D	T		K	P	X	T		Q	T	T	G		A	Z	X	T	I

H	L	Z	X		"	V	G	"	,		W	D	T		P	L	X	M

P	C	C	L	T	B	U	P	W	U	Z	K		H	Z	L

V	T	K	T	L	P	Y		G	F	L	G	Z	I	T	.

20.

C	W		1	9	3	3	,		S	C	K	V	L	H

S	Q	F	T	L	,		O	W		O	W	C	S	O	P	L	A

K	O	Y	P	Q	Q	W		K	Z	O	Y	O	K	P	L	Y	,

Y	L	K	L	C	B	L	A		8	0	0	,	0	0	0		N	O	W

M	L	P	P	L	Y	T	.

CRYPTOGRAM

21.

ZUYVMUP MVYD VG YTF

GCUXXFGY MKQPYAD VP

YTF LKAXW, LVYT U

OKOQXUYVKP KB 1000

UPW EQGY 108.7

UMAFG.

CRYPTOGRAM

22.

| Q | K | O | N | R | I | X | | R | F | | N | O | X | L | N | | R | I |

| Z | L | B | L | X | K | L | S | | L | F | | N | U | I | X | | L | F |

| P | U | J | A | | Z | L | B | J | R | O | F | | L | B | O |

| B | O | X | R | F | J | O | B | O | Q | | P | N | U | U | Q |

| Q | U | I | U | B | F | . |

23.

| T | Q | T | Z | L | | X | F | J | T | | L | C | S | | H | F | U | O |

| N | | W | X | N | J | D | , | | L | C | S | ' | Z | T |

| U | C | V | W | S | J | F | V | K | | 1 | / | 1 | 0 | | C | E | N |

| U | N | H | C | Z | F | T | . |

CRYPTOGRAM

24.

X	L	V	A		L	P	Z	L	R	A		V	I	K	C

P	B	O	V		Z	N	B	C		B	D	E	V	E	C	Q		L

F	L	H	B	.

25.

P	F	C		Q	F	B	H	V	D	C	Q	V	W

T	C	C	P	R	C		B	W		P	F	C

W	P	Q	V	H	S	C	W	P		J	H	B	Z	J	R		J	H	M

B	W		D	J	N	J	T	R	C		V	E

R	B	E	P	B	H	S		8	5	0		P	B	Z	C	W

B	P	W		V	L	H		L	C	B	S	F	P	.

CRYPTOGRAM

26.

| S | Z | U | | V | M | G | O | D | U | N | S | | K | M | K | U |

| U | H | U | F | | B | J | N | | 1 | 1 | | V | U | J | F | N |

| M | P | X | . |

27.

| Y | K | T | G | H | Q | M | | Y | J | Z | | Y | | T | Z | T | I | Z | J |

| G | W | | V | E | Z | | B | Z | Y | P | E | | W | Y | T | R | K | A | . |

28.

| A | L | F | E | N | I | F | Y | O | N | I | X | P | B | M | F | I |

| J | O | I | H | E | | D | O | I | L | | B | D | | A | P | O |

| H | Q | J | M | O | L | | 1 | 3 | . |

CRYPTOGRAM

29.

| V | I | G | W | | Y | L | B | Q | | 1 | , | 0 | 0 | 0 |

| M | T | P | P | W | G | W | Q | Y | | J | B | Q | O | C | B | O | W | N |

| B | G | W | | N | U | I | F | W | Q | | I | Q | | Y | L | W |

| K | I | Q | Y | T | Q | W | Q | Y | | I | P | | B | P | G | T | K | B | . |

--

30.

| Y | R | B | J | S | B | K | | L | C | | D | Z | R | | N | E | H | K |

| U | H | X | E | R | D | | P | Z | N | C | R | | N | B | G | L | D |

| L | C | | J | N | U | H | X | E | X | B | | P | L | D | Z | | L | D | C |

| R | F | S | X | D | N | B | . |

--

CRYPTOGRAM

31.

GKPGPXQOF GQH LSXX

IPJZ; SO ISMFGOXR

QVVFGOZ OKFSM KFQMO

QHI HFMBPCZ ZRZOFY .

--

32.

NC XPW CQQS L FQLDWII

LIRL-FQIMUQJ , NMF

FMPALBO ZNII QGTIPSQ .

--

33.

KXOE AFWOEFYD

YXHEIFHO UFOL

OYIANO .

--

CRYPTOGRAM

34.

Z	G	F	R		T	O		Z	R	F	S	Z	D	R	U

R	B	R	Z	N		O	T	Q		J	T	Y	E	D	R	O		T	Y

D	X	R		E	.	O	.

--

35.

G	O	U	H	U		X	H	U		4	5		F	V	M	U	K

S	J		A	U	H	E	U	K		V	A		G	O	U

K	W	V	A		S	J		X		O	C	F	X	A

N	U	V	A	P	.

--

CRYPTOGRAM

36.

Y	C		G	D	M	S	G	I	M	,		1	2

C	M	K	A	Y	S	C	U		K	J	Z	Z		A	M

I	J	D	M	C		E	Y		E	T	M		K	S	Y	C	I

R	G	S	M	C	E	U		M	D	M	S	F		V	G	F	.

--

37.

L	V	C		R	.	Y	.		F	T	R	M	V	L

W	U	W	Y	P	W		S	T	A		2		B	C	G	L	Y

W	G		W	B	A	C		S	A	T	H		A	R	Y	Y	O	W	.

--

CRYPTOGRAM

38.

L	S	U	D	U		Z	D	U		R	T	U	D	

5	8													

K	P	W	W	P	R	H		Y	R	O	J	
P	H		L	S	U							

E	J

--

39.

H	G	C	L	R		Q	T	D	Y		X	P	V
I	E	P	K	J	R								

J	T	K	C	W	F		S	P	I	L
B	H	H	.							

--

40.

R	Y	U	S	G		X	S	R		K
D	G	R	P							

S	W	W	Q	W		P	L		B	T	Q	X
D	I	U		U	Y	A						

D	I		1	8	6	9		F
M		S						

W	Q	I	P	D	R	P	,		X
D	E	E	D	S	A				

R	Q	A	H	E	Q	.

--

CRYPTOGRAM

41.

D T U M K B ,   L M P T C   O C   L J M

A . C . ' C   S T U L J M C L

O Q D T Q K   F B U L .

--

42.

B   M D S F   D S   I L X Z L X U L

Z N B Z   Y I   Z N L   I B A L

J S D X Z   B X F   O B U C

(S B U L U B S ,   C B H B C)   Y I

U B G G L F   B

" K B G Y X F S D A L " .

--

CRYPTOGRAM

43.

R M T   Y S C Z U ' B   S Z U T B R

J G T P T   S X   P M T Y G F H   H W N

G B   9 0 0 0   K T I C B   S Z U !

--

44.

B   F A Q I L B L H   I S W U N O X V

O X   T B W W Q U   B   H K O H .

--

45.

N S B L I H   D U   H Y B   M E X Q

B E O X D U Y   F M S N   H Y L H

B E N U   D E   H Y B   X B H H B S U

" I H " .

--

CRYPTOGRAM

46.

N	P	Y	Q	P	M	,		L	T	S	T	M	B	N	T

S	B	J	R		L	S	B	F	C		E	T		E	Z	P

F	Y	Q	P	Y	E	F	T	Y		T	U		E	Z	P

L	Z	P	P	R	P	X	A	M	D	P	M	.

--

47.

1	4	%		Y	D		M	N	N		D	M	H	S	R		M	G	J

R	S	M	S	X	R	S	X	H	R		M	F	P		V	M	J	P

B	U		M	G	J		2	7	%		Y	D		U	P	Y	U	N	P

Q	G	Y	K		S	I	M	S		D	M	H	S	.

--

CRYPTOGRAM

48.

JF "QJPMFXM WD OVM

PTBKQ", VTFFJKTP

PMXOWE (TFOVWFN

VWYIJFQ) FMZME

KPJFIQ.

--

CRYPTOGRAM

49.

LDSK WRDOJVX XJW RD

BKDNSVA J CAY PJLAK

DZ OSVSW AMAKL RYD

YAAIW DK TR YTPP

NTFAWR TRWAPZ.

--

50.

LYQ DRWFL CNBAUVXB'F

WQFLVOWVUL RU NVUVBV

GVF RU WRNYCAUB,

MWRLRFY NAXOCMRV.

--

CRYPTOGRAM

51.

1 3 %   H V   B F I L G Y B P U

B Y K C B O O A   T I O G I Q I

K Z B K   U H F I   X B L K U   H V

K Z I   F H H P   B L I   F B M I   H V

Y Z I I U I .

--

52.

P I W C L U   I U S   C   O H O C Z

H M   7 2   Y Q M M S B S L O

W I U T Z S U   Q L   U F S S T P .

--

CRYPTOGRAM

53.

A	S	D	W		G	P		Z	J	X		N	T	H	K

G	P	H	W	T	F		G	T		Z	J	X

A	W	C	G	D	D	X	W	T		Z	N		J	W	E	X		W

C	W	G	H	C	N	W	F	.

--

54.

P	Y	D	E	D		J	F		Z		1		J	T		4

A	Y	Z	T	A	D		P	Y	Z	P		T	D	M		V	I	E	W

M	J	K	K		Y	Z	N	D		Z		M	Y	J	P	D

A	Y	E	J	F	P	C	Z	F	.

--

CRYPTOGRAM

55.

| P | F | | O | I | X | E | , | | P | I | | P | D |

| P | J | J | V | L | X | J | | I | R | | D | K | V | X | M | | P | F |

| Q | M | R | F | I | | R | Q | | X | | W | V | X | W |

| Y | V | M | D | R | F | . |

--

56.

| Y | C | D | V | ' | | Z | I | X | S | F | | H | Q | G | N | V |

| Z | S | R | F | I | | C | | M | Q | C | Y | T | | Q | X | H | O | D | . |

--

57.

| J | I | G | | Z | P | R | N | | Y | G | E | R | | D | G | Y | V | Z | P |

| J | Z | | A | G | E | | D | G | S | | I | G | E | F | | Q | E | V |

| A | G | J | V | N | | Y | Z | V | V | . |

--

CRYPTOGRAM

58.

E	B	Y	N		W	B	M	F		D	B	K	N		M	D	N

D	S	P	D	N	F	M		A	B	M	N		L	I

D	L	E	L	F	N	H	R	B	Y	S	M	J		L	I		B	O	J

E	B	E	E	B	Y	.

--

CRYPTOGRAM

59.

| G | W | L | | B | W | T | X | T | B | B | T | S | L | O | | W | H | O |

| H | D | U | R | G | | 7 | , | 1 | 0 | 0 | | T | O | X | H | S | I | O | , |

| U | K | | C | W | T | J | W | | U | S | X | Q | | H | D | U | R | G |

| 4 | 6 | 0 | | H | Y | L | | E | U | Y | L | | G | W | H | S | | 1 |

| O | F | R | H | Y | L | | E | T | X | L | | T | S | | H | Y | L | H | . |

--

60.

| E | I | G | G | X | Q | | D | X | I | S | S | O | | I | Q | V |

| H | L | J | G | Z | X | O | | R | U | Z | I | J | Q | X | | I | G | X |

| D | G | T | S | L | X | G | | I | Q | V | | H | J | H | S | X | G | . |

--

CRYPTOGRAM

61.

A	D	J		S	B	H	J		Y	X		R	Q	V	U	J	B	R

F	Y	Q	A	U	S	J		R	Q		W	J	V	A	R	P	R	J	O

T	Y	Q	D	J	V	.

--

62.

G	C		C	P	Z		K	R	E	I		F	X	W	X	P	,

G	X		G	F		G	U	U	P	S	W	U		X	R		J	B	X

W	C	K		W	U	V	R	T	R	U		R	C

F	B	C	N	W	K	F		J	P	D	R	E	P		C	R	R	C	.

--

CRYPTOGRAM

63.

J K J O R U I U Q O U

V W Q U E I H U O F

Y I O I H L Q C I Q S J U G J K I

Q U O F F U L J B B O F

U Z R I I P I O W H F R A W .

--

64.

V F W M W U M C W U Z N R I G W C

Q U H R O J W J U I W V O I P W L R

M W I Q G M N V G V F G H G H L

U V F W I Q U O H V I L .

--

CRYPTOGRAM

65.

VNBKX KEQIOI SOHSZO

ZNJO, HQ EJOVEBO,

QNQO COEVG ZHQBOV

XKEQ ZOPX KEQIOI

SOHSZO IH.

--

66.

CDH DIAXF VYOS QE

RYATPQEHO YU 80%

MXCHP.

--

CRYPTOGRAM

67.

R M P U F   S S Z W K   Q M E N J B ' C

C Z U   E U L Y U B Y K   S E U T Z S U

S Z N C .

68.

B O U   H I U X H V U   S U H E

R U Z L C S   P C S S   E X H P   H

S C Z U   3 5   F C S U T   S G Z V

G X   P X C B U

H R R X G N C F H B U S A   5 0 , 0 0 0

U Z V S C T O   P G X E T .

CRYPTOGRAM

69.

| J | U | A | E | Z | Y | S | G | | P | V | S | | A | U | U | L | | Y | S |

| J | Y | C | C | X | D | X | S | R | | J | Y | D | X | P | R | Y | U | S | G |

| F | Y | R | Z | | X | V | P | Z | | X | Q | X | . | | R | Z | X | Q |

| P | V | S | | G | A | X | X | E | | F | Y | R | Z | | U | S | X |

| X | Q | X | | U | E | X | S | . |

--

70.

| F | E | D | A | | F | E | Z | | U | E | | J | C | F |

| V | U | D | D | U | F | E | | K | Z | F | K | D | Z | | C | U | D | D |

| D | U | P | Z | | J | F | | V | Z | | 1 | 1 | 6 | | F | O |

| F | D | H | Z | O | . |

--

CRYPTOGRAM

71.

QV BRZ DTMB 4000

GZTCM VJ VZP TVQSTDM

RTLZ OZZV

FJSZMBQITBZF.

--

72.

Y TCUV FYE LDS Y

BPEEVU 300 WVVB (91

T) UCES DE GPHB CEV

EDSOB.

--

CRYPTOGRAM

73.

| | U | C | | R | E | Y | J | , | | G | | ' | P | E |

| | B | T | Z | T | D | ' | | U | L | | G | | L | M | E | Z | T | | E | J |

| 1 | 0 | . |

CRYPTOGRAM

74.

QZUO SCPPMHLJBMY GZU

PZYPM IBPX PXMBH

LMMP PR LBUF RCP

IXMPXMH PXM JMZL

PXMO YBP RU BY VRRF

PR JZO MVVY RU PR SM

PXMBH GZPMHWBJJZHY'

LRRF RH URP.

--

CRYPTOGRAM

75.

A	Z	G		R	Q	N	U	H	'	K		C	Q	L	D	P	G	K	A

B	X	N	G	D	A	K		R	G	N	G		8		X	D	H		9

X	D	H		U	E	W	G	H		E	D		I	Z	E	D	X

E	D		1	9	1	0	.

--

76.

Q	X	T		Q	B	B	Q	X	V	Y	M	C	X		O	K	C

F	L	E	T	L	Q	T	S		F	L		N	X	F	L	K		F	L

1	4	9	8	.

--

CRYPTOGRAM

77.

G	Y	G	Z	R	C	M	A	F		T	M	Y	J		F	Y	G	G	Z

L	T	D		A	U	T		R	T	V	D	F		G	C	X	R

E	C	J	.

78.

U	E	G	N		E	R	I		F	Q	U	N	S	N

H	E	R	'	G		T	Q	A	X	G	.

79.

I	X	K	O	H	Y		X	Y	J		O		R	A	R	O	P

A	Q		7	2		L	B	Q	Q	J	Z	J	H	R

K	X	Y	N	P	J	Y		B	H		Y	E	J	J	N	I	.

CRYPTOGRAM

80.

Y	M	X	I	G	J	P		I	Z	S	S		O	M	E	G

K	G	M	K	S	G		D	N	R	X		K	S	R	X	G

F	E	R	P	N	G	P	.

--

CRYPTOGRAM - HINTS (1/2)

1.	R => E, U => B, H => F	**27.**	J => R, K => L, T => M
2.	O => E, H => S, L => H	**28.**	E => S, F => I, H => N
3.	U => A, L => R, B => E	**29.**	W => E, G => R, Q => N
4.	R => A, I => E, L => N	**30.**	D => T, N => O, H => L
5.	A => I, O => F, F => R	**31.**	B => V, L => K, R => Y
6.	W => D, Y => E, S => O	**32.**	Q => E, I => L, A => M
7.	B => T, K => A, O => V	**33.**	Y => C, E => T, K => M
8.	P => A, Q => I, K => E	**34.**	S => O, R => E, T => I
9.	K => W, Z => U, S => T	**35.**	N => B, K => S, A => N
10.	O => A, H => R, Z => T	**36.**	E => T, F => Y, M => E
11.	H => L, T => S, U => E	**37.**	A => R, G => N, C => E
12.	R => A, K => E, U => I	**38.**	R => O, W => L, U => E
13.	V => A, Y => E, F => H	**39.**	C => I, D => M, P => A
14.	R => S, M => V, O => E	**40.**	P => T, R => S, A => M
15.	Q => A, U => G, H => O	**41.**	B => O, C => S, D => L
16.	K => T, V => I, U => H	**42.**	Y => I, C => K, B => A
17.	S => L, F => R, M => T	**43.**	M => H, T => E, R => T
18.	Z => P, J => R, R => T	**44.**	O => I, K => W, S => O
19.	G => P, T => E, A => C	**45.**	O => G, E => N, Y => H
20.	Y => R, S => M, N => F	**46.**	T => O, Q => V, Z => H
21.	Y => T, M => C, D => Y	**47.**	Q => K, P => E, G => N
22.	O => E, F => S, L => A	**48.**	E => R, M => E, F => N
23.	S => U, X => T, L => Y	**49.**	Y => W, J => A, L => Y
24.	R => Y, A => S, L => A	**50.**	R => I, F => S, B => D
25.	T => B, W => S, E => F	**51.**	L => R, I => E, K => T
26.	S => T, P => L, U => E	**52.**	M => F, U => S, S => E

53.	T => N, H => L, J => H		79.	Y => S, H => N, B => I
54.	I => O, Y => H, M => W		80.	O => M, K => P, J => Y
55.	E => H, Q => F, X => A			
56.	Y => C, S => N, I => R			
57.	E => A, J => T, Y => R			
58.	F => S, B => A, L => O			
59.	X => L, H => A, S => N			
60.	S => T, U => C, L => H			
61.	R => I, A => T, Y => O			
62.	C => N, J => B, E => R			
63.	Z => Q, F => O, P => Z			
64.	H => N, Q => C, F => H			
65.	I => D, J => V, O => E			
66.	M => W, H => E, Q => I			
67.	P => A, S => L, B => T			
68.	S => L, U => E, G => O			
69.	P => C, R => T, X => E			
70.	J => T, F => O, Z => E			
71.	Z => E, R => H, S => M			
72.	C => O, B => T, V => E			
73.	L => S, Z => R, E => O			
74.	M => E, Z => A, R => O			
75.	A => T, W => V, L => U			
76.	L => N, X => H, Y => R			
77.	C => A, D => R, G => E			
78.	Q => O, I => D, G => T			

CRYPTOGRAM - ANSWERS (1/6)

1.	Table tennis balls have been known to travel off the paddle at speeds up to 160 km/hr.
2.	Slugs have four noses.
3.	Every person, including identical twins, has a unique eye & tongue print along with their fingerprint.
4.	The Declaration of Independence was written on hemp (marijuana) paper.
5.	The Olympic was the sister ship of the Titanic, and she provided twenty-five years of service.
6.	A Czech man, Jan Honza Zampa, holds the record for drinking one liter of beer in 4.11 seconds.
7.	Your stomach produces a new layer of mucus every two weeks so that it doesn't digest itself.
8.	Buckingham Palace in England has over six hundred rooms.
9.	The venom of the Australian Brown Snake is so powerful only 1/14,000th of an ounce is enough to kill a human.
10.	The human brain is about 75% water.
11.	The angel falls in Venezuela are nearly 20 times taller than Niagara Falls.
12.	A housefly will regurgitate its food and eat it again.
13.	The shortest British monarch was Charles I, who was 4 feet 9 inches.
14.	A spider's web is not a home, but rather a trap for its food. They are as individual as snowflakes, with no two ever being the same. Some tropical spiders have built webs over eighteen feet across.

CRYPTOGRAM - ANSWERS (2/6)

15.	Average life span of a major league baseball: 7 pitches. --
16.	Dreamt is the only English word that ends in the letters "mt." --
17.	The dot over the letter "i" is called a tittle. --
18.	In Utah, it is illegal to swear in front of a dead person. --
19.	The name Jeep comes from "GP", the army abbreviation for General Purpose. --
20.	In 1933, Mickey Mouse, an animated cartoon character, received 800,000 fan letters. --
21.	Vatican City is the smallest country in the world, with a population of 1000 and just 108.7 acres. --
22.	Dueling is legal in Paraguay as long as both parties are registered blood donors. --
23.	Every time you lick a stamp, you're consuming 1/10 of a calorie. --
24.	Bats always turn left when exiting a cave. --
25.	The rhinoceros beetle is the strongest animal and is capable of lifting 850 times its own weight. --
26.	The youngest pope ever was 11 years old. --
27.	Almonds are a member of the peach family. --
28.	Triskaidekaphobia means fear of the number 13. --
29.	More than 1,000 different languages are spoken on the continent of Africa. --

CRYPTOGRAM - ANSWERS (3/6)

30.	Mercury is the only planet whose orbit is coplanar with its equator.
31.	Chocolate can kill dogs; it directly affects their heart and nervous system.
32.	If you feed a seagull Alka-Seltzer, its stomach will explode.
33.	Most lipstick contains fish scales.
34.	Rape is reported every six minutes in the U.S.
35.	There are 45 miles of nerves in the skin of a human being.
36.	On average, 12 newborns will be given to the wrong parents every day.
37.	The U.S. bought Alaska for 2 cents an acre from Russia.
38.	There are over 58 million dogs in the US
39.	Flies jump backwards during takeoff.
40.	Sugar was first added to chewing gum in 1869 by a dentist, William Semple.
41.	Laredo, Texas is the U.S.'s farthest inland port.
42.	A word or sentence that is the same front and back (racecar, kayak) is called a "palindrome".
43.	The world's oldest piece of chewing gum is 9000 years old!
44.	A pregnant goldfish is called a twit.

CRYPTOGRAM - ANSWERS (4/6)

45.	Dreamt is the only English word that ends in the letters "MT". --
46.	Denver, Colorado lays claim to the invention of the cheeseburger. --
47.	14% of all facts and statistics are made up and 27% of people know that fact. --
48.	In "Silence of the Lambs", Hannibal Lector (Anthony Hopkins) never blinks. --
49.	Your stomach has to produce a new layer of mucus every two weeks or it will digest itself. --
50.	The first McDonald's restaurant in Canada was in Richmond, British Columbia. --
51.	13% of Americans actually believe that some parts of the moon are made of cheese. --
52.	Humans use a total of 72 different muscles in speech. --
53.	Cuba is the only island in the Caribbean to have a railroad. --
54.	There is a 1 in 4 chance that New York will have a white Christmas. --
55.	In Utah, it is illegal to swear in front of a dead person. --
56.	Cats' urine glows under a black light. --
57.	The only real person to be a PEZ head was Betsy Ross. --
58.	Male bats have the highest rate of homosexuality of any mammal. --

CRYPTOGRAM - ANSWERS (5/6)

59.	The Philippines has about 7,100 islands, of which only about 460 are more than 1 square mile in area.
60.	Warren Beatty and Shirley McLaine are brother and sister.
61.	The glue on Israeli postage is certified kosher.
62.	In New York State, it is illegal to but any alcohol on Sundays before noon.
63.	A cat uses its whiskers to determine if a space is too small to squeeze through.
64.	The people of Israel consume more turkeys per capita than any other country.
65.	Right handed people live, on average, nine years longer than left handed people do.
66.	The human body is comprised of 80% water.
67.	Frank Lloyd Wright's son invented Lincoln Logs.
68.	The average lead pencil will draw a line 35 miles long or write approximately 50,000 English words.
69.	Dolphins can look in different directions with each eye. They can sleep with one eye open.
70.	Only one in two billion people will live to be 116 or older.
71.	In the last 4000 years no new animals have been domesticated.
72.	A mole can dig a tunnel 300 feet (91 m) long in just one night.
73.	In golf, a 'Bo Derek' is a score of 10.

CRYPTOGRAM - ANSWERS (6/6)

74.	Many butterflies can taste with their feet to find out whether the leaf they sit on is good to lay eggs on to be their caterpillars' food or not. --
75.	The world's youngest parents were 8 and 9 and lived in China in 1910. --
76.	The toothbrush was invented in China in 1498. --
77.	Elephants only sleep for two hours each day. --
78.	Rats and horses can't vomit. --
79.	Humans use a total of 72 different muscles in speech. --
80.	Donkeys kill more people than plane crashes. --

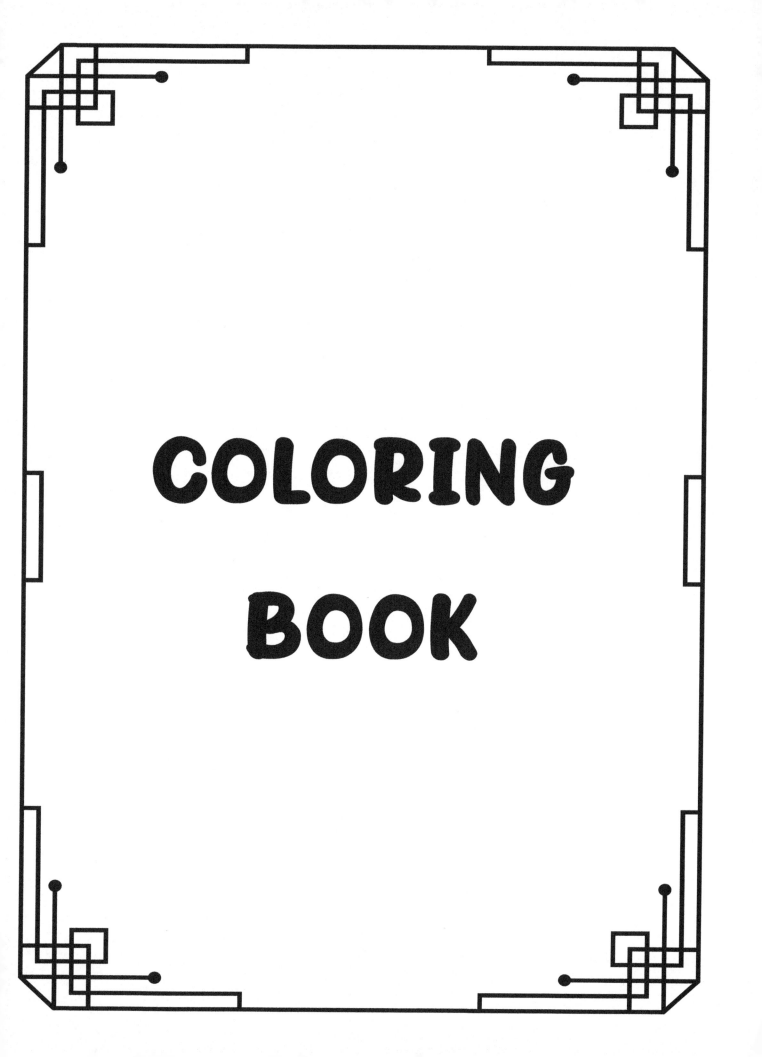

COLORING

BOOK

Made in United States
North Haven, CT
02 April 2023

34913707R00167